LINKING PARENTS
TO PLAY THERAPY

LINKING PARENTS TO PLAY THERAPY

A Practical Guide with Applications, Interventions, and Case Studies

by

Deborah Killough McGuire, M.Ed.
Donald E. McGuire, Ph.D.

Psychology Press
Taylor & Francis Group

New York London

Routledge
Taylor & Francis Group
270 Madison Avenue
New York, NY 10016

Routledge
Taylor & Francis Group
2 Park Square
Milton Park, Abingdon
Oxon OX14 4RN

© 2001 by Taylor & Francis Group, LLC
Routledge is an imprint of Taylor & Francis Group, an Informa business

Printed in the United States of America on acid-free paper
10 9 8 7 6 5 4 3 2
International Standard Book Number-13: 978-1-56032-859-9 (Softcover)
Cover design by Curt Tow.

Library of Congress Cataloging-in-Publication Data

McGuire, Deborah Killough.
    Linking parents to play therapy : a practical guide with applications, interventions, and case studies / Deborah Killough McGuire, Donald E. McGuire.
        p. cm.
    Includes bibliographical references and index.
    ISBN 1-56032-859-2 (pbk. : alk. paper)
    1. Play therapy—Case studies. 2. Child psychotherapy—parent participation—case studies. 3. Family psychotherapy—Case studies. I. McGuire, Donald E. II. Title.
RJ505.P6 M3652   2000
616.92'891653—dc21   00-044437

Visit the Taylor & Francis Web site at
http://www.taylorandfrancis.com

and the Routledge Web site at
http://www.routledge.com

To Kellye,
for giving us joy
and honor
that eclipse everything else
taken together.

CONTENTS

About the Authors   ix
Acknowledgments   xi
Foreword   xiii
Preface   xvii

1   Initial Contact with Parents   1

2   Developmental Issues   21

3   Legal and Ethical Issues of Therapy   35

4   Medical Issues in Therapy   62

5   Parent Profiles   102

6   Working With Angry, Resistant Parents   113

7   Parent and Therapist Meetings   127

8   General Homework Assignments for Parents   151

9   Special Issues   160

10 Incorporating Brief Therapy and Managed Care   178

Appendix A: Sample Professional Disclosure
    Statement and Informed Consent   190
Appendix B: Sample Play Therapy Parent
    Intake Session Checklist   194
Appendix C: Sample Child Client Intake
    Form and Authorization for Treatment   196
Appendix D: Managed Care Format   201
Appendix E: National and State Protective
    Services and Advocacy Agencies   203
Appendix F: Parenting Manual: Essential Skills
    and Practical Suggestions   208

References   222
Index   229

ABOUT THE AUTHORS

Deborah Killough McGuire, M.Ed., is a licensed professional counselor, licensed marriage and family therapist, and registered play therapist-supervisor in private practice in Dallas, Texas. She is a member of the Association for Play Therapy and the Texas Association for Play Therapy and has served on the boards of directors for both organizations. She is also a member of the American Counseling Association and a frequent presenter at conferences and workshops across the country.

Donald E. McGuire, Ph.D., is a licensed professional counselor in private practice in Dallas, Texas. He received his Ph.D. in Counselor Education from the University of North Texas. Donald is a member of the Texas Association for Play Therapy and the North Texas Chapter of the Texas Association for Play Therapy and has served on the boards of directors for both organizations. He is also a member of the Association for Play Therapy and the American Counseling Association.

ACKNOWLEDGMENTS

Special thanks go to Lloyd Mercer, M.D., pediatric neurologist, and Patti Hill, R.N., for their consultation, advice, and friendship over the last 10 years. Robert Blalock, M.D., and Tom Hartsell, JD, provided invaluable medical and legal information germane to providing therapy to children and linking parents to the process. The libraries and staff of the University of North Texas and the Center for Play Therapy in Denton, Texas were extremely helpful through our long hours of research and study. Deep appreciation goes to Emily Oe, Ph.D. for her support, input, and especially her friendship. Garry Landreth, Ed.D. offered advice, support, and encouragement. Mentor, counselor, teacher, professor, advisor, guru, and friend are all hats that he has been wearing for us. Our heartfelt gratitude is extended to our families, who believed in us, encouraged us, and made sacrifices that provided us the time and support needed to write this book.

FOREWORD

Parenting is at best a complex, often confusing, stressful process producing peaks of joy and valleys of distress and bewilderment unknown and unimaginable to those who have not experienced the richness and excitement of rearing children—a dynamic condition somewhat akin to riding a gigantic roller coaster, at other times quite like floating down a gentle stream in a canoe. And always there exists the possibility of an experience similar to being aboard a run-away train. Relating empathically to anxious, troubled parents is crucial to the overall therapeutic impact of the play therapy experience. Parents, just as any other person, want to be understood and to have their unique needs appreciated. Therefore, when interviewing parents, play therapists must not make the mistake of only focusing on the child and gathering information about the child. Debbie and Mac (I know the authors personally) have "been there," "experienced that" and relate how, through the provision of a wealth of practical suggestions, the play therapist can help parents "live through" the process of parenting which has sometimes been derailed.

By the time most parents arrive at the play therapist's office, parenting attitudes are firmly entrenched, habitual patterns of parenting are established, daily routines are set and stress is a way of life. In the face of these conditions, the play therapist must be the model of patience and understanding. Parents achieve some degree of security by maintaining established routines and patterns of behavior, even though these behaviors may be counterproductive and unhealthy. Resistance to change is to be expected and is therefore understood and accepted. The play therapist also lives out a hectic routine and must resist the urge to push for quick change. That parents must feel they are understood and their unique problems are appreciated before attitude and behavioral change is possible is an essential and underlying theme of this book. Play therapists will especially appreciate the specific and realistic suggestions for working with angry, resistant parents.

Although parents are a key part of the total therapeutic experience for children, scheduling the time needed to facilitate a working relationship with parents and maintaining the play therapy relationship with the child at the same time is a universal problem. The ideal of having another therapist work with the parent while the play therapist works with the child is seldom possible for most practicing play therapists. This book deals with the practicality of this situation and presents a workable format which play therapists can easily incorporate into their scheduling routine.

This is not a technical book which must be deciphered; this is a practical book based on practical experience, consisting of practical wisdom and containing practical, easily-applied suggestions that make the process of play therapy and the necessary process of working with parents more workable and more productive. Every part of this book is active, imparting the results of years of experience with children and parents. The authors do a masterful job of teaching through vivid descriptions of happenings with parents and their children in play therapy.

Play therapists will find the sections on typical behaviors of children at various developmental ages especially helpful as they counsel with parents. Parents who are stressed often react to normal childhood behavior as though the behavior is inappropriate. Thus they attempt to stop or suppress developmentally appropriate growth on the part of children. The authors provide an insightful peek into the developmental world of children.

The chapter on legal and ethical issues is must reading for all play therapists and will help prevent potential problems from arising. Again, the authors have accurately anticipated the needs of play therapists and have provided expert advice. The cases and play theme development described are especially instructive and helpful.

In our society, it has been assumed that parents possess the necessary parenting skills for rearing healthy, well-adjusted children who are capable of coping with the adjustments required in a highly technological, stress-induced society. It is interesting to note that similar assumptions do not exist about the skills needed to perform other jobs. We even require training and the successful passing of a test for driving an automobile. But for life's most important job, parenting, no skills are required and no training is provided on a regular basis, certainly not in educational settings. Play therapists must come to the forefront in this area and actively provide the experiences and training parents need for effective parenting. Debbie and Mac initiate this process by providing specific suggestions and assignments for parents to carry out at home with their children.

The absence of detailed information about how to work with parents has been a missing link in play therapy literature. This book fills in the gap and will make the play therapist's professional life with parents less stressful, more efficient and more effective, the result of a sensitive, caring, and insightful parent-therapist relationship. The play therapist who wants to know how to work with parents to effectively involve them in the process of helping their children will find the insights, guidelines, and suggestions in this book to be just what they need.

Garry Landreth
Regents Professor and Director
Center for Play Therapy
University of North Texas

PREFACE

What do we do with the parents? As play therapists, we have all been confronted with this question at times. Parents have a myriad of feelings about bringing their child to play therapy. Sometimes the parents are tentative and reluctant; sometimes they are hopeful; sometimes they are angry and resistant; sometimes they are anxious and worried; and sometimes they are confused about the process of play therapy. Whatever their reactions, their consent is essential for the child to be in play therapy. When their consent is coupled with involvement and support of play therapy, the child client experiences maximum benefits. Working closely with parents, the therapist may be the critical link that brings parents and children together through the play therapy process.

In order to be the link, play therapists must possess a wealth of information about many topics including, but not limited to, parenting skills, medical issues, legal issues, brief therapy, managed care, developmental issues, attention deficit hyperactivity disorder, sexual abuse, and divorce. Play therapists must also assess the child and communicate the findings to the parents while trying to protect the child's confidentiality as much as possible. Both parents and managed care companies may need or want interventions and treatment plans.

The genesis of this book began years ago when we searched, but found only very limited literature about working with parents in play therapy. We realized that most of the training programs at universities do not focus necessary attention toward working with the parents of children in play therapy, nor tying these parents into the therapy process. This book is intended as a useful text to supplement and complement play therapy courses and as a pragmatic guide for practitioners. Our goal is to provide a detailed and thorough reference book for therapists.

We have also included a separate parenting manual that therapists can either refer to themselves or give to the parents. The parenting manual has been popular with the parents we have worked with over the years. Parents have felt less overwhelmed when asked to read it because of its brevity and plethora of suggestions. The parenting manual has also been used by school districts in special education departments as well as with school counselors working with parents.

Parents are vital to the healthy development of children. Even when the children are the subject of therapy, substantial amounts of attention must be directed toward the parents. Any problems with the children are family problems. Parents need to take care of themselves and maintain their own good mental health. To assist in this, therapists need to accept, affirm, and allow parents' reactions and feelings regarding their children's characteristics.

Forming an alliance with parents can be arduous and challenging. It can also be immensely rewarding and beneficial to the child and parents. Perhaps, the following poem describes it best:

The Bridge Builder

An old man, going a lone highway,
Came at the evening, cold and gray,
To a chasm, vast and deep and wide,
Through which was flowing a sullen tide.
The old man crossed in the twilight dim;
That sullen stream had no fears for him;
But he turned, when he reached the other side,
and built a bridge to span the tide.
"Old man," said a fellow pilgrim near,
"You are wasting strength in building here,
Your journey will end with the ending day;
You never again must pass this way;
You have crossed the chasm, deep and wide-
Why build you the bridge at the eventide?"

The builder lifted his old gray head:
"Good friend, in the path I have come," he said,
"There followeth after me today
A child whose feet must pass this way.
This chasm that has been naught to me
To that fair-haired child a pitfall be.
He, too, must cross in the twilight dim;
Good friend, I am building the bridge for him."

Will Allen Dromgoole
(cited in Morrison, 1948, p. 342)

CHAPTER 1

Initial Contact with Parents

Beginnings are very delicate times—young plants are easily uprooted. The epitome of a delicate beginning is a child attending the first day of kindergarten. The kindergartner is supposed to separate from his or her parents, go into a building he or she has never seen before, and bond with an adult stranger. Parents will have various expectations for their child on this very, very delicate day. Many kindergartners are expected to gracefully and happily run inside, learn important things, and have (a little) fun. The various children will differ in their expectations, as well. Some will be going to school with friends; some will not know any other children. Of a certainty, their expectations will be colored by their imaginations, and influenced by explanations and stories from their parents and others. Very likely, children will be wide-eyed, hopeful, apprehensive, curious, scared, interested, and incredibly off-balance. In a perfect world, they would quickly begin to experience numerous small, positive events (i.e., another child's attentive smile, a friendly teacher, or a good friend in the same class).

So it is with the beginning of a child's play therapy. Balance is sought; attention is focused on minutiae; trust is being established. Ideally, a solid foundation is being built, along with a therapeutic relationship. Parents who make the decision to seek therapy services for their children will most likely experience many "new beginning" emotions themselves. As Bromfield (1992) states, "entrusting your child to any caretaker is hard. Entrusting your child to a therapist, and to the vulnerability of treatment, is even harder" (p. 46).

1

The therapist must keep this in mind and attempt to provide small, positive experiences to encourage parents and help them to believe in their decision. If a general attitude of success and confidence in the therapist can be cultivated, parents will be more likely to pursue therapy for their children. Also, the therapist's belief in the parents as a positive force in their child's life will encourage the parents to be involved and supportive throughout the therapy process.

☐ Initial Contact

Initial contact with parents is very significant in the therapy experience. The original telephone call sets the tone for the relationship between the therapist and the parents. During the original call to make an appointment, parents may attempt to tell the therapist the "whole story" about their child. A multitude of details may be provided about the child's problems and the parents' reactions to the indicated unacceptable behaviors. The therapist's first goal is to *listen*. This may be the first contact parents have ever made with a mental health professional. Inherently, contacting a therapist makes parents more vulnerable in the context of admitting the need for help. Unfortunately, and erroneously, this implies to many people a general lack of adequacy as parents.

During the original call, the therapist should be empathic with the parent. According to Carkhuff (1969), "empathy is the key ingredient of helping. Its explicit communication, particularly during early phases of helping, is critical" (p. 172). Making contact with someone's feelings is the best means of helping that person feel understood—a basic element in building rapport. Sensitivity to the parents' feelings (especially vulnerability and apprehension) can be pivotal in their decision to obtain therapy for their child and, subsequently, to participate in the therapy process themselves to increase the probability of successful outcomes for their child. If the parents' initial contact is qualified by insensitivity, lack of understanding, impatience, or a lack of acceptance on the part of the therapist, the quest may be abandoned by the parents. The parents' perception of the therapist's message is more important than the actual words or intended message. Parents need to believe that it is actually possible to improve the present situation. At this point, parents can begin to discover, and believe in, their own ability to make positive modifications in their child's life. It is tremendously helpful if the parents believe that contacting the therapist was a good idea. The therapist must try to help parents feel understood, cared about, validated, and empowered.

The initial telephone contact is not the time to give advice to parents regarding their child. There has not yet been sufficient time or contact to build a deep, trusting relationship between the therapist and parents, and the risk of offending the parents is great, especially if the parents do not like the suggestions. Giving excessive advice during the original call is very easy to do because most parents directly ask for, or at least implicitly expect, immediate information on how to deal with their problem. However, the therapist risks giving advice that may not be helpful to the parents or the child. Since the therapist has neither met nor observed the parents or children, enough information could not have been collected during this one phone call to allow the therapist the chance to give appropriate advice. At this time, it is most important to listen, support the parents' initiative in calling, and encourage them in taking the next step—whether it involves continuing with therapy, following up on a referral, or pursuing some other course of action.

☐ Making a Referral

Sometimes the only appropriate advice that can be given during the initial contact involves making a referral. Specific disorders, behaviors, handicaps, and challenges may require specialized facilities, training, or certification. Certain services may be requested that the therapist is not able or not qualified to provide. It is very possible that a therapist is uncomfortable with certain clients or issues. This does not manifest a weakness or lack of character on the part of the therapist but, rather, a healthy awareness of one's professional boundaries. Being aware of and comfortable with one's own boundaries, allows a greater opportunity for positive outcomes to the therapy process. As an example, one therapist may be uncomfortable with parents who have physically or sexually abused their children. Other therapists may find it difficult to work with aggressive, angry, or culturally different parents. The therapist needs to become aware of personal limitations and boundaries; without this awareness, it is unlikely that the therapist can provide safe and effective help or support for parents and children.

In such cases, a referral may be the only ethical option. To locate and recommend appropriate treatment and support for clients requiring referrals, the therapist should be acquainted with other professionals and services in the community. These resources can be an extremely valuable starting point for clients. If a referral is not necessary, setting the first appointment can be addressed.

☐ Setting the First Appointment

The therapist should request that parents or primary caregivers attend the first appointment, without the child. Many different family structures are common in today's society. When possible, however, both parents should be included in the initial session (James, 1997). Meeting with both parents can provide a wealth of information about the family dynamics, how the parents feel about their children, their individual and collective perceptions about the children, and how the parents relate to one another (Copley, Ferryan, & O'Neill, 1987). Valuable information can be learned about consistencies and inconsistencies in parenting styles. For example, whether or not one parent is more strict about a child's table manners than the other is therapeutic material that is more likely to present itself when both parents are present in the session. Likewise, any covert resistance about coming to therapy on the part of either or both of the parents is more likely to be evident with both parents present. These seemingly small pieces of information, taken together, can tell the therapist a great deal about the family atmosphere surrounding the children.

☐ The Intake Interview

The primary objectives of the first session are to gather data about the reason for the referral, the presenting problem, and changes related to the presenting problem (Kottman, 1995; Norton & Norton, 1997). In addition, winning the parents over to the play therapy process is vastly more important. This is done through rapport building, not interrogation. Information regarding how the parents interact, the types of discipline they use with their children, parents' enjoyment of their children, how the parents perceive the problems of the family, and how they perceive the problems of their children is often gathered by passive observation (Greenspan, 1991). Parents who feel interrogated prior to the establishment of a trusting relationship often feel resentment toward the therapist and tend to prematurely terminate the therapy process. Being sensitive and responsive to the emotional dynamics underlying the parents' reactions to each other and to the child's difficulties is a more valuable strategy at this point than strict information gathering (Guerney, Guerney, & Stover, 1972).

Reflecting the Feelings of Parents

Therapists should start intake sessions by reflecting the feelings of the parents. For example, the therapist might say, "You seem concerned about what might happen with your child." This facilitates the process of identifying parents' feelings. Touching the parents' feelings and accepting those feelings is the most powerful accomplishment a therapist can make toward building rapport and trust. The value of empathy must not be overlooked. *Reflecting* and *empathizing* are two foundational skills and two very powerful tools of the therapist.

Consider the following example: A five-year-old boy was referred to therapy because his parents caught him "playing doctor" with another five-year-old boy. Both parents attended the first session. The father was noticeably angry and agitated, his arms were crossed, he was frowning, and he kept tapping his foot. He repeatedly complained that his son needed more severe discipline, attesting that the mother was much too lenient. He insisted that his son should now be kept under constant surveillance, with at least one parent accompanying the child during all of his waking hours.

Realizing that some kind of fear is beneath all anger, the therapist chose not to focus on the father's anger or on appropriate styles of discipline. The therapist's response was, "I can see this has caused you great concern. In fact, you're so concerned that you're willing to go to great lengths to make sure this doesn't happen again. I'm wondering—what are you afraid might happen? What's the worst possible thing that could happen if your son plays doctor?"

The father stared at the floor, clenching his hands. A tear rolled down his cheek as he whispered, "I'm afraid he might be gay." Because of this information from the father, the therapist was able to empathize about his fears and reassure him that playing doctor was not an indicator that his son would be gay. If the therapist's response had been based solely upon the information that the father was *saying*, an opportunity to understand the true issue would have been missed. Most likely, further contact would not have been reached, and the father would have been less likely to trust and *hear* the therapist. Through the therapist's reflecting and attempting to touch the father's true feelings, the father became more relaxed. Feelings were validated, and the father felt accepted by the therapist. Rapport was increased, and the father began to genuinely trust the therapist. Both the father and therapist had increased awareness about what was influencing the father's reactions, behaviors, and feelings.

Again, the extended outcome of this rapport-building is a greater probability of the father's continued involvement in the therapy process. This kind of contact and trust with the therapist helps the parent gain self-acceptance, self-awareness, and self-confidence as a parent and as a person. The impact of the experience can have long-lasting benefits for the parent, as well as for the child-client and other family members.

Clarifying Expressions Used by Parents

The therapist should ask parents to describe or explain the phrases and words that they use, especially those regarding the child. As each person tends to have definitions and understanding of words and phrases pertinent to one's own experiences, the therapist's understanding of the parents' phrases used to describe the child is particularly vital. Expressions such as "aggressive" or "getting into trouble at school" will have different meanings for different people. Ask parents to be specific.

For example, if a parent says, "My daughter Susie is biting," then the therapist might need to ask, "Did Susie bite one child last week, or does she bite several children everyday?" If the parent reports, "Jason is getting into trouble at school," the therapist should clarify this and possibly ask, "When Jason is getting into trouble, is he talking defiantly to the teacher, not finishing his work, or something else?"

Other words can also carry a variety of definitions. For example, the definition of *respect* is often confused with the definition of *obey*. The expression "respect your elders" often has a lot to do with obedience, but little to do with respect. Another example is the parent who made several references to his "midwife"; upon request, he clarified the term as describing his live-in girlfriend. It is often necessary to ask parents about the meanings of their expressions; a clear understanding of parents is imperative. "What does that mean to you?" may frequently need to be asked. Through clarification of phrases and words used by parents, the therapist will learn more about the parents' perceptions of their child's problems. The more the therapist understands about the child, the more help he or she will be to the parents, and, of course, to the child. Therefore, therapists need not be shy about asking for clarification; this shows parents that the therapist cares enough about them to pay attention and strive to understand (Greenspan, 1991). If parents see the therapist putting forth effort on their behalf, it often inspires them to put forth more effort on behalf of their children.

Asking for clarification also models appropriate, respectful communication for parents. Appropriate communication is the key to understanding, and respect is the key to appropriate communication. Taken together, these are essential ingredients of healthy relationships. Hopefully, parents will increase their use of appropriate communication skills with their children.

Gathering Information

Gathering specific information is important, as are the techniques of reflecting and clarifying. There is no universal pattern or formula governing therapist responses. The therapist must use his or her professional judgment to sensitively intersperse specific questions among reflections, when additional information is needed. Many parents feel intimidated by direct, face-to-face questioning, especially during the early stages of building the therapeutic relationship.

Question, Response, Reflect Cycle

As the therapeutic relationship and rapport are developing, it may be possible for the therapist to focus more attention on gathering information. After parents begin to sense that the therapist can be trusted, they are more responsive to helping the helper. Typically, it is appropriate for the therapist to initiate this process, and most parents will be very willing to cooperate in helping the therapist. An example of how a therapist might begin is, "I want to hear more about what comes to mind for you. At this point, however, I'd like to ask several questions to help me build a better understanding of the total picture." This type of request by the therapist will usually result in willing cooperation by parents. The therapist must remember to quickly reflect parents' feelings that arise during this process. Gently, with sensitivity to the parents, the therapist can return to the previous question or ask another. This cycle of question–response–reflect can accumulate significant amounts of meaningful information to the therapist while trust and rapport continue to be built. It should be remembered that this technique is suggested for information gathering, primarily in the early stages of therapy. It is also a method of clarifying the therapist's understanding.

Client Questionnaire

A valuable source of information is the client questionnaire. Properly constructed and administered, it can be less intimidating to parents than face-to-face questioning, thereby supplying information that would otherwise be difficult to obtain. The questionnaire can be completed in the therapist's office, in the waiting room during the child's first session, or at home. Those taken home are often lost and never completed. If the questionnaire is user-friendly, it can be completed along with the other intake and consent forms in the initial meeting with the parents. During early sessions, a completed questionnaire can be a useful reference, and relevant notes can be added by the therapist. By using this instrument, more information can be obtained, the therapist's understanding can be clarified, and the relationship can continue to strengthen.

Parameters of the Therapeutic Relationship

Legal aspects and parameters of therapy are covered in more detail in chapter 4, along with information regarding intake forms, consents, disclosures, and note taking. During the initial contact and the intake session, however, parents may have questions regarding consents and exceptions to confidentiality. Therefore, parameters of therapy are briefly addressed in this section.

Confidentiality is the concept given most attention in most training programs. Therapists must ensure that client information is kept confidential, and parents must be made aware of the exceptions to confidentiality—those situations in which the therapist may be required to disclose client information to third parties. According to Bernard and Goodyear (1998), such exception situations include:

1. there is a risk of suicide,
2. the client is accurately assessed as being dangerous to self or others,
3. a child under the age of 16 is a victim of a crime,
4. the client needs hospitalization for a psychological disorder,
5. disclosure is ordered by a court of law,
6. the therapist is appointed by the court,
7. the client's or therapist's mental health is questioned in a civil (legal) action,
8. the client initiates a lawsuit against the therapist, and
9. the client expresses his or her intent to commit a crime.

When working with children and families, the therapist has complex confidentiality concerns (Corey, Corey, & Callanan, 1998). Trust in the relationship between the therapist and the parent, child, or any other client is essential for effective therapy. Thus, the child must be able to trust the therapist not to divulge thoughts, feelings, and behaviors exhibited in the playroom, especially as these may be in contrast to what the child has previously learned. However, the therapist is expected to provide feedback to parents, especially if information is specifically requested. Communications between the minor and the counselor are legal rights for the parents and guardians. Information that will or will not be shared with parents or guardians must be discussed at the beginning of therapy with both the child or adolescent and the parent (Corey, Corey, & Callanan, 1998).

According to the ethical code of the American Counseling Association (1995), the therapist realizes that family members are typically important in the client's (child's) life. Thus, the therapist strives to enlist the understanding and involvement of other family members. When alternatives to absolute confidentiality are necessary, and when developmentally appropriate, the therapist should strive to obtain informed consent from the child, that is, inform the child what is to be disclosed to the parent. Hopefully, the child can be encouraged to agree with and participate in necessary disclosures.

To protect the process of building rapport and trust, therapist responses to parents' questions may need to emphasize the professional, ethical, and legal requirements that are essentially outside of the therapist's discretion. For example, if the parents request more information regarding exceptions to confidentiality, the therapist might say, "I'm legally required to have your written consent to provide therapy for you and your child. I'm also required to call medical or law enforcement personnel if I have reason to believe the client is suicidal or homicidal. Everyone is required to report suspected sexual or physical abuse of a child. These requirements have come about to protect children." Following comments like these, the therapist should inquire about the parents' feelings and reactions. Reflecting those feelings and communicating continued acceptance of the parents is also recommended. Responses to parents' questions regarding these parameters and requirements are best kept short and simple; some therapists have the tendency to over-explain, and give parents more information than desired. As this is early in the trust-building process, it is likely that the parents may feel somewhat awkward, nervous, and inadequate in the face of lengthy explanations.

Other parameters, such as length of sessions, compensation, duration of therapy, and the nature of the therapeutic relationship, should be addressed during the intake session. Nevertheless, the therapist must keep in mind the primary goals when building trust and rapport, and always exhibit empathy and sensitivity, while maintaining clear professional boundaries.

Defining the Therapy Goals of the Parents

Parents must be asked about the specific goals and outcomes that they want from therapy—they may not have clear perceptions of what they want. Frequently, the goals are stated in terms of problems or problem behaviors. For example, a parent may say, "Johnny's depressed. We want him to be happy." This is very general information, and does not help the therapist visualize and generate a therapeutic plan. More descriptive clarification of how parents want things to be is crucial for the parents and the therapist. The therapist then might ask, "How would life look if the problem did not exist? If Johnny were never depressed, what *specific* things would be different?" Just gaining clarification of their own goals can inspire parents to implement modifications that make the achievement of those goals more probable. Awareness of the goals, in and of themselves, is therapeutic; however, parents also must understand their own goals. Parents' perceptions of the goals are far more meaningful than the therapist's reality, so both the parents and the therapist obtain clearer and deeper understanding when parents' communications are specific. Such aspects as grades, playing with friends, and interests should be addressed when identifying goals. Once the parents and the therapist understand where the parents want to go, all are much better equipped to develop plans on how to get there.

In addition to respecting the goals of the parents for their child, it is equally important for the therapist to be aware and sensitive to goals that the child may have. Goals of parents and children may differ greatly, and it is the task of the therapist to help both the parents and child to understand, accept, and cooperate in addressing one another's needs. While the therapist cannot ignore the goals and needs of the parent, neither can the therapist ignore the goals and needs of the child. Although this can be a difficult balancing act, it is actually an intrinsic element of the child's experience in the playroom and the parents' experience in regular meetings with the therapist.

Supporting the Efforts of Parents

Enlisting the help of the parents is essential to maximizing the therapeutic results for their children. According to O'Connor (1991), it is virtually impossible to expect parents continually to support a course of treatment from which they are essentially excluded. Parents must be informed regarding the goals of therapy, general nature of the sessions, and treatment progress. Parents are the primary influence over the lives and environments of their children. *With the parents' assistance*, therapy can progress faster as well as have much greater and enduring results. *Without the parents' assistance*, the child may be resistant, be chronically late for appointments, or have frequent no-shows. If the parents have negative attitudes and frequently complain about the child going to therapy, the typical consequence is resistance on the part of the child. It is preferable to have the parents as allies. Parents are the most important, and should be the most positive, in-

fluence in the life of their child; in fact, the child's positive development depends on the parents. Lockwood and Harr (1973) emphasize
that the relationship between a child and a nurturing adult is the most
important factor in facilitating the child's emotional growth. Capturing and maintaining the parents' interest and cooperation is a worth-
while endeavor that the therapist must begin early in the therapy
process. The therapist should recognize, acknowledge, and affirm as
many positive aspects as possible of the parents' skills, efforts, and,
especially, their successes.

Consider Ben, a boy who uses withdrawal to convey his animosity,
resistance, and rebelliousness. When around his parents, Ben's legs
and arms are crossed, his head is down, and he sighs loudly and frequently. Parents' attempts to communicate are ignored and, at times,
Ben stalks off when they are trying to talk with him. It can be challenging for the therapist to make positive remarks about the parenting
skills that have influenced the development of these behaviors. However, with insight and creativity, it is possible to support the parents'
struggles and efforts while clarifying their perceptions of how they
stay in control of the situation rather than give in to utter helplessness. At the same time, the therapist needs to help the parents understand Ben's possible need to feel in control and how he has learned
the skills he uses to cope with his underlying helpless feelings. This
technique can be profoundly influential in improving parents' attitudes and keeping them interested in their child's therapy. In this
situation the therapist told the parent, "I see that your son has learned
to stand up for himself. He shows some degree of respect to you—he
could be very insulting and abusive. Instead, he has learned a more
appropriate method to deal with his anger. You've helped him learn
to stand up for himself without being abusive to others. I suspect that
these are traits you hope he will have."

It is always possible to be positive and encouraging to the parent,
but creativity is sometimes needed. The skill of searching for and lo-
cating more subtle qualities to reinforce should be practiced routinely
by the therapist. Supporting the parents' efforts is a worthy pursuit of
the therapist in capturing parents' interest, building their confidence
as parents, and cultivating beneficial alliances.

☐ Educating the Parent

Parent education and training is vital when working with children in
play therapy. Through education and training, parents learn more about
how and what their child is thinking and feeling (Moustakas, 1997).

Certain levels of involvement will be more comfortable for many parents; it is helpful to remember that the least threatening strategies are usually educative (James, 1997). Along with teaching communication skills, the therapist also must teach more effective and appropriate ways for parents to deal with their child's multitude of characteristics, personalities, and developmental issues. Information should be provided to parents regarding appropriate and typical behaviors for their child. Normal developmental behaviors may seem unusual and frightening to parents, making it challenging for parents to be fully accepting of their child. For example, children will often imitate their parents and other people, even during their first year. Suppose the mother of 2-year-old Megan enjoys scented candles and generally keeps several burning. Consequently, Megan has an avid interest in matches and a demanding desire to light candles. When Megan is resistant to reprimands, her parents are fearful that their child has a developing conduct disorder, and punish her severely to "teach her a lesson" and prevent the possible conduct disorder. In this case, the therapist should teach the parents that Megan's interest in matches and lighting candles most likely is developmentally normal behavior. In addition, there is a need to explain how punishment, rather than understanding discipline, is often the groundwork for childhood conduct disorders. The therapist needs to support the parents in their efforts to divert Megan from unhealthy development while enhancing their understanding of normal childhood development, as well as appropriate modifications to their parenting style in dealing with Megan's learning process.

Children need deep, committed, and unconditional love from their parents. However, when children exhibit undesirable behaviors, parents are challenged to show their unconditional love. If parents understand that certain behaviors, such as crying, can be expected and are not merely expressions of defiance, then they will feel more capable of coping with the behaviors and still remain fully accepting of their children. Chapter 2 delves more fully into developmental stages and issues of children, and typical behaviors are discussed, providing information to help parents fully accept their child's developmental process.

☐ Explaining Play Therapy to Parents

Parents need an understanding of the treatment that their child is to undergo. If the child were to have an operation or take medications, parents would likely make themselves aware of the nature of the treatments. It is the same when children are in therapy. Information about procedures, risks, prognoses, ideal and realistic outcomes, and other aspects of therapy should be provided to the parents.

The expression *play therapy* creates a variety of images in parents' minds. Parents may be repelled by the idea of paying money for their children to play with a stranger in a room filled with toys. Parents must understand the differences between this and what the therapist actually will be doing. According to Moustakas (1997), "when parents understand play therapy and its outcomes, they become enthusiastic" (p. 42).

The therapist should convey to parents that play therapy is a valuable, credible, complex, and professional therapeutic discipline. Play therapy has developed out of the many needs of children and the complex intricacies of childhood. There are several universities with extensive programs for training play therapists. As of the writing of this book, the International Association for Play Therapy is recognized, as well as more than 40 state and regional play therapy organizations. A play therapist can earn the status of Registered Play Therapist or Registered Play Therapist-Supervisor—two processes that involve extensive education, supervised experience, and continuing education. Opportunities to improve and ensure quality and professionalism within this specialization of therapy are available through a professional journal and various newsletters, many play therapy books and journal articles, year-round conferences, workshops, and continuing education training.

Principles of Play Therapy

Young children do not have the verbal skills, the ability to comprehend the multitude of emotions, or the recognition of their own thought processes to use words sufficiently for self-expression. Consequently, traditional *talk therapy* has limited effectiveness when used as the primary treatment for children. Behaviors, therefore, are the primary means for children to express thoughts and feelings, although children most often do not deliberately choose specific behaviors to match specific meanings or feelings. For example, if a child throws herself on the ground and cries, this is frequently an expression of anger or frustration. The child has not accomplished enough, developmentally, to say, "Mommy, I am really, really mad." Neither will the child say to herself, "I want Mommy to know that I'm mad, so I'll show her this way." The behaviors are natural, spontaneous expressions of the inner workings of the child.

Play is the natural language of children (Axline, 1969; Landreth, 1991). As a consequence, play contains the vast majority of all children's experiencing. Through play, children act out what is happening in their lives, what has happened in the past, and what they hope will happen in the future. The role of the play therapist is to help children and parents understand what the child is experiencing.

The concept of play therapy itself is rather complex and can be challenging to explain to parents. According to Virginia Axline (1969), the therapist must develop a warm and caring relationship with the child and accept that child fully. The therapist uses reflection to acknowledge the child's feelings, to facilitate child's awareness and acceptance of those feelings, and to help the child understand the behavioral expressions of those feelings. The therapist maintains deep respect for children's innate ability to make positive changes as they feel safe and ready to do so. Also, limits are set, as necessary, to respect and enhance the boundaries of the therapeutic relationship and the entire therapy process. As expressed by Garry Landreth (1991),

> play therapy is defined as a dynamic interpersonal relationship between a child and a therapist trained in play therapy procedures who provides selected play materials and facilitates the development of a safe relationship for the child to fully express and explore self (feelings, thoughts, experiences, and behaviors) through the child's natural medium of communication, play. (p. 14)

Axline (1969) and Landreth (1991) addressed two very important points. First and foremost is the *relationship*. Within the therapeutic relationship, children are able to deal with physical, cognitive, emotional, social, and spiritual developmental issues. Physically, children can attack the smack 'em bag, overcome with the dart gun, master the jump-rope, or swing the snake until it dies. Cognitively, children can wonder and ponder, pretend and not pretend, explore and discover, or try and decide. Emotionally, children can play out "accumulated feelings of tension, frustration, insecurity, aggression, fear, bewilderment and confusion" (Axline, 1969, p. 16). Socially, children can play out family conflicts, stand up to the playground bully, or practice more effective ways to make and keep friends. Spiritually, children can explore the who and what of self in the context of the immediate and the more global environments. Through complete acceptance of the child by the therapist, relationships are developed that allow the child to fully reveal themselves because self-confidence is increased and the frontiers of their personality expressions are extended. Healing is the result of this complex interchange between the therapist and child. Like adults, emotional healing takes place through expression of thoughts and feelings; self-control and the ability to deal with those thoughts and feelings are heightened through expression in a therapeutic relationship. Play therapy allows children to fully express themselves by getting feelings out in the open, confronting them, and learning to control them or abandon them (Axline, 1969). The children are then freed to realize the power within themselves to move toward becoming all of whoever they can be (Axline, 1969; James, 1997).

A second point made by Axline (1969) and Landreth (1991) is the identification of play as the *communication of children*. Young children have not developed a deep understanding of feelings, thoughts, and the world. Children are continually encountering and experiencing things that are completely new without having developed the abstract and symbolic thinking necessary to verbally communicate to others what is being experienced. Words are actually symbols used to describe thoughts, feelings, actions, objects, and events. Children are very connected to the here and now and are only conscious of the noticeable, concrete things around them. Symbols are abstract. Children cannot see, touch, feel, smell, taste, or hear abstract symbols, and therefore, communication must take the form of concrete behaviors, play being the most natural behavior for children. Play becomes the language of children; toys become the words. Children use play to communicate, while adults use verbalization. Play is the natural medium of self-expression for children (Axline, 1969; Landreth, 1991).

This is not to say that all children are unable to express themselves verbally. However, to restrict children to verbalizations will significantly limit their communications. Children may not have confidence in their speech skills and may get insecure or frustrated when unable to verbalize effectively. Most adults have witnessed a child who is trying very hard to think of an appropriate word or pronunciation that will help the adult understand what the child is trying to express. The child becomes more and more frustrated and upset at being unable to make the adult understand. This can have a negative effect upon the child's self-confidence as well as continued motivation and desire to verbalize. If the adult also gets frustrated, the negative effects on the child can multiply. Parents, teachers, and even therapists frequently forget and overlook that children cannot be treated like adults. Adults often have expectations of children that are not realistic, simply due to their developmental nature.

Children have a very phenomenological orientation from which the world is viewed, only able to see their own, subjective reality. For example, a child may say, "I don't have any friends." However, the therapist has been told by Mom that the child has many friends, and, in fact, recently had a birthday party with 20 friends attending. The therapist must attempt to view the world from the child's frame of reference and experience the world of the child. It is common for Mom to say, "You have lots of friends," and not help the child process the feelings of loneliness or rejection. The therapist must explain to the parents that this *phenomenological perception* that the child experiences is an important key to the therapy process.

To help their child and to maximize positive results of therapy, parents should realize that there will be assignments and exercises for them to do. As recommended by the therapist, some of this homework will be directly with the child. Some will focus more on the environment of the child, and may appear somewhat indirect. At this point, parents should begin to accept the idea that they will be active and integral assets in the therapy process and in the welfare of their children. (More specific homework suggestions are given in later chapters.)

☐ Explaining Play Therapy to Children

The relationship between child and therapist is an integral part of the therapy process. This begins prior to the first contact in the reception area. Before the child ever comes to the first session, he or she is developing an individual impression of the therapist and what therapy is all about, relative to what the parents express. Parents need to take care when describing therapy to the child.

Parents frequently use words such as "bad," "sick," and "problem" that can increase the child's anxiety and apprehension about therapy. Parents should avoid describing therapy in ways that imply "fixing problems" or making the child "a better person." It is a good idea for parents to even resist using the word therapy. An appropriate way for parents to describe the sessions and the therapist to children is, "This is a time for you to play in a room with lots of toys and things you like to do, with someone who really cares a lot about you." If some parents need to describe more to their child, they should focus the description on details of the play. For example, "You'll be able to paint, and draw, and play with lots of toys."

Therapists should request parents not to say things to the child like, "You're going to someone who is going to help fix your problems," or "Be sure to talk about these bad feelings you've been having." This begins the process with very negative inferences. Children may believe they are inadequate and the parents want them to be different from who they are. Also, children may feel pressured to perform, as if on stage, and consequently may develop stage fright. Under such circumstances, it would be difficult for children not to be reluctant and resistant about therapy.

Although it is preferred that parents resist describing therapy to their child, especially prior to the first session, the parents should be confident that the therapist will provide appropriate information for the child as necessary. Parents should be taught some reflecting skills in the intake session so they can reflect the child's initial feelings and thoughts when being told about the upcoming therapy. The therapist's recommendation to parents should be to avoid coloring the child's perception of therapy. Ideally, it is best if the child is allowed to develop their own impressions of the therapist and what therapy is all about from actual experiences in the playroom.

The play therapist may actually conduct brief, age-appropriate intake sessions with the child before going into the playroom for the first session. For example, after introducing herself to Kevin, age 6, Miss Jensen states that they are going to stop in her office to talk about what they are going to do before going to the playroom. Ms. Jensen tells Kevin that she has a playroom where a lot of kids come to play. She also tells Kevin a little about her credentials by saying that she has gone to school for a long time and has taken big tests so she can be with children like Kevin, and that she has spent a lot of time with children like him. She then checks with Kevin as to his understanding of why he is coming to her office. When Kevin says, "I don't know," she says that his parents are concerned about him because he seems to have a hard time finishing his schoolwork and that he seems to be sad a lot of times about not having enough friends. Kevin affirms those concerns with a long face and downcast nod of his head. Ms. Jensen says, "Your parents are bringing you here because sometimes kids play and say many of the things they want to in the playroom and their feelings get better. So you'll be coming here every Tuesday at 3:30, and we'll be in the playroom for 45 minutes each time. Also, this playroom time is just for you and me, so I won't tell anyone what you say or do unless you want me to. Of course, *you* can tell anyone you want about what you do in the playroom. Sometimes I'll talk with your parents about what's happening at school and at home. I might tell them that you seem sad or happy or excited in the playroom, but I won't tell them the exact things you say and do. Now, if someone is hurting you badly or you are hurting someone else, then I have to tell someone about that because you and other people are not for hurting. So that's one time that I'll tell someone else what's happening. Do you have any questions? Okay, it's time to go to the playroom."

The therapist should refrain from pressuring the child to self-disclose. It is important for the parents and therapist to follow the lead of the child. According to Bromfield (1992), "the safety, understanding, warmth, and containment of therapy are what foster trust and ultimately seduce the child patient" (p. 41). By reflecting to children what they are doing, what they are thinking, and especially what they are feeling, the therapist and parents can allow the children to lead. One of the goals of play therapy is for the children to develop trust in themselves and to realize that confidence in their own being, thinking, and doing is acceptable.

☐ Summary

A trusting and accepting relationship between the therapist and the parents is critical to effective collaboration in the child's therapy process. One of the essential goals of the first session is to have a second session. Unless there is a respectful, accepting, and caring relationship with the therapist, parents are likely to withdraw from the play therapy process, and take their child with them. Within this chapter are techniques and strategies to build a therapeutic relationship with the parents that simultaneously help to link them to the play therapy process involving their child.

The therapist must appreciate parents for trying their best to juggle numerous balls including work, managing a household, extended family, taking care of themselves, and most importantly, being a good parent. Most parents who seek therapy already perceive themselves in a state of crisis, they are very discouraged, and they see little hope in their future. It is a very vulnerable person who will come and ask a mental health professional for help. For some parents, this is very scary, and maybe humiliating, and requires tremendous courage. Parents need to be encouraged. But first, parents need to be accepted and validated—as a person, then, as a parent.

The initial meeting with the parent is not the time for the therapist to give a lot of advice. Similar to trying to enter the child's world, and see through the child's eyes, the therapist must seek to have a deep understanding for the parent's phenomenological perspective. As we try to teach parents to be careful with their expectations of their child, the therapist must take care with expectations and assumptions about parents. Two of the essential skills that parents need are listening and encouragement. These are just as necessary for the therapist to demonstrate, in building a successful relationship with the parent. If the parents perceive that a caring, supportive relationship with the therapist exists, they will feel more involved in the therapy process, and be more motivated toward achieving the goals of therapy.

Initial contact with parents is typically via a telephone conversation.

Making effective contact with parents, at this point, is also critical in order to set up the first appointment. There are also ways to obtain information, during initial contact and in the intake session, while building a relationship with the parents. Reflecting, clarifying, and using the parent's language are among the rapport building techniques for the therapist at the onset and throughout the course of the relationship. It is not helpful if the intake session resembles an interrogation.

Subsequent to establishing an effective connection with the parent, the therapist can assess whether it is necessary to make a referral. However, even in the event that the therapist does not provide services for a particular parent, the therapist is representing the profession and also helping the parent obtain appropriate and necessary services. If the parent perceives an unpleasant contact with the therapist, it is likely that the parent will make no further effort. Consequently, the child loses.

Early in the relationship with parents, the therapist is also obligated to communicate parameters of the therapeutic relationship and the process of therapy to the parent. Parents should understand that the therapist-parent relationship and the therapist-child relationship are professional in nature and structure, yet deep, personal, and caring. There are numerous parameters that identify, define, and protect this relationship. The parent's initial goals for therapy must also be clarified. The therapist can build tremendous rapport, as well as gain deep understanding, as parents clarify what they hope to see different due to the play therapy process.

Frequently the therapist is faced with explaining play therapy to parents. It takes a great deal of courage and hard work on the part of the child to develop, change, grow up, and turn out to be who they want or need to be. Play is the most natural behavior of children and the primary mode of self-expression. Through play, children will *act out* what is presently being experienced, what has happened in the past, or what is hoped for or anticipated in regard to the future. It is the therapist's job to facilitate deeper insight and understanding of the play, and thereby help the child understand more thoroughly what is being experienced. The therapist must also communicate to the parents an understanding of the dynamics of the child's functioning, while preserving, or attempting to preserve, the confidentiality of the therapy sessions. As warranted, the therapist will give parents suggestions and assignments that will complement children's progress in therapy sessions and facilitate a carryover of the progress to the home and community. Parents need to know what the therapist will be doing, the details of the play therapy treatment process, and what to hope for and expect as an outcome. More concisely, the therapist can explain to parents that play therapy includes:

1. using play and toys to allow children to express themselves within their natural medium of communication;
2. building rapport and an accepting and therapeutic relationship with children;
3. recognizing and respecting the developmental positions of children;
4. recognizing and acknowledging the actions, thoughts, and feelings of children to help them achieve a better understanding of their behaviors;
5. setting limits that promote respect for boundaries within the therapeutic relationship as well as other relationships; and
6. using the therapeutic relationship to help children have more self-confidence, self-control, and respect for self and others.

The therapist should also discuss parents' intentions regarding explaining play therapy to the child. It is not helpful if parents take a judgmental, critical, and authoritarian approach in describing elements about therapy. Parents should avoid expressing that they perceive the child as the problem, or that play therapy is going to fix the child's problems. Parents' communications to the child can have a profound impact on the establishment of the child-therapist relationship.

Among other essential elements related to initial contact include parent education and teaching basic reflecting techniques. Reflecting the messages of parents, especially their feelings, has incredible power. Parents feel understood, cared about, and empowered, and through this process, trust develops. Reflecting parents' feelings also models a way for parents to communicate effectively with the child. When parents learn to reflect feelings and other verbal and nonverbal messages of their children, the children learn that they are valued, are important enough for their parents to try to understand them. Hence, the children learn to better understand themselves, and that what they are experiencing is okay and normal. Parents also learn more about their child, an understanding that often increases their enjoyment of their child. For both parents and child, this awareness leads naturally to increased self-esteem, more self-confidence, and, eventually, greater self-control. All in all, the ultimate aftermath is improved parent-child relationships.

2
CHAPTER

Developmental Issues

Although typical images of parenting include teaching, guiding, protecting, and providing, the most significant ability that parents can possess is that of *acceptance*. This acceptance begins during infancy, if not long before. For some parents, it comes very naturally; for others, although it is the most important skill, it may be the most difficult to master.

Frequently, parents may reject their child prior to birth. It is difficult for some parents, especially those who did not want or plan for children, to have a positive attitude toward taking on the enormous obligation and responsibility of parenting. Even during pregnancy, many sacrifices must be made. Any change is inherently stressful, and resistance to change is common. Modifications of the mother's nutritional habits, smoking, drinking, legal and illicit drug use, exercise, or sexual practices may cause tension, discord, or negativism. Financial stress due to increased medical bills and baby supplies can have a negative impact on parenting attitudes. Parenting is possibly the most challenging and stressful responsibility that anyone can take on. Hence, parents deserve and need considerable support in developing positive parenting attitudes and skills, so that they can enjoy and appreciate their children.

As children develop (e. g., turn over, crawl, pull themselves up, take their first step, walk, etc.) and exhibit the numerous other skills characteristic of childhood learning, it is common for the parents' acceptance to diminish while expectations soar. The parents' attention becomes deflected away from what the child is currently experiencing, and their *expectations* often reach heights that are well beyond reasonable levels of development for the child. These expectations inherently interfere with acceptance and focus attention on how parents want the child to be, as opposed to how the child actually is.

Attachment between the baby and the parents is important. Sears and Sears (1993) said, "Early closeness allows the natural attachment-promoting behaviors of a baby and the intuitive, biological caregiving of a mother to unfold" (p. 4). Brazelton and Cramer (1990) stress that babies have remarkable capacities for attention and interactive behavior when held and cared for by an adult.

It cannot be stressed enough how vital it is for children to feel wanted by their parents, enjoyed by their parents, and important to their parents. According to Rogers (1951), children develop positive self-regard through their perception of positive regard from others. Parents must demonstrate unconditional acceptance and positive regard for their children *in ways that the children understand.* Children must be convinced that they are valued, significant, loved, and irreplaceable. The best method parents can use to show acceptance of children is verbal reflection of what the children seem to be experiencing. As mentioned before, reflecting involves being nonjudgmental and acknowledging of what the children are feeling, doing, or communicating. A natural reaction is that children will *feel important* because parents are watching, listening, and trying to understand. Without this sense that they are significant and valuable to their parents, children struggle to develop positive self-regard. Although it becomes easier and more natural for parents with practice, the skill of reflecting requires effort and a desire to see the world through the eyes of another—in this case, the world of the child.

Parents should resist disciplining children for typical behaviors that are consistent with certain developmental positions. Frequently, parents observe undesirable behaviors in children and feel the need to correct or deter such activities. However, if the behaviors are common and expected expressions of what the child is experiencing, then disciplinary or corrective responses from parents may not be appropriate. Parents frequently punish (as opposed to discipline) a child for displaying undesirable behaviors because it is more convenient, comfortable, or face-saving than acknowledging the child's developmental exploratory, discovery, and reality-testing needs. It must be remembered that *discipline is for the children, not for the adults.* The rationale for discipline is to assist children to develop self-control, responsibility, self-respect, and respect for others. Initially, discipline may require slightly more effort than a particular parent's style of punishment. Discipline, in its truest sense, is a form of teaching, and certainly requires more effort by the parent. Nevertheless, the benefits are far greater and longer-lasting. However, as children become more responsible for their own behavior and related consequences, they learn to make more choices that are appropriate in the eyes of their parents. Thus, less effort is required on the part of parents, at least, effort devoted to the discipline of children. Additionally, children are more likely to develop positive self-regard, increased inner-directedness, and greater self-control.

Children are consistently in the midst of change. It is common for children and parents alike to struggle with these different experiences. It is not easy for children—constantly learning, changing, experiencing the unknown, and striving to please their parents. According to Weiss (1979):

> The best way to insure your ability to enjoy your child is to keep in step with his [or her] developmental needs. When you fight his [or her] needs, you damage your child and frustrate yourself. But when you take the trouble to be aware of the changing needs of your child, you work with him instead of against him [or her]. (p. 168)

At the same time, undesirable behaviors by children do not signify that parents are failing in their parenting responsibilities; rather, they may be limited in their knowledge of the developmental motivations behind the child's behaviors.

A better understanding of the world of children can increase and maintain parents' self-respect and self-confidence so that they can accept their children as they are and continue to love, cherish, and respect them through their developmental stages. The general developmental stages are outlined below according to common feelings, motivations, and behaviors of children at different points in their lives.

An individual's development is a process that is frequently portrayed in stages. This process begins before birth and continues throughout adulthood and old age. It involves the entire lifespan and becomes very complex. Any development that takes place is built upon all previous development—it spirals outward, touching larger and larger portions of the universe. Therefore, all experiences of children, even during early infancy, must be viewed as extremely important and influential to the composition of their personalities (Winnicott, 1965).

☐ Developmental Stages

General developmental age ranges are discussed in this section. Although these are presented as stages, development is more accurately conceptualized as a continuum or process. Each child experiences life differently and views his or her own experiences differently from all other children. Therefore, these stages are not concrete and are not without exceptions—it is important to recognize the innate flexibility of human development. It is also possible for overlapping and out-of-sequence development to occur. In his book *Childhood and Society*, Erik Erikson (1963) identified psychosocial aspects of development that are built upon Freud's theory of personality development. In order for healthy development to occur, the individual must work through a developmental task at each stage and establish an equilibrium between oneself and the social world. The stages are identified or labeled by these developmental tasks.

Birth to One Year

During Erikson's (1963) first developmental stage of *trust versus mistrust* (birth to one year), parents must provide for a child's basic emotional and physical needs. In babies, social trust is first demonstrated in the ease of feeding, depth of sleep, and relaxation of the bowels. Babies are dependent upon their parents, and parents must continue to be accepting, especially in face of the tremendous responsibilities and challenges. Babies who are loved, cuddled, and shown affection develop a sense of security and a sense of being wanted. They learn to trust themselves and others. As Erikson (1964) wrote:

> Defenseless as babies are, they have mothers at their command, families to protect the mothers, societies to support the structure of families, and traditions to give a cultural continuity to systems of tending and training. All of this, however, is necessary for the human infant to evolve humanly, for his environment must provide that outer wholeness and continuity which, like a second womb, permits the child to develop his separate capacities in distinct steps. (p. 114)

The sensitivity, predictability, and trustworthiness of the care given to an infant is imperative. If the care is inconsistent, haphazard, or rejecting, the child will learn to view the world with suspicion and fear. An attitude of mistrust toward the world and especially of interpersonal relationships develops (Corey, 1991). In this stage, children may either develop a sense of hope or withdraw.

What to Expect

Crying. Parents must remember that crying comes naturally and involuntarily to infants. It is their only means of verbal communication. Babies cry for various reasons, including hunger, boredom, pain, and illness. The effect that crying has on parents is remarkable. A crying baby triggers increases in parents' heart rate and blood pressure. If a baby continues to cry, despite parents' efforts at comforting, parents typically begin to feel helpless, distraught, and even angry toward the baby. Parents may then experience guilt due to the feelings of anger (Vander Zanden, 1996).

The seemingly small and insignificant activity of crying can provoke a reaction of resentment by parents. It is necessary for parents to focus on what the baby is experiencing, more than what the parents are feeling, which can be very difficult in the presence of a crying baby. However, this redirection of focus will lead to increased acceptance of the child and, ultimately, to enhanced development of the child (Vander Zanden, 1996).

Babies quickly realize that crying elicits caregiving activities by the parents. Infants have a considerable effect on those around them. They are influenced by their parents, but also the parents are influenced by them. Because infants are essentially helpless and dependent, parents must remember that crying is not an expression of rejection or an attack on their parental abilities. More importantly, again, parents must be accepting of their baby, attempt to understand what the baby is experiencing and respond to the baby's cry (Sears and Sears, 1993). This is a wonderful time for parents to begin building their listening and reflection skills, which will result in an increased recognition of different cries for different needs and the baby's increased sense of being understood and accepted (Vander Zanden, 1996).

Temperament.   A basic characteristic of babies, such as temperament, can evoke different types of behaviors from parents (Vander Zanden, 1996). Different levels of acceptance also are needed. Kagan (1994) noted, "A temperamental category refers to a quality that (1) varies among individuals, (2) is moderately stable over time and situation, (3) is under some genetic influence, and (4) appears early in life" (p. 42). Thomas and Chess (1977) describe temperament as being one's style of behavior, as compared to one's motivation, ability, or content of behavior. Temperment is the basic disposition that is inherent and relatively consistent in all people, including babies. It underlies and modulates much of their behavior. Even during the first few weeks of life, a baby can show distinct individuality in temperaments that are independent of the parents' handling and personality styles. However, as development proceeds, the nature and expression of temperament is influenced by environmental factors. Three different temperaments are identified: approximately 10% of all infants are "difficult babies," about 15% are "slow-to-warm-up babies," and about 40% of all infants are "easy babies." The other 35% display a combination of traits, and do not fall clearly into these groups.

Behaviors of difficult babies include frequent and loud periods of crying, tantrums, irregular sleep patterns, slow acceptance of new foods, negative withdrawal from new situations and new people, intense negative mood expressions, and slow adaptability to change. Slow-to-warm-up babies tend to show negative responses of mild intensity to new situations; however, they frequently develop a quiet, positive interest and involvement, if given the opportunity to repeat the new experiences. Their reactions have mild intensity, whether positive or negative. The easy babies tend to have cheerful dispositions, adapt quickly to new foods, develop regular sleeping and feeding schedules, smile at strangers, and readily accept new routines (Thomas, Chess, & Birch, 1968). Regardless of temperament, the relationship between a parent and a baby is complex and demanding. There are many ways in which the establishment of a strong and secure parent-child attachment can be jeopardized. Parents have to be educated, committed, and courageous, and they need considerable attention, validation, and support for themselves.

Love. Understanding the origins and evolution of affectionate behavior in children can be crucial. The lack of capacity to love and be affectionate tends to cultivate antisocial characteristics. According to Winnicott (1965), the meaning of love to infants proceeds through the following stages:

1. existing, breathing, being alive, and being loved;
2. appetite—no concern, only the need for satisfaction;
3. affectionate contact with parents;
4. integration of instinctual experiences with affectionate contact—giving becomes related to taking;
5. staking claims on parents and forcing them to make up for inevitable deprivations for which they are responsible; and
6. caring for parents, as their parents cared for them—a preview of the developing attitude of responsibility.

Two to Three Years

In this second stage, *autonomy versus shame and doubt,* children need to explore, experiment, make mistakes, and test limits. They develop a sense of self-reliance or a sense of self-doubt. If parents are encouraging, patient, and accepting, a child will develop willpower, a sense of independence, and an ability to rely on oneself. If parents are over-protective, foster dependency, and do not allow much freedom, then a child may develop compulsivity, self-doubt, and a sense of shame (Vander Zanden, 1996). Self-confidence and self-control are characteristic of children who succeed in doing things for themselves; those who continually fail, get punished and receive negative labels (e.g., bad, inadequate, sloppy) and learn to feel shame and self-doubt. Shaming by parents not only leads to poor self-esteem in a child, but also to secret determination to get away with things and, possibly, to defiant shamelessness (Erikson, 1963).

What to Expect

Biting.   Many toddlers will bite adults or other children for a variety of reasons. They may be angry, copying other children who bite, testing limits, or teething. On the other hand, when adults overreact, toddlers may quickly learn that biting is a way to gain attention.

The Santa Cruz Toddler Care Center (Van der Zande, 1993) suggests the following ways to help toddlers stop biting:

1. When possible, stop children before they have a chance to bite other children. For example, if two children are angry with each other and one child has a tendency to bite, the parent can firmly say, "You are really angry, but Marcy is not for biting."
2. Give children things that are okay to bite—including certain toys, teething rings, and food.
3. Talk to children about biting. For example: "Biting feels really good to your teeth, but it hurts other people. People are not for hurting."
4. Set a limit for biting and enforce it quickly, but calmly. A time-out is an appropriate limit for biting. Be understanding of the child's feelings, but firm in stating the limit. "I know you are really frustrated, but Billy is not for biting. If you choose to bite Billy, you choose to have a time-out." Be consistent and carry through if time-out is chosen.
5. Never, never bite children back in an effort to "teach them how biting feels." This is confusing to children. Also, it may escalate the aggression because it is modeled by the adults.

Tantrums.   Many parents will experience their child having tantrums. Tantrums can be frustrating, embarrassing, and exhausting for both the parents and child. Parents may see their child as deliberately "throwing fits" to cause a power struggle. However, tantrums may be the result of a child feeling out of control because of anger, frustration, or exhaustion. It is helpful to remind parents that tantrums are usually a result of a child's underlying emotions, and, although it may be difficult, tantrums should not be taken as personal attacks.

Several interventions are suggested for tantrums:

1. Children having tantrums need to have their feelings acknowledged. In a calm, neutral voice, the parent should try to show understanding and acceptance of the feelings (Reynolds, 1990; Van der Zande, 1993).

2. If tantrums occur in a safe place such as home, the parent can say, "I know you're very angry that you can't go to Eric's house. When you have calmed down, we'll talk about it. I'll be in the kitchen waiting for you." If they occur in a public place, such as a restaurant or department store, the parent can reflect the child's feelings and then stand or sit by the child quietly until the child has calmed down. Screaming back at the child will not help the child to calm down.

3. Never, never change limits if they are the cause of child's tantrums (Van der Zande, 1993). For example, if Janet is angry and throws a tantrum because she cannot go to a friend's house, do not allow Janet to go in order to stop the tantrum. If parents rescind the limits because of tantrums, the child will learn to manipulate the parents. This can be very detrimental to maintaining effective relationships between parents and children. Encourage parents to "hang tough."

Toilet Training.   The most important rule to remember about toilet training is to wait until children are ready. Parents may compare their child to other children who have been toilet trained at an earlier age, or they may be tired of changing diapers. Encourage parents to be patient and wait for their child to let them know when the time is right (Green, 1980; Van der Zande, 1993).

Short Attention Span.   Two-year-olds and three-year-olds are just beginning to develop their attention spans, so keep in mind that most children will have a very short attention span at these ages. Parents will find it more beneficial to give the child short, simple directions. For example, "Please pick up your shoes and set them by the door." Routine and structure is helpful, but should be limited to important issues (Clarke, 1978).

Autonomy.   Toddlers are taking the first steps toward independence. Often, parents will hear their toddler say, "I can do it myself" or "Let me do that." Children's efforts toward independence need to be respected and valued. This will not always be easy for parents as toddlers often are very slow when trying something new or they create a mess in the process of doing things by themselves. However, when parents do things for a child that can be done alone (however slowly or incompletely), the child may learn to be "helpless." At the very least, the child most likely will feel inadequate, incapable, weak, or unable to satisfy one's parents. Also, children only learn by doing, so parents need to be supportive of their child's efforts. It can be especially difficult for parents to let their child try certain tasks when certain schedules need to be maintained. A compromise is to let a child do it by himself or herself later when the schedule allows for more flexibility (Weiss, 1979). For example, three-year-old Peter may want to put on his shoes by himself, but Peter's mother knows they need to leave in five minutes for preschool. She can offer to help right now and then tell Peter, "You can do it by yourself this afternoon when we get home."

Imaginary Friends.   Children may develop imaginary friends around three or four years of age. Imaginary friends should be respected and welcomed by parents because they signify a child's developing imagination and are a sign of complex thinking at this age (Brazelton, 1995). In the third year, as imagination develops, the child is not yet fully capable of distinguishing between reality and wishful thinking. Imaginary friends provide a way to start bridging the gap between concrete thinking and abstract thinking.

Emotionally, imaginary friends give children a safe way to find out who they want to be and who they can be in relation to real-life friends. With imaginary friends, developing children can feel in control as they explore the complexities of building relationships. Brazelton (1995) points out that through imaginary friends, a child "can identify with children who are overwhelming to him. He can safely become another child. He can also identify with each of his parents in the safe guise of these imaginary friends. He can try out being a male or a female. He can try out all sides of his personality. This is one of the ways a four- or five-year-old gradually finds his identity" (pp. 324–325).

Imaginary friends are only a concern if children replace all social interactions with pretend friends. As long as children are developing socially with other children, then imaginary friends can be beneficial. Parents often will need reassurance about imaginary friends; they should be respectful of the pretend friends, as well as of their child. Children who create imaginary friends should never be teased, humiliated, or ridiculed in any way. Parents may tire of including the friends in daily activities, such as setting an extra plate at dinner, but they should be reassured that the imaginary friends stage will pass. In the meantime, imaginary friends can be an important phase of development for children.

Four to Five Years

During Erikson's (1963) third stage, *initiative versus guilt*, children explore beyond themselves. They are learning about how the world works, and are discovering how they can affect it (Craig, 1983). Parents need to allow their child freedom to select personally meaningful activities and, thereby, help develop a sense of initiative, self-confidence, and positive self-awareness. Otherwise, if parents curtail their child's freedom to make decisions for oneself, the child may become inhibited and develop a sense of guilt about taking any initiative. Too often, these children become passive recipients of others' decisions (Corey, 1991).

What to Expect

Need to Feel Competent.   Children need to feel competent at activities and skills at this age. The more capable they feel, the more self-confidence they will experience. Parents should encourage their child to participate in a variety of activities and be patient as new skills are mastered.

Comparing Self to Others.   Children at this age begin to compare themselves to their peers. Sometimes this will be a positive experience, as for five-year-old Linda: "I'm the only one who knew all of the words to the song today." Four-year-old Kimberly expressed a more negative experience: "Carol always runs faster than I do." When children feel "less than" their peers, parents should show respect for and understanding of the feelings, and should stress some strengths. For example, "Yes, Carol does run fast. Carol and her mother even spend time running together, so Carol gets a lot of practice. However, you're very good at soccer. The coach has you play a lot."

Teasing.   Teasing young children is often a sign of endearment and affection by adults. However, children at this age often find teasing humiliating and intolerable. They are trying to build their self-confidence and independence, and teasing undermines their self-esteem. It will be most helpful to their child if parents can eliminate teasing and find more appropriate ways to give affection.

Masturbation. Children may begin to explore their bodies any-where from two years to five years of age. According to Brazelton (1995), parents should be reassured that masturbation is normal be-havior for children, and they should not show disapproval of the be-havior or try to restrict it. If masturbation is engaged in frequently, parents need to look for the root cause of the behavior. Frequent masturbation may be the result of tension or over-stimulation; also, it is the way some children comfort themselves, similar to sucking a thumb or holding a special blanket. If parents notice any of these underlying reasons, they should intervene in an understanding and non-punitive manner. For example, tense children may benefit from parents comforting or reassuring them. Over-stimulated children may require quiet time alone or with an adult. Children who desire to comfort themselves can be offered alternative ways to do so. In any case, children should *not* be shamed, reprimanded, or punished for masturbating. Parents can set up boundaries and limits regarding the masturbation, such as allowing children to reserve the behavior for when they are in a private place. If masturbation continues to be excessively frequent or of concern to a parent, evaluation by a medi-cal doctor or mental health professional may be warranted.

Six to Eleven Years

Industry versus inferiority is Erikson's (1963) fourth stage of psychosocial development. School is a very significant entity for children in this stage. They are maneuvering into and within their first years of school. Nu-merous skills, abilities, and other information are being learned and assimilated at home, in school, and among peers. Involvement with and comparison among peers gains importance. Negative evaluation of oneself as compared to others is particularly damaging during this period (Craig, 1983). By setting and achieving personal goals as well as receiving recognition for their achievements, children realize a sense of industry and competence. Parents need to be attentive, encourag-ing, accepting, and supportive. Without this, children can develop a sense of inferiority and inadequacy (Vander Zanden, 1996).

What to Expect

Extracurricular Activities.   Children at this age begin to develop interests in nonacademic areas such as art, music, and athletics. Mas-tering skills in one or more of the extracurricular areas can help bol-ster the self-esteem and self-confidence of children, which is especially beneficial when they have trouble in academic areas. As much as possible, these activities should be made available to children.

Arguing.   Children will continue to test limits during these years. As children progress both intellectually and academically, they require more explanations and reasons for the rules and values of their parents. When a child argues, parents should empathize and explain the reasons for particular rules or values. Then, assuming the rules or values are well-grounded, parents should remain objective, stand firm, and not back down.

Peer Approval.   As children get older, peer acceptance and approval gain importance. Parents need to respect and understand the need for peer approval. If their child does not have friends, parents can try to get them involved in a social activity that may provide opportunities for friendships to develop. When parents do not like the choice of friends, they should discuss their concerns calmly with their child and try to find ways to negotiate that are acceptable to both parent and child.

Twelve to Eighteen Years

Identity versus role confusion is the developmental task in the fifth stage. This is a period of transition from childhood to adulthood, when children are asking themselves "Who am I?" Children in this age range are concurrently confronted by physiological transformation and role identification. Body characteristics, bodily functions, and hormonal balancing, as well as increased responsibility related to developmental life tasks, present turmoil that often seem insurmountable. Prior to adolescence, children learned to be in a variety of naturally-occurring roles, including those of daughters, brothers, friends, and students. Striving for more and more independence, children in this stage of development must integrate their various roles into one consistent identity in order to stand on their own. Role confusion occurs when children are unable to integrate the values and attitudes, or when there is a major conflict between major roles with opposing value systems (Craig, 1983).

Unfortunately for parents, a child's growth during this stage involves testing limits and breaking dependent ties. Many parents themselves feel rejected, disrespected, and unappreciated. It is easy for parents to lose self-confidence and believe themselves to be parenting failures. They need considerable support and reassurance when their child is in this stage so that they can remain encouraged, anticipatory, and involved in their child's therapy. Often, therapists need to reiterate for the parents that their child has natural, instinctive drives influencing behavior.

Eighteen and Beyond

Erikson's (1963) remaining stages *are intimacy versus intimacy, generativity versus stagnation,* and *integrity versus despair.* During these stages, the individuals have achieved some level of adulthood and are not required to have parental involvement in their therapy. However, the tasks remain very challenging, and positive support can prove invaluable. Parents are strongly recommended to remain involved in the lives of their offspring at any age. The skills of acceptance, reflecting, and encouragement will help parents maintain enjoyable and healthy relationships with their child throughout the lifespan. These skills also foster continued successful development of their child, and model effective behaviors for them as future parents.

☐ The Father's Role in Child Development

Traditionally, and stereotypically, primary responsibilities regarding child-rearing have been assigned to mothers. However, a father's role has a profound impact on the development of his children. For example, Jacobs (1998) states that a father's involvement facilitates cognitive development in boys, while his absence leads to boys' lack of development of analytical reasoning and deterioration in academic achievement and intellectual abilities. A father's encouragement of intellectual performance in girls leads to increased achievement, while a father's rejection is detrimental to achievement. Additionally, when a father is involved, affectionate, and helpfully interactive with his children, positive social interactions between siblings tend to develop.

Unfortunately, fathers are often physically absent due to work, separation, or divorce. Some fathers also become emotionally detached and unavailable. According to Osherson (1995), fathers often have an internal conflict involving the fear of being enveloped by the family, swallowed up, and losing their identity. Fathers also have a greater tendency to gravitate to the periphery of the family system, to feel like a nonessential part of the family, and to be of secondary importance to mothers. This typically results in persistent conflicts between parents, which lead to disruption of the entire family unit. Parents must work together to reduce these unhelpful father feelings. Therapists also must validate the role and efforts of fathers. Just like mothers and children, fathers need acceptance and emotional support.

☐ Summary

Development, by definition, is a process of change, and change cannot occur without some degree of stress. Likewise, developmental issues bring stress and challenges for both children and parents. Recognizing developmental stages and related issues gives parents insight into the motivations and behaviors of their child. Sometimes, parents are unaware that their child's behavior may be more a result of the developmental stage, than simply an inappropriate behavior. By informing and educating parents about developmental milestones as well as feelings, motivations, and behaviors that are common for children at different ages and stages, parents are better equipped to understand their child and respond appropriately. In turn, the child will likely feel validated, accepted, and valued. Expected behaviors related to developmental tasks that the child experiences should not be punished by parents. However, the child should not be "let off the hook" for inappropriate behaviors. Therefore, the therapist should provide parent education regarding the importance of discipline, limits, choices, and consequences—and how these differ from punishment.

Especially during early childhood, the child needs to feel valued, loved and irreplaceable. According to Rogers (1951), the child develops positive self-regard based on his or her perception of positive regard from others, and especially, from caregivers, siblings, teachers, peers, and others who are significant in the child's life. It is also crucial for the child to develop secure attachment to his or her primary caregivers. As stated by Bowlby (1969), without this secure attachment, the child is at risk for a life course of behavior and personality disorders.

Developmental stages, with respective motivations, emotions, and behaviors that children commonly experience, are associated with developmental tasks, which, upon their successful completion, facilitate the child's adaptive development and progress through adolescence and adulthood. Although the stages are sometimes associated with specific ages of children, a child's development is more appropriately viewed as a process that occurs along a continuum.

Finally, a fathers' role in the child's development is important. The father's role has traditionally been considered to be subordinate to the mother's, as it pertains to child-rearing. However, fathers and mothers have profound influence on the development of their child's personality.

Legal and Ethical Issues of Therapy

Defining the therapeutic relationship involves many legal and professional parameters that are essential to effectively practice therapy. The foremost guideline in providing therapy services is to focus on protecting the welfare of the client. In order to assure that clients receive the best services possible, therapists have a myriad of boundaries that identify, define, and protect the therapeutic relationship. Typically, those boundaries take the form of codes of ethics, which are mandated by licensing bodies. Local, state, and federal laws also mandate certain practices that therapists must follow. There are many consistencies among the various governing bodies such as the American Counseling Association (ACA), American Association of Marriage and Family Therapists (AAMFT), American Psychological Association (APA), and state licensing boards. However, subtle differences and a few contradictions exist among these state licensing boards, professional associations, and other governing bodies. Therapists must familiarize themselves with the laws, codes of ethics, and other sets of rules that govern their licenses, certifications, and registrations.

☐ Legal and Ethical Guidelines

In many states, professional counselors are governed by a state board and the ethical codes and standards of professional conduct are enacted into laws. Hence, a violation of the code of ethics by a therapist also may be a violation of law. Not only is the therapist's license in jeopardy, but the therapist may also face punishment within the criminal justice system. Licensing authorities can hold significant power related to the success and failure of therapists. Additionally, many states require therapists to be licensed, registered, or certified in order to (legally) practice. If someone's license is revoked or sanctioned, it could be against state law for the therapist to continue to practice. Also, there are many legal and ethical issues influencing the play therapist specifically, and parents should be aware of them.

According to Dallas, Texas attorney T. L. Hartsell (1997) these rules, guidelines, and regulations have evolved because of instances that, unfortunately, involved poor levels of care, mistreatment, abuse, and exploitation of clients. He stated that "licensing itself is a response to consumer activism." The licensing board is established to protect the consumer and not the therapist. Clients need to be protected, and these boundaries exist as an effort to ensure ethically appropriate quality care, guidelines, structure, direction, and professionalism.

☐ Protecting the Client and the Therapist

Responsibility of the Therapist

According to Corey, Corey, and Callanan (1998), when the focus of therapy involves other family members or the family system, several issues must be considered by the therapist. For whom and to whom does the mental health professional have primary responsibility and loyalty? Whose interests should the therapist serve? The child? Separate family members as individuals? The parents? The family as a whole? The *AAMFT Code of Ethics* (1991) states that "marriage and family therapists advance the welfare of families and individuals. They respect the rights of those persons seeking their assistance, and make reasonable efforts to ensure that their services are used appropriately" (Section 1.).

Clearly, two issues must be addressed regarding therapy relationships. In every relationship, even those outside of the therapy arena, the therapist has the primary responsibility of protecting the welfare of the clients or other parties. The issue of non-therapy relationships is further addressed with *dual relationships* in the following section. Not that others are more important than the therapist, rather that this also falls into the realm of responsibilities that are charged to all mental health professionals. As stated in the *Code of Ethics and Standards of Practice* of the ACA (1995), "the primary responsibility of counselors is to respect the dignity and to promote the welfare of clients" (Section A.1.a.).

Second, the therapist is responsible for the characteristics of the relationships that he or she has with each and every client. This is not intended to imply that clients should not have any responsibility in maintaining an appropriate relationship. Simply, that the therapist is ultimately accountable for defining the boundaries and maintaining them in an appropriate (professional) manner. The therapist is responsible for protecting both parties, especially in the event that the other person does not have the awareness or capability to exercise his or her relationship responsibilities.

Therapists' Fears

Epstein (1994) stated that a therapist must be able to define and maintain boundaries within the therapist-client relationship, but these boundaries require some degree of permeability. The professional must not become so fearful as to maintain rigid boundaries that prevent adaptability and immediacy to the inherent, unique intricacies presented by human clients. "A therapist who retreats behind an impenetrable barrier will become inaccessible" (p. 17).

T. Hartsell (1997) emphasizes, however, that it is important to recognize the power of the licensing board. There are strong consumer lobby groups that are much more concerned about protecting the client from the therapist than protecting the therapist.

Therapists have fears regarding credentialling authorities and affiliations with professional organizations. An angry client has the power, and the right, to register complaints with these entities, which can result in tremendous injury to the counselor. Malpractice, negligence, or ethical violations need not be proven in many instances for credentialling authorities and professional organizations to take action against a counselor. For example, the *Licensed Professional Counselor Act* of the Texas State Board of Examiners of Professional Counselors (1994) states that:

> If the majority of the board or a three-member committee of board members designated by the board determines from the evidence or information presented to it that a licensed professional counselor by continuation in practice would constitute a continuing and imminent threat to the public welfare, the board or the three-member committee shall temporarily suspend the license of the licensed professional counselor. The license may be suspended under this section without notice or hearing on the complaint, provided institution of proceedings for a hearing before the State Office of Administrative Hearings is initiated

simultaneously with the temporary suspension and provided that a hearing is held as soon as can be accomplished under this chapter and the Administrative Procedure and Texas Register Act (Article 6252-13a, Vernon's Texas Civil Statutes) and its subsequent amendments. (Section 16.A.)

If a complaint is filed against the therapist and a settlement with the board cannot be worked out, the therapist is entitled to an administrative law hearing. According to Hartsell (1997), this means that the therapist can go before an administrative law judge who makes findings of fact and rulings of law. The therapist then goes back to the licensing board and, even if the therapist prevailed before the judge in terms of good findings or findings that the therapist did not violate a specific section, the board can still revoke the therapist's license. In the code of ethics governing the conduct of professional counselors, there are many general provisions open to a broad range of interpretation by the governing board. Also, the governing board has the responsibility of ensuring professionalism among licensed counselors. The repercussions of even a temporary suspension can be extensive. For example, applications for employment, applications for credentialling in other jurisdictions, and applications to become managed care providers can all be adversely influenced.

Therapists also must protect themselves in today's litigious environment. Anyone can sue anyone else for any reason. It is not uncommon for lawsuits to be filed against therapists by parents of children whom the therapist has seen as clients. An avaricious client can file a malpractice suit in an attempt to exploit the therapist for personal gain. Therapists can be sued even though their clinical practices and motivations were innocent, moral, ethical, innocent, and appropriate (Epstein, 1994). Even if found not at fault, a defendant in a lawsuit could incur catastrophic damage. Attorney fees, court costs, license sanctions and revocations, appeals to licensing authorities, loss of clients, damaged reputations, and other similar factors can generate incredible financial, temporal, professional, and emotional liabilities. Although the rules are designed to protect clients, therapists must be able to prove their adherence to the rules. In this litigation-oriented environment, therapists face great risk, as these very powerful legal threats are poised over the therapists' careers and entire lifestyles.

Professional Judgment and Standard of Care

In therapists' attempts to maintain legal and ethical practices (and to protect themselves) they must rely on their professional judgment while always considering the standard of care. According to the *Code of Ethics and Standards of Practice* of the ACA (1995), "counselors take appropriate professional precautions such as informed consent, consultation, supervision, and documentation to ensure that judgment is not impaired and no exploitation occurs" (Section A.6.a.). This concept of professional judgment requires therapists to apply considerable discretion when making decisions. However, by consulting with other professionals and seeking supervision, therapists are able to maximize their therapeutic effectiveness while protecting clients and themselves from potential risk.

Also important for counselors to consider is standard of care. Although concrete rules cannot be found, therapists should never hesitate to consult another professional when facing legal and ethical questions. According to the *Code of Ethics and Standards of Practice of the ACA* (1995), "counselors take reasonable steps to consult with other counselors or related professionals when they have questions regarding their ethical obligations or professional practice" (Section C.2.e.).

The mental health professional is best protected if reasonable effort is made to protect others from harm. Herlihy and Corey (1997) identify safeguards and measures to minimize the risk of harm to clients that include:

1. Establish appropriate boundaries from the outset, and disclose to the client the counselor's policy regarding professional versus business, social, and personal relationships.
2. Involve the client in establishing these boundaries.
3. Discuss with the client, directly and openly, any potential problems that arise.
4. Consult with other professionals to facilitate the maintenance of objectivity and to anticipate unforeseen problems.
5. Work under supervision when any relationship is problematic, or the risk for harm is high.
6. Document interactions with clients and therapeutic efforts in clinical case notes—especially those efforts taken to minimize the risk of harm.
7. Refer the client if necessary.

Hartsell (1997) gives frequent workshops on how therapists can protect themselves from the legal threats in today's litigious mental health providers' environment. He emphasizes the need for therapists to remember legal issues. Therapists cannot be familiar with all of the laws, codes of ethics, and court findings that can be sources of jeopardy, and must protect themselves by taking the necessary steps to practice appropriately, including maintaining thorough and accurate records. Also, if therapists are worried about certain clients or practices, Hartsell cautions them to consult with their attorneys.

☐ Specific Issues of Mental Health Services

Confidentiality

One of the most sacred and beneficial tools of therapy is confidentiality. *Confidentiality* is an ethical guideline used to build trust in the therapeutic relationship. *Breach of confidentiality* is the one of the most frequent issues of malpractice suits and complaints to licensing authorities. According to Corey et al. (1998), confidentiality, privileged communications, and privacy are related concepts among which there are important distinctions. Therapists have a responsibility and duty to protect clients from disclosures of information provided within the therapy relationship. Often, confidentiality is also a legal therapist-client privilege. *Privileged communication* "is a legal concept that protects against forced disclosure in legal proceedings that would break a promise of privacy" (p. 157). *Privacy* is a legal and constitutional right that individuals have to decide what, where, when, how, and whether to share information about oneself with others. The ACA (1995) states that "counselors respect their clients' right to privacy and avoid illegal and unwarranted disclosures of confidential information" (Section B.1.a.).

Exceptions to Confidentiality.   Corey et al. (1998) define *exceptions to confidentiality* and the therapist-client privilege as specific circumstances under which information must be disclosed by the therapist. These exceptions include:

1. The client consents to or authorizes the disclosure.
2. The therapist has a *duty to warn* or protect others.
3. When reporting of certain information, such as child or elder abuse, is required by law.
4. An emergency exists.
5. If a client brings a lawsuit against the therapist, then confidentiality is deemed to have been waived.
6. Disclosure is required in order for the therapist to obtain payment or reimbursement for services rendered.

The above exceptions, 5, 6, and possibly 4, represent circumstances in which the therapist has the right to disclose information in an effort to protect oneself.

According to Bernstein and Hartsell (1998), the primary exception to confidentiality is consent. The first step in deciding whether to disclose records is to ask the parents (or the adult client). Therapists can ask for consent to disclose specific records for specific purposes and to specific people. Parents have the right to grant consent or refuse to give it.

Therapists should exercise *minimal disclosure*. Information that is extraneous, unnecessary, or unrelated to the specific circumstance should be guarded, regardless of what information is requested. The *Code of Ethics and Standards of Practice of the ACA* (1995) states "when circumstances require the disclosure of confidential information, only essential information is revealed. To the extent possible, clients are informed before confidential information is disclosed" (Section B.1.f.).

Confidentiality in Family Therapy.   Parents and children alike are often more likely to self-disclose if they do not have the fear of "everybody finding out." As with adults, it is very important for children to believe that they can trust their therapists and that the therapy sessions will remain confidential. If children fear retaliation or punishment from their parents for what they might say or do in therapy, then they will be unable to freely talk about their feelings.

According to the AAMFT *Code of Ethics* (1991), "marriage and family therapists have unique confidentiality concerns because the client in a therapeutic relationship may be more than one person. Therapists respect and guard confidences of each individual" (Section 2.). However, the ACA (1995) states that "in family counseling, information about one family member cannot be disclosed to another member without permission. Counselors protect the privacy rights of each family member" (Section B.2.b.). Also, "when counseling minors or persons unable to give voluntary informed consent, counselors act in these clients' best interests" (Section A.3.c).

Corey et al. (1998) indicate that family members that agree to become involved in family therapy can typically be expected to put the goals of therapy before their own personal goals, and they may have to relinquish some degree of confidentiality. Therapists should emphasize the need to protect the confidentiality of children when consulting with parents. Therapeutic benefits are dependent upon the therapeutic relationship that, in turn, is dependent upon trust.

Confidentiality of the Child Client.   The issue of confidentiality is based upon clients' expectations that issues discussed in the deeply personal and (professionally) intimate relationship of therapy will be kept private. Confidentiality is necessary in order to encourage child and adult clients to develop the needed trust for full disclosure and other therapeutic work (Corey et al., 1998).

Bernstein and Hartsell (1998) state that either parent usually has the legal right to access their child's mental health records. However, exceptions to this legal right may come about as a result of court orders. When a serious conflict exists (e.g., one parent demands access to the child's records and the other parent demands confidentiality and privacy), the therapist should seek a court order. A judge's ruling will decide whether or not information is to be shared or held confidential. According to Arthur and Swanson (1993), parents and guardians have the legal right to any communications between the therapist and their minor child. However, there are exceptions. If minors can legally seek or refuse treatment on their own accord, then they may be considered competent to choose which disclosures, if any, to share with others. Some judges have granted adolescents the same confidentiality rights as adults (Corey et al., 1998).

The following example, provided by Hartsell (1997), illustrates how a court can order an exception to parents' rights to their child's mental health records. After a divorce, custody of the child was split between the mother and father, with primary possession (of custody) given to the mother. The court ordered a specific therapist to continue to provide therapy as the exclusive therapist of the child. The child indicated to the therapist that his father was not mentally stable and was collecting social security disability, not working, and hanging outside the therapy office pressuring the child about the content of therapy. The child's biggest problem was dealing with the father's strange behavior. One day, the father demanded to see the therapist's session notes. The therapist refused to give the father the notes and documented the refusal in reference to her concern about what the father might to do the child if he found out what the child was saying in therapy. The father had his lawyer send letters to the therapist requesting the notes, and filed a complaint with the therapist's licensing board. The therapist filed a motion for a protective order for the child in front of the judge who granted the divorce, and asked for an order preventing the father from having access to the notes. The judge appointed an attorney ad litem to represent the child for the sole purpose of reviewing the therapist's records. Upon the recommendation of this attorney, the judge ordered only limited access to the records by the father, excluding access to therapy or session notes. The point made is that the father had an absolute right to *all* of the records until the court order was issued.

As stated by Corey et al. (1998), the therapist cannot provide minors with a guarantee of blanket confidentiality. Parents and guardians expect the therapist to supply them with requested information and feedback regarding their child's progress in therapy. Therefore, at the outset of therapy, information that will or will not be disclosed to parents should be discussed not only with the parents, but also with the child or adolescent. Hendrix (1991) states that, at times, alternatives to complete confidentiality must utilized. The therapist should seek to obtain, from the child, voluntary and informed consent that addresses potential disclosures to parents. Corey et al. (1998) recommend that the therapist informs the client whenever confidentiality needs to be broken, and invite the client to participate in the disclosure process.

Regarding adolescents, guidelines addressing confidentiality are somewhat vague and inconsistent. The therapist is forced to apply professional judgment, consult with other professionals, and carefully consider the standard of care. According to Corey et al. (1998), "in the case of adolescents, the consensus of writers and judges appears to be that they have the same confidentiality rights as adults" (p. 137). They emphasize, though, that state laws differ regarding therapy with minors, and therapists must become familiar with the laws of the state in which they practice.

To handle the issue of children's confidentiality, Hartsell (1997) recommends that "therapists who work with children try to get a consent or waiver from the parent prior to embarking on the therapy with the child, with respect to access to records." He states that parents, generally, will sign the consent if they are impressed enough with the therapist to bring their child for therapy. The therapist should attempt to help parents understand that therapy most likely will be more successful if the child is secure in knowing that the information shared with the therapist will remain confidential. It is especially important to discuss confidentiality with parents of adolescents. Adolescents have a deeper understanding about confidentiality and keeping secrets than do younger children, and often are very concerned about their parents knowing about boyfriends, girlfriends, sex, drug use, and more. They can be especially resistant and uncooperative without trust in the therapist and faith that confidentiality will be protected.

Duty to Warn

Duty to warn involves the therapist's obligation to warn an identified third party of a client's dangerousness and intent to harm that third party. The therapist must determine the level of the client's dangerousness, based on reasonable and due care, and sound judgment. Clients often may make idle threats. They may be dangerous, but no intended victim has been identified. In the eyes of the law, according to Bernard and Goodyear (1998), it is more important to make a reasonable evaluation than an accurate prediction. Ethical standards and legal practice tend to lean in favor of protecting confidentiality unless the client is clearly and immediately dangerous.

According to Corey et al. (1998), therapists, "spurred by the courts, have come to realize that they have a double professional responsibility: to protect other people from potentially dangerous clients and to protect clients from themselves" (p. 164). Therapists must struggle with determining whether a particular client is dangerous. Therapists are, generally, not liable if they fail to render perfect predictions of clients' harmful behavior. However, a professionally inadequate assessment of "client dangerousness can result in liability for the therapist, harm to third parties, and inappropriate breaches of client confidentiality"(p. 165).

The ACA (1995) states that, "the general requirement that counselors keep information confidential does not apply when disclosure is required to prevent clear and imminent danger to the client or others or when legal requirements demand that confidential information be revealed" (Section B.1.c.). In addition, if a therapist ascertains that a client has a disease that is commonly known to be *both* communicable and fatal, then the therapist "is justified in disclosing information to an identifiable third party, who by his or her relationship with the client is at a high risk of contracting the disease" (Section B.1.d.). Before disclosing information the therapist should confirm that the client has not informed the other person, nor does the client intend to inform the other person about the disease in the immediate future.

The well-used example of the Tarasoff case determined that a psychologist in California has a duty to warn intended victims of imminent physical danger (Bernstein and Hartsell, 1998). This case has been cited and is a law in some states. Each state must make its independent determination. Even then, nothing is really known in each jurisdiction until that specific state supreme court has had a case brought before it *and* made a decision on the case. However, there is no federal case.

Hartsell (1997) indicates that a mental health professional who *reasonably believes* that a client is in *imminent danger* of physical or emotional harm must contact the appropriate medical or law enforcement personnel. Likewise, if the therapist reasonably suspects that a third person is in imminent physical danger from a client, then the therapist must contact the appropriate medical or law enforcement personnel. According to Hartsell the definitions are not clear regarding what constitutes medical or law enforcement personnel; however this gives the therapist the right to call the police or sheriff, or a doctor known to be medicating the client. It would probably be permissible to call an emergency room or paramedics under the broad term of personnel. Bernstein and Hartsell (1998) emphasize the importance for therapists to become familiar with applicable laws in their state by calling a lawyer, going to a law library, or asking the state licensing board to send a copy of the statutes. Therapists should also contact their malpractice insurance carrier.

Dual Relationships

Avoidance of inappropriate *dual relationships* constitutes another legal and ethical issue that requires counselors to exercise caution and professional judgment. According to Pope (1991), "dual relationships form the major basis of licensing disciplinary actions, of financial losses in malpractice suits involving psychologists, and of ethics complaints against psychologists" (p. 25). Dual relationships occur when therapists engage in two or more significantly different relationships with clients. Multiple relationships may occur concurrently or sequentially and may not always be avoided.

Any relationship, especially a therapeutic relationship, becomes distorted and deteriorates if one party exercises a position of unequal power over the other. If a therapist is seeking personal gain by manipulating or wielding power over a client, obviously the therapist's professional judgment is unsound and unethical, and there is a conflict of interest between the counselor and client. Conflicts of interest can be defining characteristics of inappropriate dual relationships. Such conflicts interfere with the therapist's ability to maintain integrity, neutrality, objectivity, and reliability. However, in view of the various interpretations of the various codes, the therapist and client may not even realize when a dual relationship exists.

The therapist must remain aware that a power differential exists, simply due to the nature of the relationship between a mental health provider and a client. Therapists are made aware of secrets, and intensely private information regarding their clients. Clients often seek counseling in a state of feeling completely helpless—they have tried everything, and may view counseling as a last hope. This puts a client in an unequal and incredibly vulnerable position, wherein they are looking to the mental health professional for deliverance from suffering.

If a client believes oneself to be wronged within some other relationship (e.g., with an auto mechanic or neighbor) then the client has a variety of means, including court action, with which to resolve the conflict. However, if a client attempts to resolve a difficulty between oneself and a therapist, information confided to the therapist is in jeopardy of exposure, to the possible extent of being entered into public record. Clients often feel helpless because of this possible revelation.

Within the last decade state licensing boards have addressed the issue of nonsexual dual relationships more vigorously with their words—their actions have followed suit. However, there remains a lack of clear and absolute laws, ethical codes, and morals that govern therapists' decisions when facing a potentially dual relationship. This dependence upon professional judgment can be very frustrating, as well as risky, for mental health professionals.

The *Code of Ethics and Standards of Practice of the ACA* (1995) is typical and consistent with ethical codes for licensed professional counselors and other mental health professionals. The ACA code states "counselors do not have any type of sexual intimacies with clients and do not counsel persons with whom they have had a sexual relationship" (Section A.7.a.). This is direct and quite clear. However, regarding nonsexual dual relationships, the language of the code is circumspect and indirect—even in defining the parties within a dual relationship. Ethical standards of the ACA and the National Association of Social Workers (1996) refer to relationships between counselors and their clients. According to the ACA code:

> Counselors are aware of their influential positions with respect to clients, and they avoid exploiting the trust and dependency of clients. Counselors make every effort to avoid dual relationships with clients that could impair professional judgment or increase the risk of harm to clients. (Examples of such relationships include, but are not limited to, familial, social, financial, business, or close personal relationships with clients.) When a dual relationship cannot be avoided, counselors take appropriate professional precautions such as informed consent, consultation, supervision, and documentation to ensure that judgment is not impaired and no exploitation occurs. (Section A.6.a.)

Herlihy and Corey (1997) state that dual relationships range from those that have little potential for harm to those that are potentially very harmful. Therapists should only enter into dual relationships when the risks of harm are small and there are strong, offsetting ethical benefits for the client.

Sexual Abuse

Bernstein and Hartsell (1998) report that every state has a child abuse reporting statute, and most states have an elderly abuse reporting statute. This dictates that a local agency for child protective services or adult protective services is to be notified if abuse is known or suspected. According to Hartsell (1997), any citizen, not only the licensed professional, is required to report abuse of children, elderly persons, and people with physical or mental handicaps. There are also specific statutes indicating to whom offending employees of state hospitals and community agencies should be reported. According to the ACA (1995), "the general requirement that counselors keep information confidential does not apply . . . when legal requirements demand that confidential information be revealed" (Section B.1.c.).

These statutes typically protect the therapist by granting civil and criminal immunity to any person who has reasonable suspicion of abuse and makes the report in good faith (Bernstein & Hartsell, 1998). Although therapists may get sued, they will not lose if they made their reports in good faith. This is always an issue of fact even though, in many cases, abuse is difficult to document and establish. If the report is made, it is possible that the alleged perpetrator may confront the person making the report. However, the consequences of failing to make the report are much more serious. *It is a crime not to report.* If the therapist does not make the report and the person is injured, then a civil lawsuit can be brought for all of the damages that the person incurs as a result of being abused again.

Verifying Custody and Legal Right for Therapy

Bernstein and Hartsell (1998) recommend that anytime a therapist is dealing with children of divorced parents, the therapist needs to request a copy of the *most recent* court order pertaining to the child's issues. Asking only for a divorce decree may not result in the most current information. Parents may have been back to court several times, resulting in various changes in custody. Therapists' notes should reflect that they asked for the most recent court order, and they should get a copy to keep in the file. Although Hartsell (1997) contends that a therapist has the right to rely upon what their client tells them, he also recommends the therapist obtain copies of the designated court orders.

Consider the case of a father who, two years after his divorce, wishes for a change in custody of his only child. During one extended visitation, he takes the child to a therapist who recommends that the child be removed from the mother's custody. A lawsuit gets filed. Later, it turns out that the father did not have the right to consent to nonemergency mental health care. Not only does the therapist have a problem, but they are also unable to provide testimony for the father's custody case. *Safe practice is to ask for and get copies of court orders.* If the therapist is not sure what the order states, then a lawyer should be consulted.

Especially with respect to custody, the therapist should be familiar with the terms pertinent to the state of residence. According to Hartsell (1997), Texas uses the expression *managing conservatorship*. Different rights might be attached to different labels in different states. "Custodial parents" in one state might not have the right to consent to non-emergency medical care, if they are not the primary parent. Most states are moving toward joint custody, which may make it more confusing to determine who has the right to consent to either emergency or non-emergency mental health care. Again, this typically will be specified in the court orders. If not, the rights attached to the various labels will have to be determined through the statutes in the respective states. The parent with the authority to consent can allow anyone into the therapy sessions. It is up to the therapist to request that only those persons who are believed to be beneficial to the therapy process be included.

Children are often brought to therapy by a stepparent, a divorced parent (with or without custody), a sibling, a nanny, or a remote relative. The therapist must obtain informed consent from the legally appropriate guardian. Informed consent *must* be obtained from the person who has the authority to give consent. Also, the person bringing the child must have the legal authority to do so. With the permission of a legally appropriate guardian, anyone can transport the child to and from the therapy sessions.

Informed Consent and Intake Forms

Corey et al. (1998) contend that mental health professionals have the responsibility of making reasonable disclosure of all significant information to their clients. This information includes procedures, limitations, goals, benefits, probable consequences, and potential risks. The process of therapy should be explained to clients in a manner in which they are able to comprehend. "It is essential that clients give their consent *with* understanding" (p. 113). According to the ACA (1995), counselors must attempt to ensure that clients also understand such issues as fees, billing arrangements, intended use of tests and reports, and implications of diagnoses. The *Ethical Principles of Psychologists and Code of Conduct* of the APA (1995) indicates that:

1. The client has the ability and capacity to give consent for treatment;
2. The client has been informed of, and understands, significant information regarding treatment;

3. Without being coerced, the client has expressed consent for treatment; and
4. The client's consent has been appropriately documented.

Corey et al. (1998) emphasize the need for therapists to avoid subtle coercion of clients to cooperate with procedures or programs to which they have not freely consented.

An intake form can be a vehicle to obtain information from parents, as well as provide information to parents. (See appendix A and appendix C.) Corey et al. (1998) recommend that informed consent be obtained in writing. A written consent should include the name of the therapist and the client, the date that consent was discussed, a statement of the client's right to end therapy, a description of the therapy to be provided, issues and limits of confidentiality, a statement that confirms that the client understood, and the client's signature. Additional information to provide to the client may include the therapist's theoretical orientation, counseling records, fees and charges, insurance reimbursements, and managed care issues. Therapists can build consent into their intake forms wherein the client authorizes the therapist to initiate certain procedures or to withhold certain information. These consent forms are signed by the client at the outset of therapy and offer protection during the therapy process for both the client and the therapist.

Although Hartsell (1997) recommends the use of signed informed consent forms, he also indicated that public policy attorneys argue that such universal consent forms violate public policy, and are not in the best interest of clients. Public policy attorneys have also declared that they will not honor or respect these types of agreements. If therapists refuse to hold or turn over records based on such consents, these attorneys claim that they will view this action as an unethical practice. Hartsell recommends, however, that therapists obtain these consents which provide, at least, a somewhat stronger position for the therapist, than not having an informed consent.

Clinical Notes and Records

Corey et al. (1998) contend that there are essentially two purposes for maintaining appropriate, thorough, and detailed clinical notes. First, is to provide the best possible service for the client, and continuity of care in the event the client changes therapists (protecting the welfare of the client). Failure to keep accurate and thorough records can deprive the client of data needed for treatment. In addition, "it is mandatory for managed care practitioners to keep accurate charts and notes, and by law they must provide this information to authorized chart reviewers" (p. 125). In an effort to be protective of clients, many counselors and counselor educators, however, resist the practice of keeping detailed notes. Such practice is based on the belief that less detailed case notes will safeguard against the impact of potential exceptions to confidentiality (i.e., court ordered disclosure), and prevent disclosure of potentially damaging information about the client.

The second purpose for maintaining thorough and detailed records is to safeguard the therapist in the event of a lawsuit or disciplinary action (Corey et al., 1998). Many therapists believe that accurate and detailed notes provide an excellent defense against malpractice claims. Hartsell (1997) works to defend mental health practitioners in response to complaints from their clients. He recommends that therapists keep thorough, accurate, and well-documented notes in an effort to protect their license and their future in the profession. He stated that "it is hard to defend therapists when they come in with appointment calendars and one-sentence notes for each session over a two-year period. There is nothing in those notes. It becomes the therapist's word against the client's word." According to Schaffer (1997) therapists who do not maintain adequate clinical notes and records are ethically and legally at risk. A clinical record can be the most effective and least expensive form of liability insurance. Without thorough, accurate and well-documented notes, practitioners are deprived of evidence they will need to defend themselves in the event of malpractice or disciplinary actions.

By keeping detailed notes, the therapist can protect the client while protecting oneself. Of course, protecting the client is the therapist's primary responsibility. Learning good record-keeping practices about the client's progress will ideally help the therapist in conceptualizing the client's issues, keeping sessions focused on treatment goals, and providing overall quality of service (Corey et al., 1998). Clinical records should document the nature, delivery, and progress of therapy. Included in these records should be:

1. identifying information about the client;
2. an intake sheet;
3. the client's primary care physician, or explanation for omission of his or her name;
4. the client's presenting issues;
5. previous and current psychological test data;
6. an informed consent for treatment form that is signed by the client or guardian;
7. treatment plans containing specific issues and goals;

8. progress notes that are dated and signed by the therapist;
9. nature, types, and justification of services provided;
10. appointment times and dates;
11. release of information forms; and
12. a discharge summary that is completed upon termination.

In addition, the information contained in a client's record belongs to the client, and can be requested at any time. Notes should clearly describe specific and concrete behavior, and written in a style that is thorough, honest, and accurate, but never demeaning or derogatory. Finally, clinical records should never be subsequently tampered with or altered.

Getting "Set-Up" and "Dragged" into Court

Parents often wish to obtain or change their custody rights. These changes must be processed through a court. Parents will frequently take their child to see a therapist in order to obtain professional support for their views. Parents hope that they will have a stronger position in court (with the support of the therapist) for appearing to be concerned about the child's welfare, and being reasonable and not simply vindictive.

Hartsell (1997) reported that a therapist may prevent such a situation from happening. During the intake session, the therapist can have the referring parent sign an agreement stating that the therapist is to work with the child for the purpose of *therapy only* and will not be brought into any custody litigation process. This includes the parent who brought the child to therapy waiving the right to subpoena the therapist. The agreement also gives the therapist a stronger basis for a motion for a protective order, because helping the child was the sole purpose of therapy, rather than helping the parent with a lawsuit. This is not an absolute safeguard against the therapist being involved in a lawsuit because, when a child is involved, a judge can order the therapist to testify, regardless of a pre-existing agreement with the parent.

Hartsell (1997) suggests that the agreement include a provision obligating the parent to compensate the therapist for time spent producing records or giving testimony regardless of who initiates any subpoena. Without such an agreement, Hartsell refers to the therapist's position as simply being an "eyewitness to a marital wreck." The therapist may be required to donate considerable time and effort to the legal process because he or she is not in a position to bill anyone.

According to Epstein (1994), new fears have developed within today's litigious and persecutory environment. Even innocent, moral, and ethical counselors feel vulnerable to false allegations made by either unstable clients, or worse, by greedy clients that endeavor to exploit the counselor for financial gain. Therapists can be at risk of financial damages as a result of malpractice accusations, as well as having their licenses revoked or suspended.

Therapists must take precautions to protect themselves from such risks. As mentioned earlier, therapists must carefully consider the many aspects of standard of care, consulting other professionals, communicating clear boundaries with clients, and documenting their efforts in clinical case notes.

Notice of a Subpoena

A subpoena to appear in court requires the therapist to actually appear, at the least. There may or may not be an exception to confidentiality. The therapist may inform the client of the subpoena, and request the client's written consent to produce records, give testimony, or whatever the subpoena entails. If the client agrees, then protecting privilege or confidentiality is not an issue. Hartsell (1997) indicates that if the client cannot be contacted or does not consent, the therapist has two options. One, to contact the attorney who issued the subpoena and try to determine the issues of the lawsuit. Two, to also contact an attorney to file a motion for a protective order or a motion to quash the subpoena, asserting the client's privilege to confidentiality. In smaller communities, it is possible to contact the judge directly by telephone to discuss the issue of confidentiality.

The therapist may ultimately be required to give a deposition or appear in court to give testimony. In either case, the therapist should appear, and not relinquish records to anyone. Only general questions about the therapist should be answered, such as the therapist's name, length of time in practice, licensing, nature of practice, and office location. In the case of a deposition, when asked about a specific client or asked to provide any information that could possibly identify the client, Hartsell (1997) advises the therapist's response to be "I respectfully refuse to answer that question, based upon mental health privilege of confidentiality." Even though there may be considerable pressure from the attorneys to disclose more, the therapist is not obligated to do so. The attorneys then must decide whether or not to go to court and file a motion to compel the therapist to testify.

Similarly, in live courtroom testimony, Hartsell (1997) recommends that the therapist give the following response to the judge, "Your Honor, I am uncomfortable responding to questions regarding any alleged clients due to confidentiality issues." A judge may rule that there is an exception to the mental health privilege of confidentiality and that the therapist must answer the questions. At this point, the therapist is under a court order and is "off the hook" as far as confidentiality goes. The therapist should never voluntarily supply the information, and the information should never be supplied until an exception is certain, the client has consented, or a judge has issued an order.

Responding to a Complaint Filed with the Licensing Board

Most lawsuits require a formal response to a court, in which case a therapist typically contacts an attorney. Hartsell (1997) also recommends that an attorney be contacted prior to filing a response with the licensing board. For example, a therapist receives a letter that a complaint has been filed. The complaining person is identified in this notice (this information is not always provided). The board requests the therapist to file a written response within 10 days, including record specifics. Prior to contacting an attorney, the therapist files a very lengthy response, with much more information than the board wanted. Within this excessive response, the therapist tries to justify everything about his or her practice, including possibly incriminating information.

In a similar example, an investigator contacts the therapist and tries to put the therapist at ease. The investigator says, "I want to meet with you. This is no big deal. It's simply a formality. We need to clear this up. I'll be in town on this date, and I need look at your records." The investigator shows up and the therapist is off-guard, nervous, and unknowingly free with incriminating remarks. The therapist has a right to have an attorney present in an investigation. Upon notice that an attorney will be present, investigators will typically not come. According to Hartsell (1997), a therapist should not respond to subpoenas or complaints filed with the licensing board without first consulting a lawyer. Once incriminating remarks have been made in a letter or to an investigator, client testimony is no longer needed to strip the therapist of his or her license. The therapist's own words are sufficient.

Hartsell (1997) contends that, if a license is actually revoked, the therapist is permitted to appeal. There is typically at least one appellate review. It is not desirable for the therapist to be in this position. The review by the appellate court is narrow. The purpose of the board is to protect consumers, and its performance is largely measured by statistics regarding revoked and sanctioned licenses. The law has many general clauses that allow board interpretation. Even if an administrative law hearing finds the therapist did not violate an ethical statute, the board can still revoke the therapist's license. The board can argue that the code of ethics represents minimum standards, and the therapist's minimal level of professionalism was not sufficient in the given situation. Extreme caution should be exercised when responding to subpoenas and licensing complaints. It is recommended that therapists contact their attorneys prior to such responses, or if they have questions about any legal issues relative to their practices.

Videotaping or Audiotaping Sessions

Audio- and videotaping of therapy sessions should be performed only with the written consent of parents. The AAMFT (1991) states that "therapists obtain written informed consent from clients before videotaping, audiorecording, or permitting third party observation" (Section 1.8).

According to Hartsell (1997), most states prohibit surreptitiously audiotaping or videotaping sessions or conversations. There may be some clients who wish to incriminate a therapist for financial gain or other purposes, and it may be very difficult to detect and/or prove such motives or agendas. If the therapist has a flirtatious client, for example, Hartsell contends that the therapist should have a third party present or, better yet, should tape the session. Taping may be the only safeguard against illegitimate claims of sexual abuse or other alleged inappropriate therapist behavior during sessions.

Sexual Exploitation of Clients

The greatest number of complaints to professional organizations and licensing boards involve the sexual exploitation of clients. According to the ACA (1995), a therapist is prohibited from having a sexual relationship with any client with whom they have had a therapeutic relationship during the last two years or, beyond two years following termination of the therapy relationship, with any client who is emotionally dependent upon the therapist. Thus, a therapist must carefully examine the relationship to ensure that the client is not exploited, harmed, or otherwise adversely affected.

According to Hartsell (1997), therapists have lost their licenses due to sexual relationships with previous clients, even when adhering to other specifications in the code of ethics. The licensing boards often have the power to broadly define unprofessional conduct and revoke therapists' licenses. He strongly advocates that therapists never have sexual relationships with any clients, past or present. Although sexual exploitation of clients is relatively easy to avoid, this category continues to generate the largest numbers of complaints.

☐ Other Parameters of Therapy

Therapists and parents alike should be aware of how parameters may influence the therapeutic relationship and the outcomes of therapy. Inevitably, there will be subtle parameters that cannot be addressed until they occur. However, immediately identifying such parameters as length of time for sessions, frequency of sessions, and anticipated duration of therapy is very important. This will help the therapist with a sense of structure, and, more importantly, the parents will have the safety of the structure for balance.

It is preferable to address many of these boundaries with parents during early contact. Surprises can be awkward and uncomfortable for the therapist and parents. Assume, for example, that a warm, friendly, and therapeutic relationship has developed between the therapist and Mr. Jones. At the end of the third session, he is very encouraged about the progress his daughter is making and feels grateful toward the therapist. He moves to hug the therapist by the door, and the therapist holds up her hand and states, "I don't believe it's appropri-ate in our professional relationship for us to hug." This would be very embarrassing for Mr. Jones and possibly even for the therapist. The therapeutic relationship most certainly could be affected, maybe beyond repair. It is all right for the therapist to make the choice to refrain from hugging clients; however, when this choice is a surprise in the therapy session, it can have results that are antitherapeutic. Also, there may be repercussions to the therapist for going ahead and hugging Mr. Jones, especially if she is not comfortable doing so. Mr. Jones may sense the therapist's apprehension and be hesitant to return with his child the next week; the therapist may have to endure self-blame and other emotional consequences for not being assertive and protecting her boundaries. In this case, the simple act of hugging that was spontaneous, unexpected, and had not previously been addressed, blurred the quality and the roles of the professional relationship.

Therapist Compensation and Bartering

Parents and therapists must agree on the details of payment for services rendered. This becomes complicated in today's insurance and managed care environment, and when therapists sometimes provide services based upon sliding scale fees. Usually, there is little to discuss when payment amounts and procedures are dictated by managed care companies. When therapists grant sliding fees to parents, clear language should be used to reach an agreement. Whether or not to offer reduced fees and determination of specific amounts are complicated decisions. Clients' fiscal situations and responsibilities must be considered. These are sensitive issues for most people and, yet, they must be addressed in the initial contact or intake session—likely before much trust is built. Therapists should view this as an excellent opportunity to model respectful, assertive communication for parents.

Frequently, therapists include two clauses in their intake paperwork related to compensation. One states that the client is ultimately responsible for the therapist's fees, regardless of insurance coverage. This indicates that if the insurance company pays 80% then the client agrees to pay the other 20%. If there is no provision in the client's insurance policy for therapy, the client is responsible for payment. The other notifies clients that they are still responsible for the therapist's fees of missed sessions unless 24-hour notice of cancellations is provided (e.g., if they do not show for sessions). Therapists must carefully consider enforcing this clause, and consider the characteristics of specific clients. Emergencies and illnesses arise that prevent clients from attending sessions; structure and planning may be areas of weakness for some clients; and, disputes between therapists and their clients can have very negative consequences for children, parents, and therapists.

Collecting fees for missed sessions should not be used as punishment or to shame clients into making appointments, but as a sign of respect for boundaries of the relationship. An appointment, however, is actually a contract for a therapist's time with the assumption that services will be rendered. Therapists are compensated for their time. Without proper notice of cancellation, therapists are unable to offer these appointment times to others who may need them. Also, therapists show up for work but are unable to get paid. Whether involving therapists or anyone else, recurring missing of appointments may demonstrate a lack of respect as well as a lack of structure, planning, and responsibility. An important goal of therapy is for clients to develop the ability to attend the sessions as scheduled and on time. This requires self-control, responsibility, and respect for the therapist. It is hoped, of course, that these skills can be generalized and transferred to areas of clients' lives outside of the therapy session.

Bartering is defined by Merriam-Webster (1984): "to trade by exchanging one commodity (or service) for another" (p. 132). Bartering has inherent, dual relationship characteristics. In rural areas where everyone has some type of pre-existing, noncounseling (dual or multiple) relationship, the only available services to an individual may have to be provided by a familiar member in the community. The ACA discourages counselors from engaging in dual relationships, but recognizes that they cannot always be avoided. For example, the ACA (1995) ethical code discourages bartering but also provides the following guidelines when bartering is necessary:

> Counselors ordinarily refrain from accepting goods and services from clients in return or counseling services because such arrangements create inherent potential for conflicts, exploitation, and distortion of the professional relationship. Counselors may participate in bartering only if the relationship is not exploitive, if the client requests it, if a clear written contract is established, and if such arrangements are an accepted practice among professionals in the community. (Section A.10.c)

The issue of bartering (and dual relationships) is not one of total avoidance, but one of power differential. The mental health provider must avoid using any power differential that occurs in the counseling relationship for personal gain. The counselor is charged with the responsibility for using professional judgment and following standards of care to ensure that the client is not exploited or otherwise injured.

Therapists must affirm that parents understand payment parameters from the onset of therapy. This reduces unpleasant surprises that may damage the counseling relationship, or at the very least, severely interfere with the goals of therapy. Similar to the results of other disputes in parents' lives, conflicts between parents and therapists often result in the child suffering the most, and this should be avoided as much as possible.

Conducting Therapy at Home and Other Non-Office Settings

Conducting therapy sessions outside an office setting can obscure the goals of therapy by mixing practices commonly seen in professional and personal settings. It is strongly recommended for therapists in private practice to have offices or professional settings in which therapy services are provided, rather than in the therapist's home, the client's home, or other non-office settings. A more formal setting helps to clarify the nature and purpose of the therapeutic relationship. Of course, there are exceptions. Some clients have challenges that prevent them from being transported to a therapist's office. Relocation of the sessions may understandably be necessary. However, the therapist's burden of responsibility to maintain professionalism would dramatically increase within the relationship if sessions were held in the client's home or another setting that is not an obviously professional office space.

Many therapists have developed successful and appropriate practices by having offices in their homes. It is frequently argued that this requires stricter adherence to appropriate boundaries. It is a common contention that all therapists should be held to high standards of professional conduct, requiring the maintenance of healthy, professional boundaries. However, as the probability of mixing professional and personal behaviors is higher in non-office settings, suspicions tend to increase and attention is directed to the possibility of improprieties. Hence, therapeutic energy and attention may be deflected away from the specific, identified goals of therapy to defending the propriety of the therapeutic relationship. Specific communication and clarification with parents is particularly crucial to maximizing the outcome of therapy in nontraditional settings.

Length of Therapy Sessions

During the first session, or even when setting up the first appointment, therapists should establish the length of therapy sessions for the parents, and it is just as important for the therapist to adhere to this time schedule as the client. By starting sessions on time and ending sessions as scheduled, the therapist is respecting the parents' (and the child's) schedules. This practice also respects the therapist's schedule. The therapist is modeling self-respect, respect for others, and time responsibility. For example, during the intake session the therapist discussing the therapy parameters with the parent, might say, "The weekly sessions will be 50 minutes. Today, we started at 2:00 and will end at 2:50. I'll begin to wind the session down at 2:45." The therapist is able to respectfully and politely inform the client of what can be expected, thereby identifying boundaries regarding session length. Although structure is a beneficial component of the therapy process, the therapist is not advised to maintain such strict adherence to the schedule that clients' needs are not attended. Especially if there is an existing crisis, the therapist may need to vary session length to protect the physical and emotional welfare of parents and children.

Hugging

Hugging parents and children is one parameter that should be examined very closely by therapists; it can have widely different meanings for different people. Hugging occurs in many different types of relationships. Friends, relatives, spouses, and romantically involved people use hugs to express their affection. Hugging can seriously confuse the nature some relationships. The therapeutic relationship is extremely intense and personal, and requires that the therapist genuinely cares for the parents and child. It is also important that the parents and child realize that the therapist truly cares about them.

However, hugging may not be an appropriate method of communication. According to Hartsell (1997), hugging has been construed as a component of sexual relationships and sexual abuse, and has been used in lawsuits to exemplify inappropriate ethical conduct and malpractice. He recommends that therapists resist hugging all clients, especially children, because of the potential legal risk.

According to Landreth (1991), if the child suddenly "hugged the therapist, it would be inappropriate for the therapist to sit there rigid as a board" (p. 247). Responses to the child are certainly influenced if the therapist suspects that the child has been sexually abused. For example, what if a girl suddenly jumped up onto the male therapist's lap and playfully wiggled around? "Surely, the therapist would be aware of the possibilities of such behavior and would respond accordingly with 'I know that's fun for you, but I know you like me without your sitting on my lap'" (pp. 247–248). Hugging, however, has been therapeutic in many situations. Therapists must use their professional judgment, be sincere, and concentrate on serving the child's best interest.

Telephone Calls to the Therapist

To protect the professional nature of the therapeutic relationship, communications should be limited, when possible, to the therapy sessions. The therapist should encourage clients to limit telephone calls to scheduling and emergency purposes. Some clients prefer to deal with their issues over the phone or to use the phone instead of coming in for sessions because it is more convenient or less costly. Frequent or unlimited telephone contact can result in clients growing dependent upon the therapist; especially clients who have the perceived need for therapist assistance in many of their decisions. Many therapists carry pagers which alert them for emergencies (of course, services are available that page therapists for all of their calls). Similar to meeting clients outside of the sessions or in a non-office setting, excessive telephone contact can create misunderstanding regarding the roles within, and purpose of, the relationship. Emphasis must be placed upon the professional relationship being different from any other relationship and that contact should occur primarily during the therapy sessions.

Receiving and Giving Gifts

When gifts are given or received, the boundaries defining personal and professional relationships can easily become confused and unclear. Giving and receiving gifts tends to put conditions on the therapeutic relationship that imply that there will be return favors, materially or psychologically. Also, if therapists anticipate nice gifts from certain clients, attention can be focused away from the specific treatment goals. Therapists' behavior may become motivated by attempts to please these clients and keeping them happy. Hartsell (1997) advised that therapists do not accept gifts that could possibly lead to suspicion; legal suspicion especially arises or increases when therapists are the recipients of gifts from adult clients. It is less unacceptable to receive the occasional cookie or picture from a child in therapy. Altruism is a normal task of child development (Vander Zanden, 1996), and it could be detrimental to the child's growth not to accept spontaneous and genuine offerings. Nevertheless, it is not appropriate for the therapist to give gifts to a child or to be overly responsive as a recipient in order to influence the child to be cooperative in the therapy setting, to want to come back each week, to like the therapist, or to satisfy any other need of the therapist. Likewise, it would not be appropriate to accept a child's allowance money, other valuables, or expensive gifts from the child's parent (even if delivered by the child). The ACA (1995) ethical code explicitly states that counselors "avoid actions that seek to meet their personal needs at the expense of clients" (Section A.5.a.).

☐ Summary

The parameters of therapy can be viewed as the boundaries that define the nature of the therapist-parent relationship and the therapist-child relationship. Although identifying and protecting these boundaries may be seem intrusive to the therapy process, the goals of therapy are actually brought more into focus. The therapist, at times, must take special care to acknowledge the benefits of the parameters, while reducing the chance of offending parents.

It may appear that it would be difficult for therapists to build rapport with parents after informing them of these parameters. For example, arguments can be made that parents will be unwilling to disclose information due to embarrassment, feelings of inadequacy, or possible fear of being reported to child protective services. However, by identifying the boundaries, therapists are preventing later surprises from causing greater damage to the therapeutic relationship. Also, therapists can model appropriate communication techniques and the setting of boundaries for parents. These parameters actually preserve and protect the integrity and professional nature of the relationships with the parents and child. With the security of knowing where the boundaries are, the parents and child can develop a deeper trust in the therapist. They can also have more freedom to explore and express themselves, realize their own inner power, and develop greater trust in themselves.

Many of the boundaries and much of the structure involved in therapeutic relationships are expressly delineated within legal and ethical codes, by which therapists are professionally bound. These rules and regulations have evolved in an effort to protect clients from malpractice, and ensure a high level of professional care. In all situations, the therapist must focus on protecting the welfare of the client. Additionally, the therapist must consistently observe and practice with an accepted standard of care. Frequently, it is in the best interest of the client, as well as the therapist, to consult with another mental health professional.

Key legal and ethical issues include confidentiality, exceptions to confidentiality, duty to warn, sexual misconduct, dual relationships, child confidentiality, informed consent, verifying custody, clinical notes and records, and other therapeutic parameters.

Therapists must also take precautions to protect themselves. Therapists face numerous risks related to the mental health profession. Consequently, there are common fears that are shared by many therapists. Techniques and strategies are available in the event that a complaint or suit is filed against the therapist. Also, therapists can benefit greatly from understanding the governing bodies, and insight into due process regarding ethical and legal complaints.

CHAPTER 4

Medical Issues in Therapy

Behaviors are indications of how children are feeling and measurements of how children are functioning. According to child psychiatrist Ross Tatum, M.D. (personal communication, August 14, 1997), the primary indications that necessitate medication involve troublesome behaviors. Troublesome behaviors receive the most attention, and concern originates when behaviors fall outside expected patterns. These patterns are either general norms or a child's own specific norms. Behaviors can fall outside of norms due to more active or less active features. For example, Attention-Deficit/Hyperactivity Disorder (ADHD) involves more active (i.e., disruptive, excessive action) behaviors that interfere with desired levels of functioning for children. Falling outside of norms in a less active way could indicate, for instance, that children are withdrawn due to depression or anxiety.

Externalizing behaviors are those behaviors that are outwardly manifested, can typically be observed visually, and are likely to quickly attract attention (Albano, Chorpita, & Barlow, 1996). Examples of externalizing (problem) behaviors are aggression, hyperactivity, impulsivity, inappropriate running or talking, noisiness, distractibility, and inattentiveness. Internalizing behaviors are those that occur within the child, and are likely to be associated with the child's emotions. Examples of internalizing (problem) behaviors include depression, fears and phobias, somatic complaints, withdrawal, and anxiety.

Likewise, problems with externalizing behaviors are sometimes considered to be undercontrolled behaviors, while problems with internalizing behaviors are sometimes referred to as overcontrolled behaviors, or behavioral inhibition. Treatment is more frequently sought for externalized problems, because these are easily seen and very frustrating for parents. Unfortunately, behavioral inhibition and internalizing behaviors are frequently untreated because these are often unnoticed, or even welcomed and rewarded. Behavioral inhibition in young children, however, has been linked to later development of anxiety, avoidance, isolation, withdrawal, agoraphobia, and panic attacks (Mash & Dozois, 1996).

Olweus (1979), indicates that, across cultures, young boys tend to display more externalizing behaviors (e.g., impulsivity, fighting) than girls. Achenbach, Howell, Quay, and Conners (1991) indicate that young girls tend to experience more internalizing problems than do boys. Also, for children who have been referred for treatment, Achenbach and colleagues indicate that externalizing behaviors tend to decline with age as compared with internalizing problems. Mash and Dozois (1996) state that boys have more behavioral problems than girls during early and middle childhood, especially regarding disruptive behavior disorders. Girls' problems, such as depression and dysphoric mood, tend to increase during adolescence, with higher prevalence rates from mid-adolescence through adulthood.

Childhood disorders and behavior problems invariably require multiple treatment modalities. For instance, the child may require medications, while also requiring the emotional and developmental support of play therapy. In addition, general or specific parenting skills may need to be learned and applied. According to Tatum (1997), children diagnosed with depression, anxiety, or ADHD often benefit from psychotropic medications. Parents may have questions regarding the necessity, safety, and effectiveness of medication for their child. Although research and practice have evidenced the safe and appropriate use of medication when treating children, parents may remain apprehensive. Even though a physician is required to prescribe the medication, the parents most likely will see the therapist more often. Since parents will be responsible for procuring and administering the medication, they may benefit from being able to talk about their concerns with the therapist who is seeing their child in play therapy. Therefore, the therapist should develop a working knowledge of psychotropic medications, and address the concerns that parents may have.

The following sections provide information regarding various childhood disorders, including diagnostic criteria. *This information is provided solely for therapeutic knowledge and insight, and not for diagnostic purposes.* Issues surrounding how and when to provide diagnoses are very complex. In conceptualizing a diagnosis of an individual, many factors must be considered, including neurological, biological, chemical, developmental, intellectual, social, environmental, ethical, cultural, family history, and phenomenological factors. In addition, careful effort also must be given to verifying and validating the information used when conceptualizing a diagnosis. Therapists, mental health professionals, and other clinicians should *only* make diagnoses after extensive training and supervised experience. Because diagnoses can be used inappropriately, unethically, and indefinitely, extreme caution must be used when diagnoses are provided verbally, in writing, or electronically.

☐ Attention-Deficit/Hyperactivity Disorder (ADHD)

As Barkley (1996) indicates, it is common and expected for young children to be energetic, active, and to flit from one activity to another as they explore their world and experience the many novelties within their environment. As opportunities arise that offer pleasure and reward, young children are expected to pursue these opportunities without the restraint or self-control that would be expected of someone older. However, when compared to their age group, children who *persistently* display excessive levels of activity, substandard levels of attention or an inability to remain on-task, or when they are deficient in their self-regulation and impulse-control, may be seriously at-risk. These children are very likely to experience problems involving their emotional, cognitive, familial, social, and academic development. They risk falling far behind other children in facing the increasing number and variety of demands of daily adaptive functioning. They are also likely to experience harsh judgment, punishment, social rejection, ostracism, and moral denigration because they are often perceived as lazy, inconsiderate, selfish, immature, and deliberately irresponsible. According to Jacobs (1998) children with ADHD are often exposed to negative messages about their behavior, messages indicating that they are the cause of their parents' frustration, their parents' marital problems, and any difficulties within the family.

Diagnosis and Assessment Considerations

An appropriate evaluation is critical in diagnosing ADHD for children (Ogan, 1994). Developmental and behavioral pediatrician, Robert Blalock, M.D. (personal communication, August 17, 1997) reported that diagnosing ADHD in a child involves more than simply applying criteria from the *Diagnostic and Statistical Manual of Mental Disorders, 4th Edition*

(DSM-IV; APA, 1994). Although the DSM-IV is helpful, ADHD is a diagnosis based upon behavioral observations as well as the DSM-IV criteria. The symptomatic behaviors of the child can be due to more than one cause; all of the ADHD symptoms, such as impulsivity, frustration, and distractibility, may be present but also attributable to other conditions. There are three domains that must be considered when evaluating a child for ADHD: medical conditions, learning disabilities, and problems of an emotional or environmental origin. Evaluators are obligated to consider the various fundamental abnormalities that might also explain the behaviors, and not start with the premise that ADHD exists.

R. Blalock (1997) also notes that ADHD nomenclature can be misleading regarding the diagnosis of ADHD would be beneficial. For example, sometimes the behavioral characteristics of children with ADHD do not suggest a deficiency of attention but, rather, an excess of attention. Some children pay attention to everything at once, and do not adequately focus upon the most relevant or highest priority items. He describes this as more of an executive or attention management function problem, wherein higher executive skills are needed to direct attention, prioritize, and filter out distracting stimuli. This can also be referred to as a deficiency in *self-regulation* skills. These children are unable to regulate their mental energy, and expend much more mental energy attending to too many things at once, rather than too few. Blalock also emphasizes consideration of the developmental aspects of the child when conducting an ADHD evaluation. He states, "Sometimes the child's behavior is not so inappropriate as are the expectations."

Fallone (1998) states that ADHD is the most common psychiatric diagnosis most commonly applied to children, and has been the most common reason that children are referred to mental health services. According to Barkley (1996), children are diagnosed with ADHD if they are "excessively active, are unable to sustain their attention, and are deficient in their impulse control to a degree that is deviant for their developmental level" (p. 64). However, he indicates that it may be a gross understatement if one refers to this disorder as simply an attention deficit. Rather, "ADHD is most likely a developmental disorder of behavioral inhibition that interferes with self-regulation and the cross-temporal organization of behavior" (p. 64).

During the initial evaluation, child psychiatrist Ross Tatum (1997) refers to DSM-IV criteria to assess ADHD, and rule out other disorders, in a child. He performs a second evaluation a month later using the same checklist. He requests that school officials and parents also complete a similar checklist regarding their observations of the child, as having data from school officials and parents is necessary in making an

ADHD diagnosis. Parents frequently are not specific about the symptoms they want treated in their child. Therefore, some symptoms on the checklist are related to the child's attitudes and help to minimize the parents' lack of clarity regarding the child's symptoms.

Core Symptoms

As identified in the DSM-IV (American Psychiatric Association, 1994), ADHD is comprised of two major symptoms: innattention and disinhibition. Inattention may be seen as difficulty sustaining attention or responding to tasks or play activities as compared with children of the same age (Barkley, 1996). It may also be manifested as being more distracted, disorganized, and forgetful. These children tend to daydream, appear to not listen, not complete tasks or assignments, frequently change activities, and have difficulty concentrating on repetitive, mundane, and undesirable tasks. Hyperactive-impulsive or disinhibited symptoms may be seen as fidgeting, difficulty remaining seated, playing noisily, interrupting others' conversations, responding too quickly or too frequently, disrupting others' activities, impatience, difficulty waiting in line, constantly moving about, difficulty stopping an ongoing behavior, and difficulty delaying gratification and resisting immediate temptations. Impulsivity refers to the child's tendency to act before thinking—to draw, shoot, then aim. This does not involve abnormal thoughts of the child; rather it involves the tendency to act on them, with a lack of ability to inhibit these actions (Jacobs, 1998).

A child who has ADHD has enormous difficulty in following rules (Jacobs, 1998). Following rules is a skill that requires the child to conform to the expectations of others, delay gratification, and understand that he or she must conform to abstract guidelines that may or may not provide immediate rewards or gratification. A child with ADHD has difficulty maintaining his or her attention for long periods, and will tend to follow rules inconsistently. The child has trouble selectively focusing on the most important information, may not realize that the rules exist, and may not understand how the rules apply to behavior.

According to Jacobs (1998), rewards and consequences must therefore "be stronger, more immediate, and more tied to specific behaviors. . . . Rewards and consequences have to be varied more often, as children with ADHD get use to them quickly and they lose their power over the children's behavior" (p. 36).

As indicated by Barkley (1996), symptoms associated with disinhibition tend to appear first, between ages 3–4 years. Symptoms of inattention arise around 5–7 years of age, by entering school, or even later elementary school grades if inattention is the principal problem. Although disinhibition symptoms tend to decline with age, inattention symptoms remain relatively stable throughout the elementary school grades.

Managed Care Issues Regarding Assessment

According to Tatum (1997), parents wanting their child evaluated for ADHD often have an initial meeting with a therapist. Some managed care companies require an initial assessment by a therapist, and others have varying policies regarding the evaluation of children. For example, a managed care company may require that a child first be seen by a therapist to determine if a referral to a psychiatrist for an evaluation is appropriate. In this instance, the therapist is the "gatekeeper." Another company may require the client (parent) to contact a psychiatrist *first*. In this case, the psychiatrist would act as gatekeeper, and determine whether therapy (or an evaluation) was appropriate in the course of treatment of the child. Some parents have decided to send their child to a particular professional for evaluation, and incurred the respective fees. Upon contacting their insurance company, they discovered that their child needed to see some other professional as the first step. The initial expenditures were not reimbursed by the insurance company. To prevent this, parents are encouraged to contact their insurance companies and clarify their coverage at the outset of any evaluation or treatment process.

Whether the parent chooses or the insurance company approves an evaluation for a child, the therapist may refer the child to a physician, psychiatrist, or other qualified mental health practitioner for the ADHD evaluation. Nevertheless, Tatum (1997) states that the therapist's assessment and opinions regarding the child are valuable to the person performing the evaluation because the therapist may have information about family dynamics, environmental factors, and how the symptoms are manifested in the child's behavior.

Treatment and Medication Considerations

Dr. Blalock (1997) emphasizes the necessity of parents' acceptance of and involvement in their child's treatment. Presuming a proper ADHD diagnosis is reached and the family is in agreement, he believes that medication should be tried. Often, as parents learn more about the condition and the medications, their apprehensions abate. He states that:

If broken down into their individual contributions, the treatment component that has the single most demonstrable effect is medication. . . . The role of medication has become so clear that not to offer it borders on neglect. However, if the family cannot understand or accept the diagnosis and they have strong fears and reservations regarding the medications, then other lines of treatment should be implemented first.

Blalock (1997) also reports that there are three classes of ADHD medications: stimulants, antidepressants, and others. These are mentioned in the order of their effectiveness and the order in which they are prescribed. For example, if there is an appropriate diagnosis of ADHD and the child does not respond to stimulant medications, then an antidepressant will probably be tried. For ADHD, stimulants (e. g., Adderall, Ritalin, and Dexedrine) will be effective with 70–80% of the children, and have generated the fewest number of associated somatic complaints. They are short-acting, nonnarcotic, nonaddictive, and are out of the child's system in a few hours. Response to stimulants is much quicker than to antidepressants. Because there is a modest potential for abuse, they are strictly regulated and somewhat difficult to obtain. At least in Texas, prescriptions must be written in triplicate, cannot be refilled, cannot be called-in, and must be filled within seven days. Antidepressants appear to be very useful in many cases, and have a 30–50% rate of effectiveness. Response to antidepressants may take weeks to manifest itself, and, hopefully, there will be few negative side effects during this time. Many of these medications should not be discontinued abruptly because they can produce unpleasant effects if not tapered off. However, if one dose of an antidepressant is forgotten or otherwise missed, the consequences are negligible. If one dose of the stimulant class is missed results will be immediate, and possibly very noticeable or even dramatic. The third category includes a variety of medications that have been successful in isolated cases.

Parents occasionally express fears that Ritalin will stunt their child's physical growth. According to Tatum (1997), whether this problem is significant it is more controversial than the problem itself. Again, clinical lore suggests that any slowing of growth caused by the medication can be recovered on weekends or other periods when the children are off the medication. "Any shortening of stature would probably not be clinically significant. However, the benefits far outweigh this risk because, without the medication, children's self-esteem will certainly suffer." Parents also may be concerned about the "drugged" effects that ADHD medications have on their child. Tatum says, "stimulants used to treat ADHD should not make children feel drugged. They are not sedating, and there are no indications that they predispose children to substance abuse."

According to Blalock (1997), successful treatment almost always involves more than medication, and all of the treatment components are important. Only about 70–80% of children with ADHD respond beneficially to medication. Parents need to be involved enough to evaluate all of the treatment components: the diagnosis; how the condition is likely to affect their child; what the expected life pattern is; changes in lifestyle, structure, and routines necessary with medication; and what interventions are likely to help. Parental involvement in the entire diagnostic and treatment process maximizes the probability of successful treatment. Even if parents are opposed to the medications, other treatment components should be pursued. *Medications help, primarily, by making the other aspects of treatment much more effective.*

There are a number of factors that influence the ability of a child with ADHD to stay on-task, control impulses, self-regulate, and be productive. These, according to Barkley (1996), include fatigue, time of day, level of stimulation, task complexity, amount of restraint required for a given task, supervision, and immediate consequences. The child with ADHD is more likely to have difficulty when persistence in work related tasks is needed or when behavioral restraint is required and the child faces scrutiny by others (e.g., in school, church, restaurants, or when a parent is on the phone). Problems are less likely to arise during free play or when little self-control is needed. Parents and therapists must take these issues into consideration when disciplining or working with children having ADHD.

If parents request medication, and that is the only treatment modality they will agree to, Blalock (1997) reported that he is apprehensive and pessimistic regarding the outcome of treatment. With the implementation of all the treatment components, the child is more likely to lead a normal life than if some components are rejected or ignored; using medication to the exclusion of everything else reduces the likelihood of a positive treatment outcome. Blalock uses the analogy of diabetes to teach about ADHD treatment. Learning a lot about the disease, risk factors, and changes in diet and lifestyle becomes an essential part of leading a normal life, and without commitment to these other treatment components medication may not be profoundly helpful. Making sure the parents are on board with the treatment of their child is essential—parents must be committed. Even if parents are enthusiastic about medication, their child may be among the 20% who do not respond to medication. They will need to be very involved and committed to apply the other treatment modalities. The parents' positive attitude is crucial because, without their willing involvement in the treatment, maximum outcomes are impossible to achieve.

According to Tatum (1997), long-term response to ADHD tends to be broken down into thirds. Approximately one-third of children find that their symptoms resolve by adulthood. The second "third" of children continue to experience some symptoms into adulthood, but these are less (i.e., inattention being the symptom that is most persistant). Medication for these symptoms continue to be beneficial. The last third includes people whose symptoms were not well-controlled during childhood and continue to be not well-controlled in adulthood. These people continually struggle, often developing substance abuse or antisocial behaviors. Complaints of symptoms that tend to go away first involve impulsivity and hyperactivity; inattention tends to stay the longest.

Parenting Skills and Techniques to Help Children with ADHD

When children are diagnosed with ADHD, the parents of these children face special challenges. Children's behavioral expressions of ADHD can have overwhelming and calamitous effects on the families. The mother usually has the responsibility for the day to day care and, therefore, will often experience the greatest difficulty and hardship. Often, the mother is the person who first notices the behavioral symptoms of ADHD, but it can take years after the onset of behaviors to decipher whether the child actually has ADHD (Friedman & Doyal, 1992). Fathers have a tendency to attribute ADHD behaviors to normal, active behavior, especially in young children. Fathers often are less accepting of the counselor's suggestions, express more doubts, and anticipate more pitfalls (Jacobs, 1998). Regardless of whether there are differences between parents, or if they have assumed separate and disparate roles, the therapist must be sensitive to both mother and father. Both parents' feelings must be acknowledged and validated by the therapist.

Blalock (1997) emphasizes that the entire family is affected when a child is diagnosed with ADHD. Parents need support, understanding, and encouragement in order to cope with their child's behavior and difficulties. Parents will experience stressful periods as they face the long-term, ongoing challenges of raising a child with ADHD.

A diagnosis of ADHD can cause conflicting feelings in the parents regarding their perceptions of their child, themselves, and their parenting abilities. Parents respond to the diagnosis in one of three ways: denial, tolerance, or acceptance (Whitman & Smith, 1991). "Denial can manifest itself in one of two ways: (a) with a complete malabsorption of what the diagnosis implies and a resultant failure to respond in any way to the child's needs, or (b) with anger and defensiveness" (p. 206). Parents who respond with anger and defensiveness fail to recognize the neurological difference, and maintain that their child can control his or her behavior but deliberately does not. Parents who get immersed in the nature of the diagnosis respond with unawareness and indifference, ignoring rather than responding to their child's needs. They also tend to blame others, such as the schools, for their child's behaviors. According to Gupta (1999), parents who are in denial often make the following types of arguments against their children having ADHD: "My child is able to play on the computer or watch television for two hours"; "My child sat appropriately in the doctor's office for 20 minutes"; "My child acts okay at home"; "Maybe his teacher just doesn't like him."

Children with ADHD are often able to focus on what interests them, with discrepancies, inattention, and activity level due to interest level and attentional demand (Woods & Ploof, 1997). Some parents of ADHD children do not see the more renowned symptoms because there is no structured demand at home. Often, being at school is not as much fun as being at home for these children; they have fewer interests at school, and there is a greater demand for them to be attentive. Blalock (1997) emphasized, "not only is this not a disqualifier for the diagnosis, but it comes close to being characteristic. Hyperfocus, the ability to become absorbed in a chosen, stimulating, salient pursuit for hours at a time and possibly shutting out the world, is a very commonly observed behavior in the most floridly affected children."

Parents who tolerate the diagnosis are often relieved that someone has identified what is wrong with their child. However, the parents fail to recognize the complexity of the diagnosis and what it means in relation to their child's behaviors and needs. Therefore, parents are inconsistent in their expectations of their children and inconsistent in their responses to them. The children may or may not feel accepted, and are often unclear about parameters regarding their behaviors (Whitman & Smith, 1991).

Parents who are accepting of the ADHD diagnosis usually are relieved and hopeful that treatment will improve their child's life. Accepting parents have known their child was different and feel validated when the diagnosis is formally presented (Whitman & Smith, 1991). Accepting parents also realize the diagnosis is permanent and that treatment, in some form, will be ongoing. The focus is on the diagnosis and not on blaming the child.

According to Whitman and Smith (1991), "parents' level of acceptance of the ADHD diagnosis impacts their feelings toward their child's behaviors and the impact of these behaviors on the family" (p. 207).

Even accepting parents will experience difficult periods with their child and should be reminded that management of ADHD is an ongoing process. The therapist can be instrumental in helping parents who deny or tolerate the ADHD diagnosis move toward more acceptance. These parents benefit most by learning how to manage the symptomatic behaviors of their ADHD child and by having their feelings legitimized regarding the ADHD diagnosis of their child.

Tatum (1997) stresses the importance of therapists working closely with the parents whose child has been diagnosed with ADHD. "If a therapist does not work closely with the parents and pay attention to them, then I will not refer ADHD patients to that therapist." Tatum recommends that the therapist teach parenting skills and filial therapy to the parents. He gave the following example to show the benefits of involving the parents in the treatment of children with ADHD. A father whose son had been diagnosed with ADHD and depression was instructed by the therapist to have two uninterrupted, 30-minute play sessions with his son each week. The father later complained that the child's behavior had not improved, and the father's frustration had drastically increased. As the therapist probed into the details of the play sessions, the father revealed that the play sessions involved watching television with his son sitting in his lap, or the son accompanying his father to work. The father was then coached by the therapist on how to conduct the play sessions. Several weeks later, the father reported dramatic positive changes in the child's behaviors and in his relationship with the child. Whitman and Smith (1991) said, "parental views of, and responses to, this child impact on treatment efficacy and outcomes" (p. 209).

Interventions

The greatest challenge for parents and therapists is to aid children with ADHD in developing more internal controls. However, there are several interventions which are effective in helping these children develop and master the internal controls necessary to maintain behavior which are acceptable in their milieu.

Intervention 1: Pharmacology

About 70–80% of children with ADHD require medication. Medication improves social behavior, decreases impulsivity, motor restlessness, and indirectly improves academic performance (Gupta, 1999). Refer to the previous ADHD section: *Treatment and Medication Considerations,* for information regarding medications utilized in the treatment of ADHD.

Intervention 2: Antecedent Phase of Behavior

By observing and becoming aware of what things happen *just before* problem behaviors are exhibited, parents increase the chances of ameliorating the unwanted behaviors of their child. Actions taken during the antecedent phase of behavior can foster resolutions for the behaviors, as well as prohibit emotions such as anger and frustration, of both parents and child, from escalating. By teaching parents to carefully observe the progression of their child's behaviors, the parents can understand the patterns and triggers of the behaviors. A greater understanding of the child's behaviors, especially the catalysts for the behaviors, fosters more acceptance by the parents for the child and provides opportunities for quick, effective intervention (Braswell & Bloomquist, 1991).

Six-year-old Clayton was diagnosed with ADHD in the first grade. Clayton's mother, who was a medical doctor working long hours, was overwhelmed and frustrated by Clayton's behavior at night and on the weekends at home. The therapist asked her to list the behaviors that most frustrated her. At the top of the list was Clayton arguing and hitting his 3-year-old brother. The therapist told Clayton's mother to carefully observe Clayton's behavior the next week, especially what happened just prior to the arguing and hitting between Clayton and his brother, and asked her to write down her observations. The following week, Clayton's mother was surprised at the similar patterns that preceded the arguments and hitting. She discovered three main triggers: Clayton was tired, "alone time" with his father had not been available, and Clayton wanted more of his mother's attention. The therapist told Clayton and his mother to plan a special date and time to discuss the behavior and triggers. Clayton and his mother were also asked to write down the triggers and possible interventions, such as separating Clayton and his brother when Clayton was tired, planning ahead for Clayton to have alone time with his father right after dinner and at certain times on weekends, and scheduling specific one-on-one times for Clayton and his mother.

While Clayton's mother tried to implement the interventions on a regular basis, both she and Clayton agreed to try to be more aware when Clayton's feelings of anger and frustration were building. When either of them recognized it, they were to look at the list of interventions and select one. Clayton's mother reported two weeks later that the arguing and hitting was greatly diminished. Another benefit was that Clayton told his mother that he felt happier because she was "not always taking my brother's side." Clayton's mother said she felt closer to Clayton, and realized that she had been blaming him for the arguing and hitting because he was older.

Intervention 3: Structure, Routine, and Consistency

Structure is one of the primary nonmedical treatments for children diagnosed with ADHD (Rief, 1997). When children are diagnosed with ADHD, parents quickly become aware of the importance of structure. With or without medication, children with ADHD require substantial structure to maximize their functioning and to minimize their frustration. For example, without structure, homework is frequently incomplete or forgotten, resulting in negative repercussions for the child and possible impaired attitudes in future school performance. With repeated failures, children often learn not to bother putting forth effort (Blalock, 1997).

Setting up and implementing structure for their child can be formidable for some parents. Ogan (1994) offers the following suggestions for more effective plans for structure with their children.

Task Structure

When presented with a task, be sure the child:

- Understands what needs to be done.
- Is not overwhelmed by the size and complexity of the task.
- Is given sufficient cues to minimize frustration.
- Can successfully complete the task with a sense of accomplishment and pride.

How to accomplish this:

- Select tasks that are either well within the child's range of capabilities or only slightly more difficult than those that can be successfully performed independently.
- Be sure to elicit the child's attention before explaining the task. Either establish eye contact with the child or focus the child's attention on the task.
- Explain the instructions slowly, using simple words and short sentences. Patiently repeat the instructions if necessary; some children have auditory lag.
- Supplement verbal instruction with picture cues or actual demonstrations. When using demonstrations, proceed through each step slowly.

- Break down complex tasks into sequential parts. Be sure the child understands each part before presenting the next one.
- Help the child actually move through the performance of a task if necessary. For example, when learning to draw different shapes, guide the child's hand (manually or with templates) through the movements that produce the shape.
- Offer supportive reassurance whenever the child's attention or motivation begins to decrease.
- Monitor the child's performance. With noncritical comments, guide his or her efforts toward successful completion of the task.
- If a child is unsuccessful with a task, praise his or her efforts and provide the opportunity to try again.
- While repetition or practice is important, do not make excessive demands of the child at any one time.
- Remember that there is more than one way to reach a goal. Most skills, such as various social or educational skills, may be taught in a variety of ways. Do not persist with a particular task or procedure if it always results in frustration, failure, or a power struggle. Be prepared to select alternate tasks or procedures that will develop the same skills, but in a more harmonious way (pp. 101–102, reprinted with permission).

Helping the Child to Complete Homework.   A child with ADHD typically has deficits in attentional and behavioral persistence (Jacobs, 1998). Likewise, this child tends to have difficulty with, and low motivation for, tasks that are viewed as uninteresting, unstimulating, and repetitive—such as homework. For the child with ADHD, homework places heavy demands on his or her organizational abilities. At a young age, the child with ADHD learns that avoiding demanding tasks protects against failure and humiliation. Therefore, a child with ADHD typically does not finish homework, and often does not begin, without adult supervision. This can be very confusing and vexing to parents who realize their child knows the material or has the intelligence to learn it. Even more disturbing to parents is the child who completes the homework, but fails to turn it in. It is necessary for parents to keep their focus on the traits of ADHD, and prevent themselves from seeing their child's behavior as a reflection on themselves and prevent the related power struggles.

A child with ADHD will work best on a task that is new, but the effect of the novelty is short-lived. For this child, Jacobs (1998) recommends working for 10 or 15 minutes and then taking a short break. The child that works until bored, distracted, or tired will associate negative feelings with the task and resist returning to it. "The mention of homework will then elicit a negative psychological and physiological reaction in the child" (p. 141). However, if the child pauses while attentive, energetic, and productive, then he or she will be much more motivated to return to the task. Positive feelings of productiveness will be experienced, as well as receiving a reward (i.e., the break) for effort. The child needs help organizing the work, especially with the initial formatting of homework time. Parental help will also be needed in breaking down long-term responsibilities and large projects into nonoverwhelming tasks, and then scheduling these tasks. Lists and charts that can be copied, modified, and reused are invaluable to helping children with ADHD maintain organization and succeed. Adequate time for homework (and short breaks) should be allotted, and recreational activities can serve as rewards for completing the work efficiently. The child will also realize that homework time is a priority before recreation time.

Helping the Child Turn in Homework.   A child with ADHD may actually complete all of his or her homework, then forget to turn it in. Parents become very aggravated when this happens and have great difficulty understanding that *this is a characteristic of ADHD, and not just a deliberately defiant child.* To help increase the frequency that homework is turned in, develop a contract with the child that specifies desirable activities, privileges, or rewards for turning in assignments on one's own (McCarney, 1992). Provide verbal rewards, as well. As the child increases his or her success, gradually increase the number of times required to receive the reward. Also, allow for the occurrence of natural consequences when assignments are not turned in (e.g., the child does not get to participate in a desired activity).

Helping the Child Need Fewer Reminders.   According to McCarney and Bauer (1990), if a child has to have several reminders before completing tasks, then rules for following directions can be established. These rules must apply to everyone in the home. Examples include listening carefully to directions, asking questions when directions are not understood, and following directions without being reminded. Directions should not be given from another room. Rather, the parent should go to the child, get his or her attention, and then communicate the directions. Reward the child (and others in the home) when directions are followed without reminders. Possible rewards include verbal praise (e.g., "Thank you. You knew how to complete that job, and you did it."), desired activities (e.g., watching a favorite movie, going to the playground, having a friend over), and hugs and kisses. Give directions at the time for which the task is to be done, not for some future period. For a reoccurring task, a behavior contract can be written that clearly specifies the task and includes the reward. This contract must be written in language that the child understands, and should address only one task at a time. Parents can benefit the child greatly by helping to get a task started, such as homework or cleaning his or her room. The child should not be punished if he or she forgets or is interrupted. However, allow natural consequences to occur (e.g., toys left in the street may be run over by cars), or administer logical consequences (e.g., bedtime is one minute earlier for each required reminder). *Consistency is essential.* The child should not be expected to follow directions one time, then permitted to fail to follow the directions the next time. Also, expectations of the child must be appropriate for his or her developmental level.

Helping the Child Monitor One's Own Behavior.   Eventually, children must be able to effectively respond, on their own, to the multitude of demands presented by their environment (Jacobs, 1998). As children learn about choices and consequences, as they internalize values, rules and limits, checklists that identify series of manageable tasks can be of tremendous benefit in helping to monitor their own behavior. Children should be involved in the process of constructing checklists (Rief, 1997), and the checklists should specify rewards and consequences related to completion or lack of completion of the tasks. For example, a "morning checklist" that includes the following items could be posted in the child's room: 1) get out of bed on time, 2) wash face, 3) comb hair, 4) get dressed, 5) get school materials in backpack, 6) eat breakfast, and 7) brush teeth. A new copy could be used each day to allow the child to actually cross off or check each item with a favorite pen. Self-monitoring techniques typically involve keeping track, in writing, of specific behaviors. For children with ADHD, pre-established checklists provide needed structure and consistency.

Intervention 4: Situational Structure

According to Ogan (1994), the parameters of the situation for expected behaviors must be well-defined.

- Do not expose the attention deficit child to situations where failure is anticipated.
- Prepare the child in advance for every situation that is not part of the usual daily routine.
- Explain clearly to the child what can be expected in a situation.

- Explain the expected behavior, limits, and consequences in a supportive, nonthreatening, yet decisive manner.
- The duration of an experience should be determined by the child's tolerance.
- Reward appropriate behavior.
- Avoid setting goals that are unrealistic, vague, or will not be applied.
- Limit the choices that the child must make.
- Provide structure through the use of established procedures.
- Follow a relatively consistent daily schedule at home and at school.
- Monitor the child's behavior in each situation (pp. 102–103, reprinted with permission).

Helping the Child with Sequencing Skills. Sequential processing is an ability that involves linear and logical (cause and effect) thinking and development of a future orientation. Development of sequencing skills is greatly needed by children with ADHD (Jacobs, 1998). Learning to cope with changes and transitions helps children to develop sequencing skills. However, children with ADHD have tremendous difficulty dealing with transitions—changes in their routines or environment. Change may be the only universal constant. For children to learn to cope effectively with their world, they need skills in adapting to the flow of events over time. They need to be able to predict and anticipate changes and to modify their behavior (choices) in response to changes in expectations, rules, and consequences. Some changes are radical and obvious, and some, such as social norms and mores, can be very subtle.

Letting the Child Have Control. Ironically, it is often helpful to give the child control over an issue that he or she seems unable to control. This often can eliminate a struggle between the parent and the child. This technique, adapted from recommendations by Jacobs (1998), involves assigning a goal to the child, but giving him or her the freedom and choices in pursuing the goal. For instance an assignment might involve telling the child, "I realize that you and your parents argue a lot. There seem to be too many arguments to keep track of. I want you to write down on a chart how many arguments you have with your parents. Your goal is to have a lower number of arguments than you had on the previous day. Don't worry if the number increases, just remember that your goal is to have fewer arguments on the next day. Do whatever you need to do to have fewer arguments." Assuming that the child protests or is otherwise resistant, reassure him or her that no one is to blame, that the parents also have assignments, and that the child's perspective and judgment is highly valued.

Jacobs (1998) contends that children, especially those with whom specific behavioral interventions have not previously worked, respond well to specifying a goal without assigning specific behaviors. This method frees the child to attribute the arguing and subsequent improvement to whatever is useful to him or her, and whatever is helpful in pursuing the goal. Prescriptions of specific behaviors limit these attributions related to behaviors and improvements.

Intervention 5: Relationship Structure

Structure will be more acceptable and more understandable if the child has opportunities to see behaviors and outcomes in action by someone whom the child trusts and believes.

- Demonstrate or model the kinds of behavior that will enable the child to cope successfully with his or her feelings and needs.
- Through careful observation of the child, learn to recognize the early stages of emotional upset; intervene quickly.
- Use honesty, fairness, consistency, and nonvindictive interventions to build a trusting relationship with the child.
- Share with the child some of the difficult experiences or fears you have had in your own life.
- Model appropriate behaviors for the child.
- Verbalize cause-effect relationships for the child.
- Acknowledge and praise the child's efforts and his or her progress.
- Explain to the child that he or she has trouble tuning in (use TV and adjustment of antenna as an example) (Ogan, 1994, p. 103, reprinted with permission).

Helping the Child to Control Impulsivity.   Silver (1999) described impulsivity as "being unable to stop or having difficulty stopping to reflect before speaking or acting. Some individuals have difficulty stopping to think before speaking; others have difficulty stopping to think before acting. Most individuals have problems with both" (p. 55). Children with ADHD often know what to do and what not to do. The problem is that they sometimes do not bring their knowledge to bear. They know that if they do not do their homework they will get in trouble, or if they run out in front of a car they will get hurt. *It is not a failure to know what to do. It is a failure to do what they know.* The problem is that they run out in front of a car without thinking, or forget their homework and leave it on the bus. They regret it just as much as the next child; they are also graded and berated just the same as the next child. At this point, it is too late to do anything about it. A typical statement from the child with ADHD is, "I really want to, but I can't." Unfortunately, parents turn this statement around and perceive, "I can, but I just don't want to." Parents often add discipline to make a point with the child. However, the child already knows the lesson the parents are seeking to teach. The problem has to be with remembering (Blalock, 1997). Barkley (cited by Blalock) emphasized that dealing with ADHD is not a matter of knowing what to do; rather, it is a matter of doing what is already known. Management of behaviors should be aimed first at helping children remember and then developing the skills to follow through on that knowledge. Ogan (1994) reinforced that premise:

> Even when a child may be able to tell you that an action would be wrong, they may do that same action before realizing they are in the process of doing it. There is no consideration of any consequence that may befall, although at a later time, they may be able to tell you what such consequences might be if "someone" performed such an action. At the moment they are engaged in the action, they are oblivious to those same potential consequences. In such instances they don't realize that their own response has been inappropriate. Often they may say they didn't do what the parent just saw them doing . . . this can be more than frustrating! (p. 113)

Consistency with Limits, Choices, and Consequences. A child who has ADHD is driven by the present moment, unable to delay gratification, and unable to anticipate future rewards or consequences (Jacobs, 1998). Therefore, there is little value in parents' attempts to talk through problems with their child and use language to change their child's behavior. Language should be used to briefly explain why the consequences occur—to tie the consequences to the behavior. A child with ADHD is affected much more by real-world consequences than by parents' words.

Positive consequences, rewards, and negative consequences must be administered (or naturally occur) immediately, frequently, specifically, and consistently if a child with ADHD is to associate making a choice with a corresponding consequence (Barkley, 1997). Nelsen (1981) emphasizes the importance of consequences also being related, respectful, and reasonable. Although a child with ADHD may have a life-long challenge with impulse-control, he or she can learn to improve decision-making skills. However, because this child is challenged with inattention and disinhibition, there is a limited ability to associate delayed consequences and rewards with choices (Rief, 1997).

Jacobs (1998) and Barkley (1995) recommend that parents communicate consequences without emotion, long explanations, justifications, or negotiations. Although this appears to contradict some beliefs about emotional development and parental bonding, it is typically more important for the parent to remain in control and to structure their child's environment. Nelsen (1981) indicates that if the parent can communicate limits and consequences to the child without anger and without shaming the child (emphasizing that the child chose the consequence when he or she chose to break the limit), then the child will feel accepted, understood, and respected by the parent. Parents must not lose sight of exploring with their child what he or she wants, and not simply imposing what the parent wants. This way, the parent-child relationship will be enhanced rather than damaged.

Many necessary parenting skills, especially with children having ADHD, are counterintuitive or seem to run counter to what parents believe are good parenting practices (Jacobs, 1998). For instance, a parent who is concerned about public appearance and sensitive about personal displays in public might have difficulty administering a time-out in a restaurant or department store. A parent who believes in the importance of understanding the child's emotions and explaining things to the child might find it difficult to adopt authoritative, no-nonsense limit setting. Regardless, parents need to develop an understanding of how the child sees the world, and how the child sees himself or herself. In addition, it is essential that parents create an environment that provides structure and consistency for the child.

Team Concept in Parenting.   Whenever there are two (or more) guardians for a child, these guardians must function as a parenting team. Different parenting styles often result in power struggles between the parents (Jacobs, 1998). For example, a boy's parents may have differing opinions about how to handle a bully at school. One parent may believe the best course of action is to fight back, while the other parent may believe the boy should walk away and tell a teacher. Such a difference can lead to a breakdown of the parental relationship, dysfunction in the family system, and severe damage to the emotional well-being of their son. If parents support each other, then each is reinforced in the parental role which makes each more effective and self-assured in communicating limits, following through with consequences, and providing a healthy role model for the child. Children (and family systems) need the comfort provided by parental consistency. They need both parents to be in positions of authority and guidance, and both parents working together (Woods & Ploof, 1997).

Differences in parents' perspectives, opinions, and expectations can provide tremendous benefit to the child, as well as the marriage and the family (Jacobs, 1998). Different people cannot be expected to be void of differing personalities and values. However, parents must use these differences to complement each other, rather than to undermine each other.

Reducing Arguments and Fighting.   Arguing, fighting, and bickering often characterize families that have one or more member with ADHD (Jacobs, 1998). Children (and adults) who face repeated criticism, punishment, shaming, and ridicule typically develop patterns of argumentative, oppositional, and defiant behavior. Jacobs states that arguments, themselves, tend to take on consistent patterns over time, with predictable patterns of "intensity, interaction, build-up, crescendo, and resolution" (p. 131). Although family members may believe that specific arguments actually involve specific issues (e.g., bedtime, chores, discipline), examination of patterns reveals that arguments usually are more often because of a need to engage in a control struggle. Therefore, it is very important that parents and therapists look at the *process* of the arguments, and not simply the *content*. These patterns also need to be examined in order for parents to avoid the related traps. Parents need to be aware of their own roles in the initiation and continuance of control struggles with children and spouses. For example, if a parent wishes that the child learns better self-monitoring skills, then the parent must also learn and demonstrate these skills.

Special Play Time with the Child.   Barkley (1997) emphasizes the importance of parents having special play times with their child who has ADHD. He describes these brief, 10–15 minute periods of uninterrupted play time, in which the activity is directed by the child, with few limits. During this time the parent focuses attention on the child, and acknowledges appropriate behaviors.

Joining a Parent Support Group.   Parent support groups can provide parents with a network of social and emotional assistance. A large national-international organization for parents of children with ADHD is known as CHADD (Children and Adults with Attention-Deficit Disorders). CHADD usually conducts meetings for parents and professionals on a monthly basis. For a list of additional support groups and advocacy agencies, see Appendix F.

Practicing Forgiveness.   The principle of practicing forgiveness with the ADHD child is important, but often difficult for parents to do consistently. Barkley (1995) says practicing forgiveness involves three steps for parents. First, at the end of each day, parents should take a moment to review the day and forgive the child for transgressions. They should strive to let go of the negative emotions such as anger and resentment that was experienced throughout the day. Remember the child cannot always control what he or she does and deserves to be forgiven. Second, parents need to concentrate on forgiving others who may have misunderstood the child's inappropriate behavior and acted in offensive ways. Third, forgiving oneself for mistakes in the management of the ADHD child that day is important.

☐ Depression

Tatum (1997) reports that, for many years, general opinion maintained that young children were not capable of having depression. Support of this opinion included the belief that their egos were not yet structured enough. Current opinion proclaims that children's biological makeup is similar to that of adults, thereby supporting the probability of children having depression similar to that of adults. As Green (1980) indicates, younger children have not developed the understanding or verbalization skills to describe what they are experiencing. Therefore, *changes in behavior patterns and physical symptoms are what trigger suspicion that children may have conditions that require treatment.*

Diagnosis and Assessment Considerations

The same criteria used to diagnose depression in adults can be applied to children. A few symptoms, especially irritable mood and grumpiness, are more likely to be present in childhood depression than in adult depression. Children are also more likely than adults to exhibit somatic complaints, separation anxiety, phobias, and behavioral problems. Children are less likely than adolescents and adults to experience anhedonia, and exhibit vegetative symptoms. Symptoms of depression also may be presented as loneliness, frequent crying, perfectionism, feeling unloved, feeling persecuted, feeling worthless, having fear impulses, being self-conscious, being suspicious, feeling unhappy, feeling nervous, feeling guilty, and frequent worrying (Hammen & Rudolph, 1996).

Most behaviors and physical symptoms of depression and other disorders are typical and common for all children at different times, so they may or may not mean that a child is depressed. According to Tatum

(1997), the key to determining whether the behaviors and symptoms are related to depression is to look for *changes* in behavior and physical symptoms in the child. Intensity, frequency, and duration of the observed behaviors also indicate whether concern is warranted.

According to the fourth edition of DSM-IV (APA, 1994), diagnosis for major depression involves meeting five or more symptoms out of nine during a period of at least two weeks. At least one of the symptoms must be depressed mood, or loss of interest or pleasure. In diagnosing children, irritable mood may be substituted for depressed mood. The nine symptoms are: depressed mood; significant decrease in interest or pleasure in all or most activities; significant weight loss, weight gain, or decrease in appetite (in children this can present as not achieving expected weight gains); excessive or lack of sleep; psychomotor agitation or retardation; lack of energy or fatigue; excessive or inappropriate guilt or feelings of worthlessness; difficulty concentrating or making decisions; and recurrent thoughts about dying or suicide. The presence of three of those symptoms, for at least one year, signifies dysthymia in children. *Dysthymia,* according to Tatum (1997), is a low-grade, long-term, depression. Both major depression and dysthymia symptoms may manifest themselves as changes of attitude, increased irritability, withdrawal, and a decrease of self-esteem. For example, these might be evidenced by a child saying, "I can't do anything" or "I'm no good."

According to Blatt & Homann (1992), the expression of depression in children may include dysphoric mood, sleep disturbances, anhedonia, suicidal thoughts, as well as the "multiple forms of defense that children, especially adolescents, often use against depression, such as denial, mania, and displacement in various types of enactments" (p. 82). Family history is another aspect that can have a large impact regarding a child's depression and can influence whether a diagnosis of depression is given. Green (1980) indicates that children can have a genetic predisposition for depression, and there is a greater chance that depression will present itself in children for whom there is a positive family history. There is also a greater chance that depression will show up at a younger age.

Tatum (1997) states that psychiatrists and physicians use **SIG E CAPSS**, a common mnemonic based upon medical vernacular, to help determine if a person is depressed. It symbolizes the symptoms that psychiatrists look for when screening for depression, symptoms referred to as the *neurovegetative signs of depression.* **S** represents changes in sleep patterns, which can be either up or down and are labeled as excessive, or as three types of insomnia. Initial insomnia involves difficulty falling asleep, intermittent insomnia refers to waking up throughout the night, and terminal insomnia signifies waking up during the night without falling back asleep. I represents loss of interest in things that the child normally enjoys and is frequently referred to as anhedonia. G represents feelings of guilt that may be accompanied by feelings of helplessness and hopelessness. E CAP represents increases or decreases in energy level, concentration, and appetite that may be symptoms of depression, as well as changes in psychomotor, or physical activity, levels. The first S represents a decrease in libido, or interest in sex, which is a strong sign of depression for adults but is not important for young children. The final S represents increased thoughts of death, dying and suicide. Such thoughts are very serious, and must always be carefully considered.

Medication Considerations

Regarding treatment of depression, Tatum (1997) states that clinical experience has shown medication to be tremendously beneficial. In addition, the newer antidepressants also are much safer to use, generating fewer and milder side effects. Clinical lore upholds that antidepressants are very effective for children, although there are few research studies that document this. Conducting research with children is very difficult, as the majority of parents are reluctant to subject their child to medical research studies.

Tatum (1997) describes a 4½-year-old girl who had severe symptoms consistent with separation anxiety disorder and depression. She had been going to therapy, but was not progressing. Tatum prescribed an extremely low dose of Prozac and described the positive results as being "absolutely dramatic." For about six months the girl did very well. However, the mother grew tired of hearing from relatives, friends, and rumors that she was a terrible mother for putting her daughter on Prozac. She discontinued giving the medicine to her daughter without consulting the doctor. Within one week the girl again was exhibiting rages, tearing things up, shouting, and scratching siblings, with noncompliance and unresponsiveness to appropriate parenting interventions. Tatum said that they "restarted the Prozac, and it evened her out—just like magic." The daycare workers at the church even commented regarding their surprise at the sudden and immense changes. Tatum kept the child on the medication for nine months, then tapered off the dosage. The symptomatic behaviors resumed, so the medication dosage was again increased; the behaviors changed for the better. This is one of many examples that Tatum says demonstrate how dramatic improvement can be achieved with the use of antidepressants.

Parenting and Therapeutic Considerations

According to Kennedy, Spence, and Hensley (1989), children with depression consider themselves to be less socially skilled, more submissive, and less assertive as compared to nondepressed children. Hammen and Rudolph (1996) report that children with depression tend to be unpopular and rejected by other school children, and to isolate themselves from their peers. Their coping skills tend to have less of an active, problem-solving focus, and more of an avoidant, passive, and emotionally-driven focus. In response to interpersonal and academic challenges, depressed children tend to have increased levels of helpless coping. Academic achievement tends to be negatively affected by depression, but there is less affect on actual intellectual potential. Thus, depression interferes with children's motivation or ability to reach for their full potential.

Helping the Child with Social Successes.   Cole and Cole (1996) express the need for the child to have *islands of confidence*—areas in which the child has experienced success. Small successes build courage and confidence needed to strive for larger successes. McCarney (1992) suggests providing the opportunity for the child to experience varied social situations and varied groupings of children. This will allow parents and teachers to determine the type of setting and people with which the child has the most comfort. When possible, make adjustments in the environment to prevent the child from experiencing stress and frustration. For example, separate the child from a classmate who stimulates sudden mood changes. Also, the child may need guidance regarding appropriate self-expression, especially socially acceptable expressions of feelings.

Helping the Child with Academic Successes.   Consistent routines enhance the child's sense of stability. Give the child advance notice of upcoming changes, such as the termination of a routine activity, beginning a new activity, or special events. A calm and pleasant environment can reduce the probability of sudden or dramatic mood changes. Flexibility in completing assignments may be required if the child demonstrates such mood changes (McCarney, 1992).

Help the Child Learn Ways to Deal with Conflict.   A depressed child needs the safety of a warm and caring adult, to discuss ideas for handling situations with success and without conflict (e.g., walking away from potential conflicts, changing activities, and seeking help; McCarney, 1992). The depressed child is typically motivated by emotions, and often acts impulsively, before thinking. McCarney indicates that the child needs to learn to inwardly ask such questions as "What am I doing?" "What is happening?" "What would be my best choice?" According to Barkley (1997) and Nelsen (1981), immediate, related, respectful, and reasonable consequences will also help the child to learn how to catch oneself before acting impulsively.

☐ Anxiety

Diagnosis and Assessment Considerations

Albano, Chorpita, and Barlow (1996) contend that anxiety disorders are the most common and prevalent category of psychiatric disorders that affect children and adolescents. However, less than 20% of children that require mental health services actually receive necessary treatment. This is largely due to the fact that children with internalizing the disorders, such as anxiety, suffer mostly in silence, and are frequently not identified as problematic. In its most disabling forms, anxiety is manifested by the child's avoidance of activities such as attending school, socializing with peers, and performing autonomous activities. Anxiety disorders frequently have an early onset in childhood that run a chronic course well into adulthood. Childhood anxiety is frequently accompanied by other disorders, such as ADHD and depression, and tends to have a significantly negative impact on academic and social functioning.

According to the DSM-IV (APA, 1994), there are nine anxiety disorders with which children can be diagnosed. These include generalized anxiety disorder (previously referred to as overanxious disorder in children and adolescents), separation anxiety disorder, social phobia, panic disorder, obsessive-compulsive disorder, agoraphobia, acute stress disorder, and posttraumatic stress disorder. Although a detailed discussion of all nine anxiety categories is beyond the scope of this chapter, the following sections address generalized anxiety disorder, separation anxiety disorder, social phobia, panic disorder, and obsessive-compulsive disorder.

Generalized Anxiety Disorder (GAD).   In the DSM-IV (APA, 1994), GAD is characterized by excessive anxiety and worry, about a number of activities or events. The excessive anxiety and worry must be difficult to control and must have been present for the majority of the days in the past six months. At least one of the following physiological symptoms must be present:

1. restlessness, feeling keyed up, or feeling on edge;
2. irritability;
3. difficulty concentrating;
4. being easily fatigued;
5. sleep disturbance; or
6. muscle tension.

The focus of the worry and anxiety must not be confined to aspects of another disorder, such as being embarrassed (as in social phobia), being away from home (as in separation anxiety disorder), or being contaminated (as in obsessive-compulsive disorder). The worry, anxiety, and physical symptoms must cause clinically significant impairment or distress in social, academic, work related, or other important areas of functioning.

Separation Anxiety Disorder (SAD). For a child to have a diagnosis of SAD, according to the DSM-IV (APA, 1994), he or she must experience, for at least 4 weeks, excessive and inappropriate anxiety about separating from home or from those with whom the child is attached, as shown by at least three of the following:

1. repeated and excessive distress related to the occurrence or antici-pation of separation from home or major attachment figures;
2. persistent and excessive worry about losing or harm coming to major attachment figures;
3. persistent refusal or reluctance to go to school or elsewhere due to fear of separation;
4. persistent and excessive worry that an event, such as being kid-napped or getting lost, will cause separation from significant at-tachment figures;
5. persistent and excessive fears or reluctance to be alone or without significant attachment figures;
6. persistent reluctance or refusal to sleep away from home or with-out being near major attachment figures;
7. recurring complaints of physiological symptoms (e.g., nausea, headaches) related to the occurrence or anticipation of separation from major attachment figures; and
8. repeated nightmares that involve the theme of separation.

The disturbance must begin before the age of 18, occur for at least 4 weeks, and cause clinically significant impairment or distress in social, work related, academic, or other important areas of functioning. In addition, the disturbance must not occur exclusively during the course of a psychotic disorder or pervasive developmental disorder, or be better accounted for by panic disorder with agoraphobia. Early onset is considered to be before 6 years of age.

Social Phobia.   Vasey (1995) contends that social phobia is most often diagnosed for adolescents, and only rarely is it diagnosed for children younger than 10 years old. According to the DSM-IV (APA, 1994), social phobia is characterized by marked and persistent fear of one or more social or performance situations in which the individual is exposed to possible scrutiny or unfamiliar people, and that he or she will act anxious or otherwise in a way that will be embarrassing or humiliating. For children, there must be evidence of the capacity for developmentally appropriate relationships with others, and the anxiety must occur in peer settings, not only with adults. Exposure to the feared situation almost invariably invokes anxiety, which may take the form of a panic attack. In children, anxiety may be displayed by freezing, crying, tantrums, or hiding. The feared situations are avoided or else endured with intense distress or anxiety. The anxious anticipation, distress, or avoidance related to the feared situation interferes significantly with the person's social, academic, occupational, or other important functioning. The fear or avoidance must occur for at least 6 months for individuals under the age of 18 years, and must not be better accounted for by another mental disorder.

Obsessive-Compulsive Disorder.   As indicated in the DSM-IV (APA, 1994), obsessions are characterized by recurrent and persistent impulses, images, or thoughts that are inappropriate and intrusive, and cause marked anxiety of distress; these impulses, images, or thoughts do not simply represent excessive worrying about real-life problems; the individual makes attempts to suppress or ignore the impulses, images, or thoughts; and the individual realizes that the impulses, images, or thoughts are from within his or her own mind (not from without, as in thought insertion).

Pediatric neurologist Lloyd Mercer (personal communication, September 30, 1997) stated that anxiety can manifest at any age, including childhood, but the effect on the behavior will vary with the age of the child. Anxiety is manifested in emotional responses that become triggered in settings in which no real threat, or only a minor threat, exists. In the young child out of the infant stage, anxiety may manifest as a developmental regression, such as a decline in a child's toileting skills, speech, or play behaviors. The older child may demonstrate social withdrawal, excessive preoccupation of thoughts, daydreaming, unrealistic fears, and sometimes even paranoid ideation. A child may develop excessive concern about the safety of parents or guardians. More subtle behaviors that can occur with anxiety include hyperactivity, repetitive behaviors, easy distractibility, and emotional overreaction.

For anxiety, DSM-IV (APA, 1994) includes the following symptoms: excessive anxiety, and worry occurring more days than not, about multiple events or activities; difficulty controlling worry and restlessness; prevailing fatigue; difficulty concentrating; irritability; muscle tension; and sleep disturbance. These are the symptoms which are most easily targeted and for which treatment responses can be most readily measured. Tatum (1997) asserted that anxiety is the most common disorder in the general population of children. However, disorders such as ADHD receive more treatment attention because "the squeaky wheel gets the grease," and ADHD symptoms may be more apparent than anxiety symptoms. Tatum also stressed that children are just as biologic as adults, and therefore medications may be very helpful in treating children with anxiety.

Medication Considerations

According to Mercer (1997), many of the medications that are used for anxiety and depression in adults are equally effective for children but may require modification of the dosage or the manner in which the medication is administered. Some medications such as hydroxyzine (Atarax) are well-known to parents since they are used for other purposes (e. g., an antihistamine) and are readily available in children's preparations. As in the case of hydroxyzine, other antihistamines can produce modest improvement in anxiety, but must be used mostly at night or in low doses because of the significant sedative effect they can have on children.

Mercer (1997) also reports that some of the longer-established medications still used for both depression and anxiety in children are from the group of medications called tricyclic antidepressants. The more familiar names from this group are imipramine (Tofranil), amitriptyline (Elavil), and doxepin (Sinequan). These medications have also been used for other purposes such as improving sleep, treating headaches, and reducing enuresis. With the exception of doxepin, they are not generally available in liquid or chewable forms and can be difficult for young children to take. As with the antihistamines, sedation is a concern with this group, and often treatment is started with bedtime doses. The less sedating medications of this group can be used at lower doses during the daytime if necessary.

A group of medications that is less often used in children but commonly used in adults, according to Mercer (1997), is the group related to diazepam (Valium). This group is called the benzodiazepines and includes Tranxene, Klonopin, Xanax, and a variety of others used for the treatment of both anxiety and insomnia. The drawbacks of this group for children are that physiological dependency can occur; the clinical response tends to diminish with continued use, necessitating an increase in dosage to achieve the same effect; and a tendency toward withdrawal occurs if the medication has been used for a prolonged period and is abruptly discontinued. For these reasons, benzodiazepines are not used as frequently to treat childhood anxiety as other medications, but are sometimes necessary when other medications have not been effective.

Mercer (1997) states that an alternative to benzodiazepines has been Buspar, which has some definite advantages. Buspar is not noted for its risk of dependency or its withdrawal effect when discontinued. It can be effective in a single daily dose and may not need to have the dosage increased over time. Buspar is not available in a liquid or chewable form, but the tablets are small and easily crushed.

There is a group of medications classified as major tranquilizers such as risperidone (Risperdal), thoridazine (Mellaril), haloperidol (Haldol), and many others, that Mercer (1997) reports as being used for depression and anxiety. These may be reserved for refractory cases since these medications can carry a risk of long-term, potentially permanent, side effects on a person's physical movement. When these medications are used, short-term use and low dosage are generally safer.

Mercer (1997) says a newer group of medications to emerge in the treatment of both depression and anxiety in children is the group of selective serotonin reuptake inhibitors (SSRI). The most common agents in this group are Prozac, Zoloft, Paxil, and Luvox. New studies are emerging in their use with children that will likely result in these medications actually obtaining FDA indications for treatment of mood disorders in children. These medications are often well-tolerated, with minimal risk of side effects, and are the least likely of all the medications mentioned to produce sedation. This would make these medications particularly advantageous for children of school age.

Parenting and Therapeutic Considerations

According to De'Amico and Friedman (1998), the child may have deficits such as depression and low self-esteem that increase one's vulnerability to fear and anxiety, and decrease his or her repertoire of adaptive coping skills. These additional (or primary) deficits, with their effects and history, should be addressed in (play) therapy.

Play.   Play is the primary means in which children gain mastery regarding their activities, skills, behaviors, fears, and themselves over-all. Landreth, Homeyer, Glover, and Sweeney (1996) credit Milos and Reiss (1982) for their study of play therapy with young children experiencing separation anxiety. Results of this study included a dramatic reduction of anxiety associated with children's opportunity to play with toys that were relevant to their anxiety, in the presence of a nonjudgmental adult. Also, the individual child's amount of emotional involvement in the play was associated with anxiety level. Thus, higher level or quality of play was directly related to lower anxiety levels.

Gradual Exposure to Fear-Evoking Stimuli.   In parents' and therapists' attempts to assist the child to gain mastery over his or her fear and anxiety, avoidance of the anxiety- and fear-evoking stimuli tends to maintain the phobic behavior (De'Amico & Friedman, 1998). Treatments that appear to be most effective, are those that promote exposure to the fear-evoking stimuli, while ensuring that the feared outcome does not actually occur. A *fear hierarchy* should be used to plan the gradual exposure. "Identifying multiple specific fearful situations on a continuum from not very fearful to very, very fearful aids in charting the path for the progression of systematic extinction" (p.56). Additionally, the child can be taught coping skills such as relaxation, direct observation of others, emotive imagery, and cognitive self-instruction.

Parents, Teachers, and Peers as Co-Therapists.   A child with fears and anxiety will naturally avoid the fear-evoking stimuli. D'Amico and Friedman (1998) contend that the goal of any intervention is to alter the existing environment, attempting to reduce the probability of the related problem behavior. Parents can help to alter aspects of the child's natural environment, which allows for gradual, appropriate exposure to the stimuli, and thus permits the development of adaptive self-control and coping skills. McCarney (1992) suggests that alternative activities be provided for the child who has difficulty or fear performing the assigned activities. However, gradual removal of the alternative activities should take place, as the child's fear decreases and success increases. Also, classmates, friends, or siblings can often provide tremendous support and demonstrate appropriate modeling for the child with anxiety. Direct observation of another child being exposed to a scary situation (with a safe and positive outcome) can help to deflate the threat of anxiety-inducing stimuli and reduce the fear experienced by the child with anxiety.

Parents' Resistance to Medication

The decision to treat or not treat with medication, as stated by Mercer (1997), ultimately rests with the parent. Helping parents understand the use of medication can sometimes help them make this decision. Parents should be allowed the opportunity to consider the advantages and disadvantages of medical treatment and ultimately make the decision with which they are most comfortable for their child. Mercer (1997) explained:

> The unknown is often more frightening than the known. The more that a physician can inform parents about the medication, the more comfortable parents may be with the idea of its use. Parents are often concerned about long-term effects of medication administered to children, and it is helpful to describe the extent to which the medications have been used and the experience that we have after years of use. It is often helpful to emphasize to the parents that the medication is not looked upon as a "cure" but rather as a tool to temporarily change the spectrum of mood while modalities of therapy are given the opportunity to effect a more permanent change in behavior and adaptation of the individual.

Mercer (1997) further offered a necessary word of caution in discussion of the use of medication prescribed for improvement of mood disorders in children: Very few pharmaceutical companies have invested the expense necessary to obtain an approved indication for prescription of newer medications for mood disorders in children. These studies are often very expensive in money and resources. Similarly, most of the longer-established medications are not of enough economic interest to the companies to invest the money to obtain an FDA-approved indication. As a result, most medications effective in the treatment of anxiety and depression are not FDA-approved for use with children, but rather are prescribed at the discretion of the physician by "off-label" usage. This is confusing for parents at times, since the lack of an FDA-approved indication is construed to mean that the medications are not equally safe or equally effective for children as they are for adults. Parents must understand that FDA-approval only fulfills the legal requirements of a pharmaceutical company to sell a medication. It is up to the physician's experience to know how to use the medication.

☐ When Parents Have Depression or other Disorders

Fallone (1998) reports that the therapist may face an additional challenge: immediate family members of the child with ADHD are significantly more likely to have ADHD themselves, as compared to family members of a child without ADHD. Therefore, the therapist must be prepared to work with parents that have symptoms consistent with ADHD. In addition, immediate family members of children with ADHD have increased likelihood of having other forms of psychopathology such as mood disorders.

Adult disorders are typically associated with a pattern of childhood problems and adverse conditions (Mash & Dozois, 1996). Parents of children with ADHD, depression, or anxiety are likely to experience tremendous stress, frustration, guilt, a repeated sense of failure, and a sense of hopelessness. Continual exposure to these elements easily leads to emotional difficulties, even depression. As addressed in other sections, a child with depression or anxiety may display symptoms consistent with ADHD. Regardless of diagnosis, the child who experiences the persistent ridicule, shame, punishment, and rejection common for children who display these symptoms, is likely to develop feelings such as a sense of failure or inadequacy, shame, guilt, isolation, and hopelessness (i.e., depression). Likewise, a parent who has a child with ADHD, depression, or anxiety is likely to already have or to develop symptoms of depression. Whether the parent has ADHD, depression, anxiety, or another disorder, the *demands and skills needed for effective parenting are likely to be pushed* aside as the demands of surviving and coping with the related symptomology take priority. Therefore, parental depression and related effects on parenting are important issues to discuss.

Studies clearly show that depression also tends to run in families (Hammen, 1991). However, on a case by case basis, it is difficult to determine whether transmission across generations is due primarily to genetic or psychosocial influences or both. Determination of specific causes of depression can be hampered by its variety or heterogeneity (Hammen & Rudolph, 1996). Regardless, families with depressed members are very likely to experience significant disruption within the family unit. Children in these families are therefore at risk for environmental as well as genetic factors.

It is evident that childhood development is a very complex phenomenon. There are many needs that children must have met in order for their adaptive development. Likewise, there is a tremendous amount of responsibility associated with effective parenting. The many skills, strengths, endurance, and perseverance required of parents is incredible. Unfortunately, parents with depression often do not have the needed energy and attention to offer their children. This can lead to maladaptive development, expressed through a variety of emotions, behaviors, and disorders. Consistent and positively responsive parenting is essential to adaptive child development. Depression precludes consistency, largely due to its episodic nature. Children are likely to experience their depressed parents as unpredictable and inconsistent. Due to the fact that confusion and preoccupation with oneself are common symptoms of depression, children are also likely to experience their depressed parents as unresponsive, as well as physically and emotionally unavailable (Radke-Yarrow, Cummings, Kuczynski, & Chapman, 1985). According to Bowlby (1969, 1980), children that fail to develop secure social and emotional attachments with significant others, tend to develop a life course of emotional, behavioral, personality, and relationship disorders, as well as physical health problems.

The depressed parent is the primary feature of the environment in which the child develops. The conditions of parenting will reflect the symptoms and impairments (e.g., sad affect, irritability, emotional unavailability, hopelessness, and confusion) that constitute the disorder (Radke-Yarrow et al., 1985).

Davenport, Zahn-Waxler, Adland, and Mayfield (1984) recognize eight patterns of child-rearing in families with a bipolar parent. These are:

1. massive denial in an effort to avoid feelings of loss, grief, anger and affection;
2. dependency and helplessness in close and intimate relationships;
3. unrealistic standards of conformity and self-expectations;
4. displacement of low self-esteem by parents onto their children;
5. a tendency toward isolation, excluding anyone outside of the family;
6. fears of the heritability of the illness;
7. fears of the recurrence of episodes, despite medication; and
8. passive or absent fathers.

Parenting factors that lead to normal healthy development in children include emotional warmth, availability, stable parent-child relationship, and tolerance for assisting the child to deal with intense feelings such as rage, frustration anxiety, and sadness. A bipolar parent typically exhibits inconsistent parental behavior. In this environment, a child never knows what to expect or whether one's needs will be met, and may even perceive life as dangerous (Davenport et al., 1984).

Depressed parents tend to be less sensitive to the developmental needs of their child. These parents demonstrate little involvement in their child's ongoing activities and low sensitivity to their child's expressions of inhibition, wariness, and distress. They tend to be negative and hostile towards, or likely to withdraw from, interaction with their child. Parenting behaviors of depressed parents often include a lack of encouragement, a lack of encouraging the child to explore the environment, a lack of encouraging the child to interact with new people, and an angry, critical style used to influence the child. The greater the severity of parents' depression, the more likely they are to use the angry, critical style of interaction with the child. Parents are models of behavior for their child. Depressed parents often model behaviors that include being anhedonic, passive, withdrawn, and anxious (Kochanska, 1991).

Zahn-Waxler, Cummings, McKnew, and Radke-Yarrow (1984) report that families with bipolar members tend to create conditions of "environmental deprivation" that are detrimental to the healthy development of the child members. Parenting deficiencies in bipolar parents include: lack of awareness of others; lack of empathic abilities; taking, but refusing to give; difficulty in dealing with hostility; difficulty maintaining friendly social relations; difficulty maintaining balanced moods; and, due to the parents' own dependency needs, lack of abilities to promote stable and secure attachment with their children. These deficiencies increase the risk of their children developing depression or other emotional and social problems.

How Children Are Affected

Being reared in an affectively disturbed environment contributes significantly to the development of emotional problems in children. With parents having the intense needs associated with depression, children often develop into the role of caretaker, and have increased risks for depression, anxiety, isolating, sleep problems, excessive anger, aggression, and other psychopathological symptoms. Hyperactive, disorganized, aggressive, hostile, uncooperative, cautious and undercontrolled patterns of behavior are also characteristic of children with bipolar parents. Other problem behaviors include shallowness in interpersonal relations, inability to empathize, taking but refusing to give, difficulty dealing with conflicts or losses, overreaction to stress, dysphoria and anhedonia. Since children tend to look to and be guided by the emotional expression of their caregivers, especially during times of emotional uncertainty, children with bipolar families are likely to develop ongoing emotional uncertainty (Zahn-Waxler et al., 1984). However, Kochanska (1991) reports that, in rare cases, children of bipolar parents might become "supercompetent" (p. 251). According to Zahn-Waxler and colleagues (1984), 2-year-old boys from bipolar families tend to show more undirected aggression than girls, while also showing more altruism toward their mothers than girls.

Blatt and Homann (1992) report that organismic, constitutional, and environmental factors interact and affect development and create vulnerabilities to depression. These vulnerability factors include characteristics of the child, characteristics of parents, the family, the social environment, as well as the impact of stressful life experiences (e.g., death of a parent). They describe "the normal infant's developing sense of the self as capable, coherent and positive as deriving from consistent interactions with a responsive, attuned mother" (p. 77). "Experiences of parental lack of care, nurturance, or support and excessive parental authority, control, criticism, and disapproval are associated with the later development of depression" (p. 76). If a depressed parent is unresponsive or controlling, a child is likely to develop anger and resentment toward the parent. This can lead to a negative sense of self due to feelings of guilt, shame, and inadequacy.

Children tend to look toward or go to their caregiver for guidance, information, or reassurance when exposed to distress. The caregiver's response, as teacher, empathizer, and model is pivotal in the child's emotional development. If a parent is dysfunctional, the child may learn to not look toward the parent for guidance, and thus, the child is deprived of a very important source of learning related to emotional development, and dealing with emotionally arousing situations (Zahn-Waxler et al., 1984).

Transmission Across Generations

According to Radke-Yarrow and colleagues (1985), "[d]epression is known to aggregate in families, to be transmitted from one generation to the next. Significantly higher frequencies of psychopathology have been reported among children of parents with affective disorders" as compared to children of normal parents (p. 884).

Children of bipolar parents often show increased levels of distress and preoccupation with conflicts and suffering of others. They exhibit difficulties in sharing, helping their peers, and maintaining friendly social interactions, as well as maladaptive patterns of aggression toward adults and toward their peers. These characteristics, being similar to characteristics of persons with bipolar disorder, indicate that the disorder can be transmitted from parents to their children (Zahn-Waxler et al., 1984).

Radke-Yarrow and colleagues (1985) report that behavior problems are also known to aggregate in families and be transmitted from one generation to the next. Significantly higher frequencies of psychopathology have been reported among children of families with mood and behavioral disorders as compared to children of families without these problems. Thus, there is an intergenerational transmission of behavioral and mood problems. Children that do not experience basic needs of acceptance, warmth, attention, love, permissiveness, and appropriate limit setting are likely to grow up and pass their problems on to their children.

Attachment

The behaviors and mental status of a depressed parent interfere with one's functions and responsibilities as a caregiver, as well as the development of a healthy, affective attachment between parent and child (Radke-Yarrow et al., 1985). Certain biological and temperamental qualities in a child can also increase the risk that insecure attachments will develop, due to the impact of these qualities on parents and parents' capacity to adequately care for their children (Blatt & Homann, 1992). These characteristics that develop in children can also interfere with the parents' acceptance of, and attachment to, their children (Radke-Yarrow et al., 1985). Due to the fact that depression and other disorders tend to run in families, it is very possible that both parent and child have symptoms that interfere with the parent-child relationship.

Insecurely attached children tend to exhibit behavior problems, including social withdrawal, anxiety, difficulties in relationships with peers and adults, and more dependency on adults. Insecurely attached children also develop a view of themselves as being unlovable and a view of others as being rejecting and unresponsive. Other behaviors that tend to develop in children with depressed parents include sadness, extreme avoidance, distress, affectlessness, and other signs of depression. Young children frequently mimic and match parents' affect and responses. Since a depressed parent is likely to be self-deprecating, such views are likely to extend into the perceptions of one's child (Blatt & Homann, 1992).

According to Mash and Dozois (1996), most adult disorders can be traced back to childhood problems, conditions, and experiences. Bowlby (1969, 1980) has contended that children who do not develop secure social and emotional bonds have increased likelihood of developing lifelong personality, emotional, behavioral, relationship and physical health problems.

Socialization

Barber and Olsen (1997) reported that those children that are able to (a) experience consistent and positive emotional bonds with significant others, (b) experience consistent and fair limits that regulate their behavior, and (c) experience, value, and express their own thoughts and emotions are more likely to experience healthy development, including a stable sense of self and identity. Thus, children that experience connection, regulation, and autonomy are able to meet a basic requirement of healthy human development—socialization. Socialization conditions are relevant to a variety of childhood functioning, and family relationship experiences predict future mental health—including depression.

Depressed parents tend to have decreased encouragement and fostering of their children's overall exploration and play. These parents also tend to speak less with their children, and tend to avoid effortful socialization activities (Kochanska, 1991).

Zahn-Waxler and colleagues (1984) indicate that children of bipolar parents have decreased likelihood that they will engage in social interaction with playmates. Even children between 1- and 2-years-of-age who have a parent that is bipolar are likely to exhibit difficulties in establishing friendly social and sharing interactions, aggressive and conflictual behaviors, a lack of altruistic prosocial behaviors, and a development of insecure attachment patterns.

Inhibition

According to Kochanska (1991), parental depression tends to increase the likelihood that their children will develop an inhibited, timid, or fearful personality style. Extreme inhibition in children is a bellwether of oncoming developmental maladaptation, which includes patterns of withdrawal, restraint, anxiety, and depression. Most caregivers recognize the fact that their child's ability and willingness to explore and respond positively to new environments and people is an important goal of social and emotional development. If they perceive their child as withdrawn or inhibited, they seek to reduce these behaviors and discomfort by fostering and facilitating social interaction and exploratory behaviors in their children.

There are several reasons that a child of a depressed parent has an increased risk for developing maladaptive levels of inhibition. Depressed mothers, according to Kochanska (1991), "have difficulties in getting involved in day-to-day parenting—in maintaining the level of energy and positive affect necessary to provide a young child with adequate stimulation, play, and opportunity to explore new environments" (p. 251). These parents also tend to have low levels of activity, vocalizations, and spontaneity.

Kochanska (1991) reports that boys of depressed parents are more likely to demonstrate inhibition when facing a new environment. In contrast, girls of depressed parents tend to demonstrate inhibition when facing a new person. Evidence clearly shows that mental health, behavioral, and biological disorders are transmitted from one generation to the next. Parents face tremendous responsibility to provide for many of their children's needs. These demands are complicated by parents' own issues. Consequently, children suffer from the effects of their parents' struggles.

☐ Summary

Children diagnosed with depression, anxiety, or ADHD frequently require multifaceted treatment strategies. For example, a child may benefit from psychotropic medications and require the emotional and social support of play therapy. However, parents may have questions and apprehensions about administering the medications to their child, and often need to process their concerns with the child's play therapist. Medications are rarely the only treatment modality, and are typically used to facilitate other therapy and parenting strategies. Consequently, to best serve the client, the therapist needs a working knowledge of psychotropic medications, as well as, relational, supportive, structural, and behavioral techniques.

The therapist also needs to help parents focus on the characteristics of their child's disorder, rather than personalizing the issues, which results in control struggles. This process exacerbates the child's, as well as the parents', existing challenges. Parents often see their child's behavioral issues as laziness, willful defiance, and disrespect. These perceptions lead to power struggles among the child and the parents. Such struggles then become the object of focus, rather than accepting and coping with the traits associated with the disorder. Parents often get stuck in their belief that the child *can, but doesn't want to* rather than accepting that the child *wants to, but can't*.

This chapter provides information regarding diagnostic criteria and characteristics related to several common disorders. Caution is necessary whenever diagnostic labels are associated with real people—especially children. Possible risks of providing a diagnosis include a child's development of an identity based on the diagnosis (i.e., a self-fulfilling prophecy). Also, especially in today's information age, diagnoses may follow a child indefinitely. Unfortunately, diagnoses are sometimes misused, and can cause considerable, unnecessary harm, to someone who is likely to be struggling enough, already.

Specific information is also provided regarding ADHD, depression, and anxiety. Details related to medication interventions are included, along with common parent concerns. Additionally, interventions that involve therapy are described, along with issues that address parenting strategies. For example, parents must consistently administer immediate consequences and rewards, emphasizing how the child chose the outcome when he or she chose the antecedent behavior. Although parents need to be accepting of their child's challenges, the child must learn to be accountable for his or her behaviors. Parents should not be encouraged to let their child "off the hook." However, they need to have reasonable expectations and administer reasonable consequences, without emotion and without shaming their child. Various suggestions of how to involve peers, school, and the child are also presented.

Therapists must be prepared to work with parents who have their own emotional needs and disorders. Recent research clearly identifies the fact that mental health, developmental, and behavioral disorders become transmitted across generations. Thus, the biological, genetic, behavioral, and personality factors of ADHD, depression, and anxiety tend to run in families. Regardless, parents frequently have issues that significantly impact their parenting skills, interactions, and the relationship with their child. Consequently, parents' issues have tremendous influence upon the development of their children. Parents who present for therapy, with their child already identified as the patient (or problem), are often reluctant to work on their own issues. Therefore, the therapist may need to reframe how parenting deficits are addressed, and only refer to special parenting needs of their specific child.

Parent Profiles

The therapist's understanding of the parents is a necessity in the therapy process. Reflecting and probing questions can lead to a deeper comprehension of parents' motivations and influences. This chapter provides various parent profiles to assist the therapist in developing more discernment about parent characteristics. These profiles, of course, are general outlines that must be tailored to reflect the characteristics of specific parents. Caution must be exercised whenever assumptions are being made regarding an individual's personality. Intuition and speculation can be valuable assets to a therapist, but they can also distort, influence and lead understanding away from reality. These profiles are recommended for use, along with the therapist's professional judgment, to better understand the parents who present their child for play therapy. Understanding is instrumental to making deeper contact, building greater trust, and optimizing the therapeutic relationship.

Within the various sections of parent profiles are strategies for relationship building. Effective tools for working with specific personality types are suggested. These sections provide suitable platforms from which to demonstrate the techniques; however, the strategies can be generalized and implemented with multiple parent profiles.

☐ The Resistant Parent

The resistant parent is the one who is opposed to therapy. In most cases in which this profile presents itself, the father fills the role. This is not intended to be a biased remark, but an observed behavior in many fathers of play therapy clients. Fathers are typically less willing to delve into their innermost feelings and beliefs than mothers; fathers are typically more uncomfortable disclosing their thoughts and emotions, especially to a stranger. Frequently, however, the mother is more resistant to many of the aspects of therapy. Therapy often involves sharing intimate and sensitive information about the family. The resistant parent likely believes that therapy is useless, and that he or she probably was "dragged" to the session, and fears airing the family's "dirty laundry." Certainly, receiving advice from strangers is undesirable for this parent. The therapist may hear phrases such as, "We can solve our own problems"; "No one is going to tell me how to raise my child"; "We keep our problems private"; or "Our child just needs more discipline."

The power of reflecting cannot be overemphasized. Reflecting will help the therapist reduce the opportunities for power struggles with parents. Therapists should refrain from agreeing or disagreeing with such early statements from the resistant parent. For example, the therapist might reflect: "You've tried everything you can think of, and nothing has worked very well. You're also very upset about having to seek help from outside your family."

Communications must be framed appropriately by the therapist. In other words, *how* the therapist conveys information is vital, especially when conveying advice. In addition to reflecting, the *back door technique* can be very beneficial when attempting to provide information to the resistant parent. This allows the therapist to give advice gently and indirectly. This is not to be used with the intention of minimizing the importance of messages, being manipulative, or being deceitful. On the contrary, this is a system of paying close attention to the parent's position and acceptance rate in the therapy process, and then tailoring communications appropriately.

The *confused technique* is very helpful in increasing the therapist's and the parent's understanding. As an example, the therapist would say, "I'm confused about what you said. Can you help me understand?" This combination of statement and question puts responsibility for understanding on the therapist, not on the parent's ability to express him- or herself. Also, asking for help reduces the chance that the parent will feel criticized.

When using these strategies, tone of voice is critical. The therapist must exhibit genuine compassion for, and interest in, the parent. A patronizing or shaming tone will be very damaging to the trust level of the parent in regard to the therapist. If necessary, the therapist can simply clarify that genuine interest and gaining understanding are the exclusive motives. However, if the therapist has genuine interest and empathy for parents, explanation rarely will be necessary.

Consider the 6-year-old boy who was referred for therapy because he was hitting and pushing other children at school. The father was verbally harsh, almost abusive, to his wife (the boy's mother) and the therapist during the intake session. He accused his wife of being responsible for the boy's behavior, stating that she was always too lenient. He insisted that their son just needed more discipline. He then turned to the therapist and sneered, "I'll bet you don't agree with that, do you? Well, discipline is important. Kyle just needs more spankings. Dr. Dobson said spanking is necessary."

At this point, his wife spoke up and said, "But we've tried that. It hasn't helped." The father snapped, "He needs more spankings. We haven't spanked him enough."

The therapist leaned slightly toward the father and said quietly, "Tell me more about this, Alex. How often have you tried spanking?" He said, "Recently, Kyle probably gets spanked three or four times per week. He needs one every day. Don't try to tell me I'm wrong about this. That's what Dr. Dobson says."

The therapist replied, "I'm confused about this. I've read some of Dr. Dobson's books, but I need to go back and look at them again. I know he believes in spanking, but I didn't think he recommended it to this extent." This reply let the father know that the therapist realized that he was exaggerating. It was also framed in a way that did not corner the father and did not cause a power struggle. It indicated the therapist's responsibility to obtain more information. At this point, the therapist left the subject with the intention of returning to it later.

Toward the end of the session, the therapist said, "Maybe we can try some other discipline techniques with Kyle for a while. If these don't work, you can always go back to doing what you have been doing, such as spanking. But for now the spanking does not seem to be working." The therapist was aware that the mother was eager to change the current discipline strategies, while the father was still resistant. By suggesting other strategies "for a while," the father did not feel as threatened by cooperating.

Reflecting, empathizing, and *avoiding power struggles* go a long way with the resistant parent. Typically, the resistant parent expects to be met with unacceptance by others, and lacks the capacity to trust. Reflecting and empathy build trust by demonstrating acceptance and understanding. These are what the resistant parent needs most.

☐ **Parenting as a Career**

Career parents are usually evidenced in the parent who does not work outside the home. Most often, it is the mother who is depicted by this profile. If problems exist in the family, or especially for the child, this parent will feel like a failure. Achieving and maintaining happiness, harmony, and well-being in the home is this person's job—this person's career. Parenting is the largest responsibility in this job. Often, being a parent reflects more about the core identity of this person than his or her other roles or job responsibilities. This parent may reach an incredibly low point and may have difficulty calling in an outside expert to help their child.

The parent with this profile needs a lot of reassurance. The therapist should reflect feelings and show empathy, but this parent also needs to hear several compliments during the first session. The therapist should extol the importance of the parenting efforts, and how these efforts make up a large part of the parent's significance and identity as a person. The parent needs reassurance that this is the most important, yet most difficult, job anyone can have—and that the therapist understands.

For example: Shay, age 7, was referred for therapy by her second-grade teacher. She was withdrawing and becoming very isolated at school. Shay's parents attended the intake session together. Donna, Shay's mom, was tearful as she explained the changes they had seen in their daughter. At one point, she could not talk because of the tears. The therapist said, "Shay's welfare is so important to you, Donna. You don't understand why this is happening, and you feel responsible. It's even harder because this is your full-time job. Being a stay-at-home mom is your career, just like banking is your husband's career." Through the tears, she whispered, "Yes, and my husband doesn't need counseling to be a vice-president, like I do just to be a mom." This gave the therapist the opportunity to reflect more of her feelings and to mention several positive things that had been observed about her relationship with Shay. "It took a lot of courage to come here today. I can see that it's so important to you that Shay is happy and well-adjusted at school and at home. You try really hard to spend quality time with her." Donna kept her head somewhat bowed, but nodded, indicating the accuracy of the therapist's contact. The therapist said, "There are far more skills needed in this career than any other. This job requires the ability to be a security guard, chef, teacher, accountant, janitor, nurse, carpenter, policeman, secretary, chauffeur, and much, much more." Her head began to raise, and her back slowly straightened. Donna's husband had not realized that she was taking Shay's difficulties personally. He became more aware of his wife's feelings and as a result, was able to be more supportive.

☐ Two-Career Parents

When both parents work full-time, often in high-level careers, they fit the two-career parent profile. They both may want to work, possibly more than 40 hours per week. Both parents have invested considerable time, education, energy, and money into building their careers. The therapist is likely to see one of two reactions. First, these parents are often irritated that they have to deal with problems their child is experiencing. The parents view themselves as successful, and should therefore be impervious to all of these problems. Secondly, the parents may feel guilty and responsible for the difficulties that their child is experiencing. They may blame themselves.

A good response to the irritation is, "I think play therapy can be very beneficial. Hopefully, I can make some suggestions that'll be very helpful, yet at the same time won't alter your lifestyle significantly. It's amazing how much of a difference small changes can make." The *small change technique* is necessary and effective with parents who are very busy and feel threatened by additional items in their schedules. Small changes might include: the parent having a special "date" with the child for 15 minutes a week; the parent giving the child a "30 second burst of attention"; a sandwich hug; and other parenting skills suggested by the therapist that would take the parent only a minimal amount of time to incorporate. Small changes can alter the paths of people's lives, and over time the individuals end up in very different places than if the changes had not taken place. Also, immediate results can be observed. Being able to actually see positive change provides tremendous encouragement, inspiration, strength, and courage available for making additional changes. Some parents who are very invested in their careers simply do not want to change their lifestyles; they may fear losing all they have put into building their careers, or jeopardizing the "good life" that their careers support. In fact, they also may believe that change is truly impossible.

An effective response regarding the guilt is, "It's hard to balance it all. Your child and your careers are both very important to you. I'll try to help you make some small changes that won't interfere significantly with your schedule." The therapist should emphasize and encourage anything positive about their parenting skills or about their parent-child relationships. If the therapist can win over the parents and help them make small changes, the parents will be able to see the positive impact on their child—the result for their efforts. This will typically encourage them, and potentiate increased efforts and bigger changes.

To give an example, Todd's mother, a surgeon, brought him to therapy because his grades were falling. Todd played-out and later talked about being lonely at home. He had a nanny, but really missed being with his parents and wanted more time with them. The therapist asked Todd's mother if she or Todd's dad could sit down with him at night while he worked on his homework. She started detailing her day, as well as her husband's day, and complained about how tired they were at the end of their 12-hour days. The therapist sympathized and suggested she sit down with Todd for just 15 minutes at night, whenever possible. The mother described how much homework Todd usually had and said that 15 minutes would not begin to cover it. The therapist had to be persistent, and said that this might give Todd a little encouragement and could be surprisingly helpful to him. The doctor agreed to try. Two weeks later, the mother reported that Todd was doing much better in school and that both of them looked forward to their homework time together. Todd had been trying to let the nanny help him with the hard subjects, so he could save some of the easier homework for when his mother could sit down with him. Consequently, Todd was motivated to get more work finished before his mother got home, and the mother-son relationship grew stronger and closer at the same time. To her amazement, the mother realized that she truly enjoyed her son. All of this was the result of the "small change" she made.

☐ The Single Parent

The single parent is invariably feeling overwhelmed and inadequate. Whether it is the mother or the father who is bringing the child for therapy, the single parent very likely has high anxiety. It is also likely that the anxiety is being passed on to the child. The therapist must first reassure the parent by recognizing the high level of responsibility and pressure in being the primary caregiver or sole provider. This is another scenario that requires the small change technique, since this person cannot accept an extensive number of assignments and added activities. *The therapist must attempt to avoid overwhelming the parent further.* A good response is, "We'll try to understand more about what's going on with Sarah and make some small changes for her that'll make a big difference." This statement de-emphasizes the interruption of existing schedules or the need for change in the parent's method of operation. If the parent can actually begin with a small change, then the parent can ease into bigger or more numerous changes.

The therapist should implore the parent to take care of him- or herself. This also should involve small changes. The parent should be advised to set aside and protect special time that is only for the parent. Fifteen minutes is a good allotment that can help the parent relax, increase self-confidence, and feel rewarded with little or no guilt for using the time for self. Whether the parent prefers reading a magazine, taking a bubble bath, meditating, or something else, the parent must prevent anything from invading this time. Anticipating and relishing the time has therapeutic value in itself even before the time really occurs. If the parent takes the special 15-minute break when the child is awake, this parent behavior is also good modeling for the anxious child. It communicates the parent's belief and own self-importance. The child, as well, can possibly use this time for his or her own special self-indulgence.

The single parent may experience guilt associated with the inability to spend more time with the child. The therapist should help the parent to focus on the atmosphere when spending time with the child. Young children experience life primarily on an emotional level, and are more motivated by feelings than cognitions. *The child will remember the mood during an experience with the parent, rather than the actual number of minutes spent together.*

☐ The Recently Separated or Divorced Parent

It is typical for the recently separated or divorced parent to also experience high levels of anxiety. This person's life is likely to be very chaotic. If the parent feels like he or she is drowning, the child probably does too. The therapist should emphasize that the early period of separation or divorce is a very real crisis. An enormous loss is being generated and experienced, simultaneously. As opposed to the immediate and complete loss with theft or death, this loss involves a process that may be perceived as neverending. The parent is experiencing shock, pain, depression, anxiety, and the other emotions associated with grief. These feelings need to be reflected, acknowledged, and accepted by the therapist. The parent should be reminded that the fears and uncertainties of being lost that are being experienced are new and uncharted territory for the parent.

Because the parent may feel hopeless and helpless during this initial period, reassurance that life can and will improve literally may be critical. The therapist may need to say, "I'll believe for you, until you can believe for yourself, that life will get better, for you and your child." Suggestions that can be implemented immediately must be provided by the therapist to make this period more manageable for both parent and child. Emphasis must also be placed on the fact that this is a period in time—with a beginning *and* an end.

The child needs the opportunity to safely express emotions resulting from the parents' behavior. Although it may take time for the child to believe it, the child needs assurance that responsibility for the divorce falls on the parents. Children will typically blame themselves if their parents divorce or separate, believing themselves to not have been "good" enough. Play therapy will provide an arena in which to, at least partially, satisfy these needs. The parents, as well, need to provide safety for the child's self-expression. Parents should be encouraged by the therapist to emphasize that blame is not attributable to the child.

A recently divorced parent is likely to be under considerable stress and to be experiencing a storm of emotions. It is asking a lot to request that special attention is focused on the child. Nevertheless, the commitment to nourish and protect the child was made long before the divorce or separation, and the current and future mental health of the child is dependent upon this devotion.

☐ Parents Who Are Not Seeking Counseling

To differentiate from otherwise resistant parents, these parents are required to bring their children for therapy. The requirement may be the result of a court order, a school order, the children being expelled from daycare or school, suspected abuse, or numerous other reasons. It is natural that the parents will be resistant and irritated, at least initially. Hopefully, the therapist will be able to link them to the therapy process. This may require superb skills and incredible luck, or it may occur easily.

When parents have no investment in therapy, and possibly no emotional investment in their child, it can be difficult for the play therapist to remain objective. *Countertransference* is likely to arise during therapy with these parents. Countertransference is the therapist's unresolved feelings for significant others that may be transferred to the client (Gillilard, James, Roberts, & Bowman, 1984). The therapist must monitor his or her own feelings that surface. Primary focus must remain on the child, and the therapist's own feelings must be kept in perspective. Any undesirable messages that the parents perceive will result in even more resistance. The goal is to help them see how they can benefit by bringing their child to therapy. The parents need to see how the required changes could very well prove to be advantageous. For example, the therapist might say, "I realize that your child must attend daycare, and this is the second one that has expelled him. It would probably be a relief not to talk to the director every day, and not be required to take off work to pick him up. There's a lot that can be done to improve his behavior, and I'll genuinely try to help."

Very likely, the child's best chance for emotional health will depend upon whether or not the parents continue bringing him to therapy. Giving small and sincere *compliments* can build rapport between the therapist and the parents. The parents have repeatedly received criticism regarding their child's behavior and their parenting skills, so compliments are not likely to be expected. They can capture parents' attention and make a lasting impression. Everything that can possibly be viewed as successful parenting should be glorified. The therapist should praise anything that generates benefits, even if the parents' behaviors were not intentionally directed toward those results. The small changes technique is recommended for these parents. They are already resistant, and probably the only changes they implement will be small ones. Even if the only attention the child receives is in response to misbehavior, the therapist can acknowledge it in a favorable light. For example, "You have a strong ability to really focus on your child at times. Focused attention can be one of the greatest gifts any parent can give their child. I think it'll be very helpful if we can find a few more times for you to show your child attention."

☐ Grandparent in the Parent Role

More and more grandparents are raising their grandchildren. This is a huge responsibility and often a big shock for the grandparents—as well for the child. As with the recently separated or divorced parent, one will likely see chaos and crisis in the family setting. As ecstatic as grandparents are with their children's children, grandparents are often disappointed and discouraged to become the primary caregivers for their grandchildren. The prospect of long-term child-rearing is typically inconsistent with the dreams that people have for themselves at this stage in life. Retirement, travel, leisure, recreation, and vacation homes are only a fraction of the possible dreams. Becoming a parent again frequently prevents these dreams from coming to fruition. Clothes, food, school supplies, and medical bills are among the obligations that dip into retirement funds. Numerous grandparents who had successfully tucked away enough for retirement have had to return to work because of the added responsibilities of parenting. They also may feel incredible despair because they view themselves as failures. In their minds they must be terrible parents, since their own children have not been able to take care of the children. They may have limited self-confidence in facing another round of parenting.

Grandparents need reassurance and encouragement. There may be incredible differences between what were generally accepted parenting practices when these clients were actively parenting or being parented, and the professionally accepted practices of today. They also may need help with very basic parenting skills. The therapist must determine what is specifically needed and prioritize those needs.

Highlighting some of the positive parenting techniques that the grandparents incorporated with their children is another valuable technique. The therapist can search for and highlight aspects of parenting that brought the grandparents joy and success in the past. This will identify areas in which the grandparents have confidence, as well as the possibility of generalizing these strengths into other parenting skills. The grandparents' perception of success is often far more important than the actual outcome. This also identifies areas to compliment, which provides encouragement for the grandparents.

The small changes technique can be very useful with these parents. They very likely are established in their lifestyle, and can be overwhelmed by a large number of new practices. Experience and evidence of success will be more influential than simply quoting theory. The therapist must take care to view the world through the eyes of these newly commissioned parents.

☐ Summary

Building a relationship with the parents is the therapist's key to enlist their cooperation and enliven their motivation regarding the child's therapy. The outcomes will be tremendously enhanced, occur earlier, and be longer-lasting. Understanding the parents greatly facilitates building the relationship with them. To facilitate the therapist in understanding parents, several profiles of parents that are often seen in therapy are described in this chapter. However, the therapist must remember that every parent is unique, with an unique phenomenological perspective. These profiles can expedite a therapist's conceptualization of parents, but the profiles are simply a beginning. Therapists must use their own professional perspective and intuition to more fully understand individual parents. Even though the world sometimes seems small and individual characteristics can be seen in many different people, each person must be accepted, appreciated, and understood as a unique human being.

Parent profiles described in this chapter include:

1. the resistant parent;
2. the parent for whom parenting is a career;
3. two-career parents;
4. single parents;
5. recently separated or divorced parents;
6. parents who are not seeking therapy; and
7. grandparents in the parenting role.

Regardless of profiles or individual characteristics, all parents are in the process of fulfilling the most important and difficult responsibility possible, and they require understanding, support, and reassurance, as well as, celebration of their efforts. In addition to therapy for the child, these aspects of communication are, in themselves, therapeutic; therefore, the therapist must find ways to incorporate them into the relationships with parents whenever possible. The therapist can also make great strides in building the therapist-parent relationship when ways to compliment the parent are discovered. In addition, parents need to be encouraged—as people, as parents, and as therapeutic agents for their child. These strategies will greatly help the therapist to enlist the support of parents.

Along with the various descriptions of profiles, specific techniques are provided that can be applied with a variety of parents. These techniques further help to connect parents to the play therapy process, while maintaining and fostering the therapist-parent relationship. The *small changes, back-door, highlighting,* and *confused* techniques are among those described. Reflecting feelings and empathic understanding are also universal and powerful techniques, and can be relied upon to build trust and rapport.

6
CHAPTER

Working With Angry, Resistant Parents

Resistance is defined as opposing; using force to prevent something from happening or being successful. Anger is defined as a feeling of displeasure, rage, wrath, fury, indignation, and intensity (Merriam-Webster, 1984). When working with angry, resistant parents, the therapist may face challenges ranging from exasperated, irritated parents to raging, opposing parents. Parents may be direct or indirect with the anger and resistance. A direct approach might include a parent saying to the therapist, "No one is going to tell me how to raise my child; therapy is useless; you don't know what you're doing." An indirect approach might be worded more softly, but the impact on the therapist and therapy process can be as powerful as the direct approach. An indirect approach might include a parent saying to the therapist, "Elise has been coming three weeks now, and we haven't seen any changes at home. How much longer do you think this will take? We're a little unsure about therapy."

Whether the resistance and anger are mild or severe, working with this type of parent often takes a greater toll on the therapist than working with any other type. Therefore, the angry, resistant parent profile is singled out in this chapter because it is crucial to be prepared to work with such parents, who may so easily and significantly limit or deny access to therapy for their child.

113

☐ **Consistent and Persistent Reflection**

If it is early in the play therapy process, reflecting the parents' feelings often will help dissipate the anger and resistance. The parents may project their anger toward the therapy process, toward the therapist, or toward the child's behavior or problem. The therapist and the therapy process are prime targets of blame for raging, antagonistic parents. Reflecting these feelings can be helpful because, in the first few sessions of therapy, parents may not be convinced that therapy will be helpful for the child. There is a period of winning parents over to the therapy process. The more resistant parents are when bringing the child to therapy, the longer winning them over can take on the part of the therapist. Reflecting feelings of parents, including negative suspicions about the therapist and therapy process, can help them to feel safer, less threatened, and more encouraged.

For example, Les, 8 years old, was referred for therapy after the death of his father. Les' father dropped him off at school on a Tuesday morning and drove to work. Thirty minutes after arriving at work, Les' father fell out of his chair and was pronounced dead by the paramedics minutes later as a result of a heart attack at the age of 36. The family had no prior warning of any health problems.

Les sat sullenly on the sofa in the waiting room. His tall, slender, and attractive mother sat erect on the sofa reading a magazine. When the therapist greeted the two of them, the therapist was met with total silence from Les. His mother, who insisted Les be present at the initial session, informed the therapist that she wanted to speak to the therapist alone. In the therapist's office, Les' mother proceeded to do most of the talking, tersely declaring, "I don't know why we're here. I can't see how counseling can help, but the teacher and school counselor insisted we come. The children and I are doing fine. It was a shock about John, but it's time get on with life. It's been three months now since he died, and I expect Les to start focusing on his grades and baseball again. We have our faith, and I keep telling him this was God's will and we must go on about the business of living. So, since we're here, I'd really appreciate it if you could get these points across to him. He's an excellent baseball player and he's not playing to his full potential. He's also quiet and withdrawn all the time. I'm tired of that, too. His sister and I don't sit around moping all the time."

As you can imagine, Les' mother maintained her position for several weeks. Each therapy session, she reminded the therapist about Les' grades and baseball performance. Since she appeared to be in shock and denial herself, she had little understanding or tolerance for Les' grief and pain about his father. Les' mother, as often is the case, projected her pain toward the therapist and toward Les' grades and baseball performance. The therapist reflected her feelings about the therapist and about Les' behavior. Many sessions later, Les' mother did gain some insight into her reaction toward Les, but in the beginning of therapy she was unable to understand or tolerate Les' feelings. With empathy and understanding, the therapist met Les' mother where she was at the time and along the way. A more confrontational or direct approach by the therapist in the first few sessions almost certainly would have caused her to pull Les out of therapy.

☐ Acknowledgment of Parents' Agenda

Therapists cannot ignore the agenda of angry, resistant parents because they will use such behavior as leverage against the therapist and therapy process. Remember that your primary goal with angry, resistant parents is to win them over. In order to do so, you must buy some time for the relationship to develop rapport and trust. Parents, especially resistant parents, will be more likely to give the therapy process a chance if the therapist gives time and attention to the goals of the parent.

Les' mother, in the example above, was clear about her agenda for Les. She wanted him to be more focused on his grades and his baseball performance and to stop isolating himself from others. It would have been unsuccessful, as well as detrimental to Les, if the therapist had focused on these goals with Les in play therapy. However, the therapist did reflect the mother's feelings and offered to talk to Les' teacher about his grades and to his coach about his baseball performance. The mother agreed and signed a release of information for the therapist to talk to them. The therapist explained to the teacher and coach that Les was still very much in the grieving process. The teacher and coach were understanding and set up a plan to modify his schoolwork and baseball practices for two months. Les' mother saw her goals as being addressed, and the therapist had protected the integrity of the play therapy with Les.

If the suggestions you make regarding the goals of the parents do not work, *try something else*. Keep giving parents ways to work with their child. Resistant, angry parents will be quick, and often harsh, when reporting that the therapist's plan did not work. Try to keep their comments separate from your self-esteem by visualizing a wall between you and the words of the parents. Reflect their feelings and set up another plan for their agenda.

Four-year-old Jamie came to therapy because she was having temper tantrums at home and school. Jamie's mother and father were angry with Jamie, and projected their anger toward Jamie and toward the therapist. They demanded that Jamie's temper tantrums stop immediately and the father informed the therapist that he had a list of three other therapists that he would contact if he did not see results quickly. The therapist noticed that the parents, especially the mother, were very inconsistent in their discipline with Jamie. Sometimes the mother would give a time-out, sometimes she would spank, sometimes she would ignore Jamie's behavior, and sometimes she would try to bribe her with a treat. The therapist suggested that the mother consistently give Jamie a 4-minute time-out (1 minute for every year of age) when she behaved inappropriately.

Very angrily, Jamie's mother reported the next week that when she started to give Jamie a time-out, Jamie had kicked her. She then pointed to the bruise on her leg and told the therapist the time-out was a "stupid" idea. The therapist reflected the mother's anger and frustration and then asked the mother to describe more about the time-out. The mother revealed that she had been doing the time-outs for 20 minutes by putting her daughter in the guest bedroom that was isolated from the other bedrooms and den. The therapist reiterated the importance of the time-out being limited to four minutes, and also suggested that Jamie's mom sit with Jamie in the room where she was having the time-out. Jamie's mother was suspicious of this plan, but reluctantly agreed. At the next session, Jamie's mother described Jamie's behavior as improving and acknowledged that the time-outs were working much better. Jamie and her mother were both calmer. Jamie's mother was able then to give Jamie time for the therapy process without making undue demands of the therapist or Jamie. Jamie's father never attended another session after the first.

☐ Targeting Areas of Change

Sometimes parents get discouraged and frustrated when their child regresses to old behavior, or if they have not seen more progress. Parents need to be reminded of the changes that they have made with their child and the changes the child has made alone. Look for positive differences in the child's or parents' efforts outside therapy and help the parents focus on them.

An example to use with parents is to remind them of a history lesson with which they are probably familiar, but may have forgotten. Many years ago, when the Soviet Union was building its empire, with the intent of taking over the world one nation at a time, their philosophy was "two steps forward and one step back." This meant that they kept their focus on their destination or goal to take over the world, but were not overly concerned with every battle or every nation. Rather, they believed they were moving toward their ultimate goal even if they made progress, and then either regressed (lost a battle) or did not move forward for a while. They were able to concentrate on their primary goal of taking over the world without getting sidetracked by defeats they believed to be temporary.

This analogy can help parents focus on the utmost important goal that they have for their child without weekly having to evaluate the success or failure of the therapy, the therapist, the child, or themselves. When parents are able to delay a final conclusion about their child's behavior or problem, everyone involved in the process will be able to relax more and let the child move at the pace needed to move ahead in therapy.

☐ Appealing to the Less Resistant Parent

If one parent is more favorable toward the child being in play therapy, appeal to that parent to keep the child in therapy. Remind the parents that it did not take 3, 4, or 5 weeks for the child to develop the undesired behaviors or problems, and change of the behaviors or resolution for the problems may require a considerable amount of time.

When one parent is *overtly* resistant, the therapist can help the parent who supports therapy to confront the resistant parent. The task of helping one parent confront the other parent must be executed carefully. The overtly resistant parent, when confronted by the other parent, very likely will terminate therapy if a power struggle ensues. A nonthreatening approach is to request more time from the resistant parent for the therapy process.

The *covertly* resistant parent must be handled differently by both the therapist and the supportive parent. The covertly resistant parent probably will give a variety of justifications for premature termination of therapy, such as, "Therapy is too expensive," "The child's too busy with school and other extracurricular activities," "Therapy is interfering with the child's schoolwork," and "Therapy is inconvenient now, but we will resume it in a few months."

Help the supportive parent point out the positive changes since therapy started and address the excuses gently. Focus on the investment already made and request more time for therapy before terminating it. Try to work out a plan for the scheduling and financial difficulties with the parents. The therapist and supportive parent may be tempted to confront the "real issue" with the covertly resistant parent—a plan doomed to fail because the covertly resistant parent most often will deny being resistant and will have very logical reasons for terminating therapy. The child will have a better chance of continuing when there are solutions to his excuses.

☐ Recommending Individual or Marital Therapy

Resistance to therapy for the child may be a protection against revealing deeper issues in the family system. The therapist has an ethical responsibility to focus the play therapy sessions on the child. However, there are times when the therapist cannot ignore other issues in the family; these issues will often surface as resistance by one of the child's parents.

Alex, age 6, was referred to therapy because of behavior and academic problems seemingly related to his diagnosed ADHD. Both parents attended the initial session with the therapist, and both were favorable toward therapy at that time. At the 15-minute parent meeting after Alex's first session, the therapist gave the parents a 10-page parenting manual, and both agreed to read it. Alex's father explained to the therapist that he traveled frequently and worked long hours, so he would not be attending the sessions each week. Nevertheless, he attested that he would read the book and follow through on any other suggestions made by the therapist. However, 3 weeks later, during the 15-minute session with the therapist, Alex's mother started crying as she reported that she had read the parenting book, but her husband had not. She added that Alex's father had even suggested that maybe therapy was too stressful for Alex and should be postponed until summer. The therapist recognized that there was a covert attempt on the part of the father to terminate therapy, and, in light of the mother's tears and general decorum, she suspected something much deeper and more secretive was going on in the family.

The therapist addressed a plan to continue therapy with Alex that would lower his stress, although neither she nor the mother had sensed additional stress for Alex while in therapy. Therapy sessions would be moved to Saturday mornings, and Alex would miss a week of therapy when he had a Saturday baseball playoff game. Next, the therapist asked Alex's mother to talk about her feelings regarding her husband not reading the parenting book. She said she was sad and disappointed, and then revealed that her husband was an alcoholic, and the reason he had not read the parenting book was because he started drinking immediately when he came home from work and continued until bedtime. She said she had talked, begged, and pleaded with him to cut down on his drinking. Alex's father insisted that he did not have a drinking problem and that drinking helped him relax in the evenings. He justified drinking because he held an executive position with a major corporation that included long hours and much pressure. Alex's mother said the alcohol was a major issue between her and her husband, but that he did not want to discuss it with her or with anyone outside the family.

The therapist suggested Al-Anon and individual therapy for Alex's mother. Even though the therapist reflected her deep pain and concern regarding her husband's drinking, Alex's mother was reticent about both Al-Anon and therapy because she had so much invested in keeping the family secret. The therapist gave her some referrals for individual therapy and gave her the Al-Anon phone number to call just in case she changed her mind.

The next week Alex's mother reported attending an Al-Anon meeting and scheduling an appointment with another therapist for her own therapy. She was more hopeful, although still very sad. Alex's father reluctantly agreed to the Saturday sessions, and Alex's mother said he was anxious and worried when she told him she was going to therapy for herself, although he did not try to stop her from going. The therapist pointed out to Alex's mother that it was a positive sign. In the following weeks, the mother was able to focus on Alex and his ADHD in the 15-minute meeting with the therapist. Alex's Saturday appointments were soon changed back to a weekday because Alex did not like giving up sleeping late and playing with his friends on Saturday. Alex continued play therapy for 13 more weeks with resulting improvement in his schoolwork and behavior. When Alex's therapy was terminated, his mother was still in individual therapy and frequently attending Al-Anon meetings. Alex's mother called the therapist 6 months later to report that her husband had started attending Alcoholics Anonymous meetings.

The therapist must stay aware that the child is the client and that the child's therapy should not, if possible, be meshed with other therapy issues that will take away from the child's time. Of course, family issues, such as alcoholism, certainly affect the child and need to be addressed. However, it is preferable that these issues be addressed through separate therapy and community resources.

☐ Gentle Confrontation

Confronting resistant parents can be challenging, but sometimes is necessary. Confrontation does not have to be harsh or discordant. It can be beneficial when the parents are invited to inspect their attitudes and thoughts toward their children. The therapist can point out incongruities, especially between the verbal expression and the non-verbal expression (Corey, 1991).

In addition, confrontation does not have to be directed at unfavorable traits of the parents or negative discipline techniques; resistant parents can be challenged to identify the strengths and positive qualities that they possess as parents. The therapist is wise to notice positive traits about the resistant parents and frame them in a manner that facilitates hearing and identification by the parents. If the therapist points out their positive traits and qualities, especially in conjunction with parenting skills, resistant parents can gain a fuller awareness of themselves and become more open to suggestions and interventions of the therapist in the future. Corey (1991) provides a basis for such confrontation:

> Perhaps one of the most essential ingredients in effective confrontation is respect for the client. Counselors who care enough to make demands on their clients are telling them, in effect, that they could be in fuller contact with themselves and others. Ultimately, however, clients must decide for themselves if they want to accept this invitation to learn more about themselves. (p. 248)

"Clients" in the above quote is directed at the resistant parents in this case. The therapist will have a greater chance of breaking through to the parents if the therapist is respectful and exhibits genuine concern for the resistant parents. According to Bergman (1985), the therapist's qualities should include "warmth, charm, caring, forthrightness, wanting to help, and charisma" (p. 196).

☐ Reframing

When working with resistant parents, reframing can help the parents see their child's behaviors and emotions in a different way. Reframing is a technique that has been in use for a long time. Bergman (1985) explains:

> Reframing occurs most often in psychotherapy when a therapist offers a new way of looking at something—a way that is different from the way in which the patient has perceived the same phenomenon. If the reframing is presented to the patient in a way that is consistent with the way he thinks, organizes his life or perceives his world, the reframing is more likely to be accepted. Reframing in itself has enormous therapeutic power. Patients react to an effective reframing with responses such as surprise,

startle, and sometimes, excitement. When a reframing is accepted, not only the perception but also the affect associated with the perception change. And often, one finds that changes in behavior follow this change in perception. (p. 41)

Reframing may be the avenue to help parents change parenting techniques or skills in ways that are more effective in communicating with the child. Finally, reframing may help resistant parents see themselves differently which also results in a positive impact on the child.

☐ Looking for Windows

Positioning is a concept that gained popularity and notoriety in 1972 when authors and lecturers Al Ries and Jack Trout wrote a series of articles entitled "The Positioning Era" for the trade paper *Advertising Age* (Ries & Trout, 1986). Positioning is a technical phrase that means a "new approach to communication" (p. 1) used to help advertisers, by positioning the product, influence the consumer to one brand of a product, such as toothpaste, over another brand. There are a number of elements in positioning that can aid the therapist in working with angry, resistant parents.

Positioning begins with a product (Ries & Trout, 1986). "But positioning is not what you do to a product. Positioning is what you do to the mind of the prospect. That is, you position the product in the mind of the prospect" (p. 2). Through positioning, advertisers influence consumers to buy a particular product by finding a unique aspect of that product. Advertisers usually communicate this unique perspective through a short, simple slogan such as "Seven-Up: The Uncola" or "Nyquil: The Nighttime Medicine." These types of slogans, which market something unique about the product, influence consumers to buy these products.

So, what does this have to do with working with angry, resistant parents whose child is in play therapy? *It means that the therapist must continuously look for unique ways to reach difficult parents, or any parents, for that matter.* Some other points about positioning will explain this further.

Advertisers realize that people will reject information that does not compute with information already in their minds. The mind filters out new information that is not congruent with already established information that it possesses. The human mind dismisses information that does not match its prior knowledge or experience (Ries & Trout, 1986).

Most parents come to the parent meeting with preconceived ideas about parenting and about their child's behaviors or problems. Many of the parenting concepts and skills are based on how the parents were raised as children and on information they have acquired over the years. For instance, one parent might advocate spanking and another might be adamantly against it—all because ideas and experiences about spanking have influenced them before they bring their children to play therapy. It is not easy to change their ideas.

Advertisers also know that, when trying to influence consumers to buy a particular product, the advertising slogan and marketing must be kept simple. Consumers cannot assess and integrate massive information about products; there is not enough room in their minds or enough time to focus on so much input. That is one reason advertisers make up short, simple slogans; consumers remember the slogan, and when they go to buy a product, they are influenced by what is in their minds, by what they remember (Ries & Trout, 1986).

It will be helpful to therapists to try to think and communicate in simple terms about parenting skills and suggestions regarding the child in play therapy. Limit the amount of information you are giving parents weekly. Give the parents time to process and try out ideas and suggestions before making more suggestions. By keeping the information simple and concise, the parents will be more inclined to actually incorporate new parenting skills that will be continued long past termination of play therapy with the child.

Advertisers know the importance of *prioritizing*. Advertisers want the consumer to remember what is most unique and most important about a particular product. For instance, "Nyquil, The Nighttime Cold Medicine" had to give up the daytime market where cold medicines were concerned (Ries & Trout, 1986). The makers of Nyquil subsequently began producing and distributing "Dayquil" to capture part of the daytime medicine market. When working with a child in play therapy who is experiencing many problems, or when there are resistant parents, internally ask, "What is the most important concept I can communicate to these parents today?" Do not overload or overwhelm them with information. Keep it simple, and prioritize the skills and information they need to have regarding their child.

A therapist taking a weekly graduate class was observing a professor conducting filial therapy with several mothers. One week, the professor gave the mothers a homework assignment. The mothers were to have 15-minute play sessions with their children and report about the experience the next week in the group. The mothers returned the next week and began to share information and feelings regarding the play sessions. One mother, LeAnne, talked about her play session in an annoyed and irritated tone and basically described it as a negative experience. LeAnne had not been reflective, empathic, or accepting of her child. The professor listened, reflected LeAnne's feelings, and then made *one* suggestion for her to try the next week. Later, when the graduate students were discussing the session they had observed, several brought up questions about LeAnne. They asked the professor why he did not make more suggestions to LeAnne and confront her more. He explained that LeAnne was overwhelmed and would not be able at this time to process more suggestions or tolerate more confrontation. The professor then spent some time reviewing the previous filial sessions and charted for the students "Where LeAnne Started" to "Where LeAnne is Now" regarding her parenting skills. The professor highlighted the positive changes LeAnne had made with her child. Although these changes were minimal when compared with changes made by other mothers in the group, for LeAnne the changes were very significant, when keeping in mind from where she began. LeAnne shared with the group in the first session about her own childhood, which was dysfunctional and painful. She was starting from step 1, whereas some of the other mothers started from step 3 or 4. The students learned a valuable lesson that day about working with parents: Keep it simple for parents and prioritize what is most important for them to work on in regard to their child.

Advertisers, when trying to market and sell a product that is similar to another well known and well-established product, search for something unique about the product. This is a simple idea, yet is difficult to incorporate. Sometimes, the position of the product fails time and time again and advertisers must keep trying a new position. The advertisers must *keep looking for a new window* to open whereby they can reach the consumer.

The therapist may make suggestions, assign homework, and explain concepts only to have the parents not follow through with the suggestions or homework assignments and reject information the therapist provides about their child. When this happens, keep looking for windows—keep looking for a new way to explain the information; look for a different way to reach the parents.

Frankie, who was 6 years old, was brought to therapy by his father. Frankie was having trouble adjusting since his parents divorced 7 months earlier. Frankie was in second grade, and typically made A's. Before the divorce, he had not had behavior problems in school. His parents had joint custody. He spent Sunday through Wednesday with his dad and Thursday through Saturday with his mom. Although they were divorced, Frankie's parents were amicable and even attended the intake session together. Both were concerned about Frankie; they took turns bringing him to therapy, and both attended the parent meetings. The therapist was impressed and encouraged at how well the parents worked together as a team in regard to their son. During the first few sessions, Frankie was very aggressive in the playroom and did not adhere to the limits set by the therapist. He was angry and frustrated, which was apparent from his play in the sandtray. The therapist explained to the parents that Frankie was angry and suggested ways for them to reflect his feelings, demonstrating a structured play exercise for them to do with Frankie at home. Later, the father reported that he had not tried the structured play exercise and "couldn't get into reflecting" his son's feelings. In the third parenting meeting that Frankie's dad attended, he told the therapist that he thought Frankie was "just being a boy" and everyone was making too much fuss about Frankie's behavior. He pointed out that he and his ex-wife were "nice" to each other and that Frankie got to see them both during the week. He concluded that Frankie's behavior was temporary and not at all connected to the divorce.

Frankie continued to play out his anger, and his unacceptable behaviors escalated at school. As you might guess, the father concluded from Frankie's escalating behavior that it must be the therapy that was "making him worse." Frankie's dad rejected the idea that Frankie was angry.

The therapist kept reframing and explaining Frankie's behavior, and finally, asked Frankie's dad if he would try an exercise. The therapist asked him to close his eyes and to think back when he was a little boy, "Now take a deep breath and keep your eyes closed. Visualize the school where you went. Also visualize your house. Keep seeing yourself as a little boy. Keep breathing deeply. Now, think back on a time when you were mad at your mom or dad. Keep breathing and take your time."

Frankie's dad sat for a couple of minutes, and the therapist noticed his body tensed. A tear welled in the corner of his eye. The therapist asked him to open his eyes and tell what he was thinking. Frankie's dad related an incident when he was 8 years old and his parents thought he had stolen some candy from the store. He said he was so mad because he could not convince them that he had not taken the candy; in fact, to that very day, he believed that his parents were still convinced that he had taken the candy and just never admitted it. The therapist made the connection between his feelings and Frankie's feelings, to which dad responded, "I guess I don't want Frankie to be angry, so I've tried not to see him as angry. I sure don't want him to carry something around for years and years like I have—or resent me." Frankie's dad then sighed and said, "Okay, tell me again some of those things to do at home with him." Because the therapist kept looking for *windows*, eventually a window opened that Frankie's dad could connect with in relation to his son.

☐ Taking Care of Yourself

Therapists may experience sessions with resistant parents that leave them drained, frustrated, and even angry, so much so that when driving home at the end of the day they may find themselves contemplating a career change! *Taking care of oneself* can be helpful in managing feelings and reactions toward difficult, angry, and resistant parents.

Sense of Humor

Keep a sense of humor about oneself and one's work as a therapist, do not take yourself too seriously and do not judge each parenting session as a success or failure. Therapy is a process—and so is working with parents. Find humor and share it with the resistant parents. Humor can help lift the despair and pain that the parents may be experiencing. It also lightens the moment and gives everyone, including parents and therapist, a chance to take a deep breath and begin again. Of course, humor must be used judiciously and never in a mocking or ridiculing manner. Genuineness on the part of the therapist is important here, just as it is in reflection, reframing, supporting, and other interventions.

Boundaries

Therapists are not required to suffer abuse from resistant parents. Some therapists, especially new therapists, will sacrifice their own boundaries in an effort to keep the parents engaged in the therapy process. The therapist may fear, and justifiably so, that parents will terminate the child's therapy. However, there is a balance between trying to keep parents engaged and conceding personal boundaries. For instance, the therapist may be sensitive to yelling or intimidated by verbal attacks. The more the therapist knows about oneself and what is needed in terms of boundaries, the more successfully he or she can set and preserve those boudnaries. All mental health professionals are encouraged to look closely at themselves and the boundaries they need. For example, the therapist should carefully consider difficult sessions with parents and the related feelings and reactions that the therapist experiences. That is a warning sign that something is wrong, and needs to be delved into further until what is going on in relation to the therapist is addressed and managed appropriately.

Seeking Advice

Contact a supervisor if possible, or consult with a colleague. If frustrated and unsettled frequently after the parent sessions, the therapist may need to be in an ongoing supervision or peer-supervision group. Input from other professionals can help with treatment goals and help gain insight into the dynamics between the therapist and resistant parents (Kell and Mueller, 1966). Discuss ways to confront or talk to the parent along with assigning appropriate homework.

☐ Summary

When working with resistant parents, the therapist must endeavor to reach the parents and to win them over to the play therapy process. The more prepared the therapist is to use a variety of interventions with resistant parents, the greater the chance for successful therapy with the child and the parents. The therapist will have to rely heavily on his or her relationship building skills to link angry and resistant parents to their child's therapy.

Presented in this chapter are several strategies and related intervention issues, including:

1. appealing to, and engaging, the less resistant parent;
2. targeting areas for change;
3. gentle confrontations;
4. reframing;
5. whether to recommend individual or marital therapy; and
6. the therapist taking care of him- or herself.

The therapist will need to deal with the parent's resistance, as well as anger. Along with reflecting the parent's feelings, there is a need to acknowledge and appreciate the parent's underlying or unspoken agenda. However, the therapist must also focus on following, or returning to, the expressed goals of therapy and remember that the child is the principle client in the play therapy process.

Parent and Therapist Meetings

By meeting with the therapist, parents are more connected to and involved in the therapy process. They are less likely to feel threatened and less likely to withdraw the child from therapy. Parents have the ultimate power over the child's environment, and can be very beneficial in achieving positive therapy outcomes. By meeting with the parents, the therapist is able to learn more about the child, factors influencing the child's behavior, and meanings behind the child's play. Also, the therapist is better equipped to offer suggestions and assign homework to the parents. Meeting with the therapist also increases parents' accountability for their efforts toward the goals of therapy, and can provide the therapist with valuable information about barriers to success. Regular meetings with parents can greatly affect their attitudes toward therapy and the therapist, and are the strongest force in linking them to their child's therapy.

☐ Weekly 15-Minute Parent Meeting

Scheduling

Ideally, the therapist meets with at least one parent every session. This can be during the first 15 minutes of the session, before the play therapy with the child or during the last 15 minutes, after the child's session. This ideal may not be possible with some parents. Occasionally, parents will have someone else provide pick up and delivery service to get the child to therapy. For example, sometimes a babysitter, nanny, or friend may bring the child to therapy. Remember that consent for mental health treatment of the child must be given in writing by the parent who has authority to give that consent. Also, to schedule appointments, the therapist should only communicate with a person who has such authority. After that, anyone can pick up and deliver the child with the parent's permission; although, the therapist is recommended to obtain written permission to release a child to anyone other than a legal guardian. Some parents have considerable difficulty being available on a regular basis, and the therapist can try to meet with them every few weeks for the entire session.

Children's Involvement

A child must feel as comfortable as possible about the meetings between the therapist and the parents, and that comfort level is largely dependent upon the trust developed with the therapist. Much of this trust comes from a child's belief that confidentiality of the play therapy sessions will be protected. Even if a child claims not to care, often he or she will want to know what is being discussed in these meetings. The therapist should assure that the parents will not be told things that were asked to remain private; in other words, the therapist will protect the confidentiality of what is done and said in the playroom. An explanation is helpful so that the child will know what to expect. The therapist might say, "I'm going to meet with your mom each week either before or after our time in the playroom. I won't tell your mother what you do or say, but I will tell her things that you may need. I may even make suggestions to your mom about how to try to make things better at home or school for you. Please ask me any questions you have about this. I'd like for you to decide if you want your mom to go before or after our playtime."

Notice that the child is given the choice about when the therapist will meet with the parents. Choosing between the first 15 minutes of therapy or the last 15 minutes of therapy will allow the child to feel more involved in the decision and usually less anxious about session details being disclosed about the therapy. When the 15-minute parent meeting occurs the child will need a place to stay during your meeting. If the therapist's office or playroom is near the waiting room, the child can sit in the waiting room while the therapist meets with the parents. It is advisable to leave the office door cracked so the child can see the parent and therapist, but cannot hear the conversation. Have toys in the waiting room and ask the child to knock on the door if something is needed, including reassurance. It is not recommended to let the child stay in the playroom for any reason during the parent meeting. It could affect the therapeutic process that goes on in the playroom, or if the child were to get hurt or the toys get broken, it could raise some liability questions.

Parents' Involvement

The general format of the weekly 15-minute parent meeting is three-fold: parents sharing weekly highlights, including homework assignments; therapist sharing session themes; and making new homework assignments. Parents are encouraged to call prior to the session if they are very upset, sad, or angry about something that has happened during the week with their child. This protects the child from seeing or hearing parents being very upset about something regarding him- or herself. Even if the child is waiting in another room, when the parent comes out of the parent meeting and was upset, the child often knows or the parent might be loud enough for the child to hear.

The parent meeting is not intended to be a time to punish a child by "tattling" or reporting about them in a negative way. The parents should be encouraged to share the highlights of the week—the positive aspects as well as the negative aspects of the parent-child relationships, including the results of any homework assignments. This is a prime time for the therapist to listen carefully, be accepting, and support the parents for their sharing. Then, the therapist can talk about the themes the child seems to be playing out in the playroom. The therapist must remember that the *child is the client,* and must protect that relationship as much as possible within the realms of the state's laws regarding the confidentiality of child clients. Specific homework assignments can be given based on what the therapist has observed in the playroom and similar themes at home as determined from the parents' sharing.

When the 15-minute meeting does not seem to be long enough, look for reasons why. This is especially crucial if it is *not* the first two or three sessions of therapy, when there is naturally more information to share. If the therapist is constantly stressed after the parent meeting or if the therapist has difficulty limiting the parent meeting to 15 minutes, then the therapist should look at possible underlying issues in the family system. In addition, the parent's insight may increase and resistance may decrease after a few sessions. In this situation, the parent likely has more comfort and trust in the counselor, along with increased awareness of underlying issues.

Some parents may need to schedule a separate appointment for individual or couples therapy (at another time) to deal with issues that are beyond the scope of the 15-minute parent meeting. The following example illustrates this point.

Hannah brought her 7-year-old son, Josh, for therapy because of severe behavior problems that he was having at school. He was having angry outbursts, not following school rules, and arguing with his teacher. Hannah would sit in the waiting room with Josh's twin brother during the play therapy session and then come to the office for the 15-minute meeting. At the beginning of the fourth session, Hannah entered the waiting room with tears in her eyes and sniffling. She made little eye contact. At the end of the play therapy session, she entered the office and started sobbing hysterically. It was several minutes before she could start to talk about what was upsetting her. She said Josh had gotten angry with her the night before when she told him it was time to go to bed. He wanted to watch one more television program. Since Hannah and the therapist had been working on her and her husband being more consistent with their sons, she said, "I know you really want to stay up and watch this show, but the rule is bedtime at 8:30 on school nights." Josh became very angry and started yelling, "I hate you. You are the worst mom in the whole world. I really, really hate you." Hannah replied, "I can hear how angry you are at me. You think this is unfair, and it really upsets you. But, it's time to go to bed."

Josh then proceeded to start kicking Hannah. Josh's anger escalated, and he began kicking Hannah repeatedly while yelling and crying for approximately 40 minutes. Hannah shared with the therapist about being angry with Josh and afraid, too. Her husband was out of town on business, and she felt so alone and helpless. She then started telling the therapist how difficult Josh had always been for her and that she felt sad much of the time and overwhelmed. As she talked and cried, it was obvious that Hannah was struggling not only with parenting issues, but with depression and anxiety as well. The therapist suggested individual therapy and referred her.

Filial Therapy and Parent Training

Throughout numerous research studies, filial therapy has demonstrated tremendous effectiveness in helping children and parents. Studies have shown filial therapy to be helpful for children and parents with such populations as single parents (Bratton, 1994), incarcerated mothers (Harris, 1995), Native American on the Flathead Reservation (Glover, 1996), and children experiencing learning difficulties (Kale, 1997). One of the earliest studies was by Guerney (1976), wherein filial therapy was shown to be effective in working with disturbed children.

The procedure of Filial Therapy Training involves teaching parents child-centered play therapy skills and practices: nonjudgmental and empathic understanding, unconditional positive regard, and self-congruence. By using these skills, parents can become therapeutic agents of change for their children (Landreth, 1991; VanFleet, 1994). Parents learn how to create an accepting, nonjudgmental, understanding, and supportive environment in which children experience safety and an absence of emotional threats. Through this safe relationship children are able to explore themselves, their feelings, gain trust in themselves, and learn new ways of relating to their parents. According to Landreth's (1991) model, 6 to 8 parents and the therapist meet once a week for 2 hours and engage in lively interaction and discussion regarding their concerns and experiences as parents. The therapist introduces training information and teaching points related to the parent's experiences. After the third session, parents also meet once a week for 30 minutes with their child and practice their new skills. Parents videotape the play sessions and review the tape during the parent group meeting. Each parent thereby gives and receives support, encouragement, feedback, and supervision from the group and the therapist.

According to VanFleet (1994), filial therapy is an appropriate and effective intervention with a wide array of children's issues. Examples include children with depression, adjustment difficulties, anxiety, school problems, as well as abused children and children of divorce. There are very few children's issues with which filial therapy would not be appropriate and effective. It would be easier to address some of these conditions than to attempt a list of all childhood issues for which filial therapy *is* appropriate.

Conditions where filial therapy *might not* be effective include:

1. severely traumatized children;
2. children with severe mental health disorders (i.e., schizophrenia);
3. children who have been, or are currently being, severely sexually abused; and
4. children whose parents are unable to give what it takes to complete the filial training and develop the essential parenting skills.

The effectiveness of filial therapy is largely due to its focus on the parent-child relationship. This relationship is seen as the primary influence in the development of the child and the child's difficulties (VanFleet, 1994). The parent has the capacity to develop skills to become a therapeutic role for the child. The skills the parent learns in filial therapy are those skills needed for effective parenting. The enhanced interacting and relationship provides a vehicle for both parents and child to use throughout the child's life to work through and deal effectively with problems. Other attributes of the parent-child relationship that make filial therapy effective include:

1. the therapy or training process closely resembles reality;
2. the child is able to experience acceptance directly from the parent (rather than from the therapist);
3. the parent feels less excluded and views the therapist as an ally;
4. the parent feels less defensive and resistant; and
5. the process uses the existing parent-child relationship which facilitates therapy.

The structure of the filial therapy training also facilitates success in the program. The parent is to use new skills only during 30-minute, once-a-week play sessions with the child. Other parent training programs have parents practice new skills in all interactions, which can be very overwhelming for the parent. The group format in Landreth's (1991) model also increases the effectiveness of filial therapy. The natural processes of the group, including support from others, feedback, diverse ideas and opinions, and the realization that others have similar problems can be very encouraging for the parent.

Parents are the most significant adults in the lives of children. Through the process of filial therapy (VanFleet, 1994), parents experience many benefits, including:

1. increasing the parent's understanding and acceptance of oneself;
2. increasing the parent's understanding and acceptance of the child;
3. helping the parent to recognize the importance of play and emotion;
4. helping the parent to communicate more openly, especially with the child;
5. enhancing the parent-child relationship;
6. helping the parent model appropriate expression of feelings;
7. decreasing the parent's feelings of frustration;
8. developing a positive attitude toward self and child;
9. developing appropriate limit-setting skills;
10. increasing confidence in self and parenting abilities;
11. increasing feelings of trust and warmth toward the child;
12. permitting the child to direct self;
13. rediscovering the joy of parenting;
14. providing a safe environment (group session) for the parent to process one's own feelings and issues regarding parenting;
15. helping the parent learn how to allow the child to grow as a unique individual, including emotional and interpersonal development; and
16. helping the parent develop realistic expectations of the child.

Through the filial therapy process, the child is likely to experience numerous benefits. These include:

1. improving understanding and perception of parent's feelings, thoughts, and behaviors, especially how these relate to the child;
2. increasing the child's trust and confidence in the parents—the child views one's parents as fully accepting when the parents reflect empathic understanding of the child's feelings, desires, and needs; and
3. helping the child develop self-responsibility, self-control, mastery, and positive self-regard.

☐ Determining Play Themes

Identifying play themes and interpreting underlying issues can be very complicated. Not all play therapy theories stress interpretation—especially interpreting to the child. According to Brody (1997) and Landreth and Sweeney (1997), developmental play therapists and child-centered play therapists usually do not make interpretations. Carroll and Oaklander (1997) state that the Gestalt play therapist may offer an interpretation as a "tentative possible way of viewing the child's work, or the therapist's associations or thoughts. The child can verify or reject these ideas" (p. 195). Most importantly, the therapist should determine a theoretical framework with which he or she feels best aligned, and adhere to that theoretical view.

Repetitive, sustained, and recurring play behaviors indicate possible themes within the child's play. The therapist should ask oneself, "What's the meaning behind this play?" According to Ryan and Wilson (1996), the therapist forms hypotheses about the meaning of the child's play in order to understand and respond to it. Play themes can also provide meaningful information to share with parents in the parent meetings, and can form the basis from which to assign the parents related and appropriate homework. If the therapist has some ideas but does not feel very confident about the themes, the parent can be asked questions that might help to clarify the child's play behaviors.

Norton and Norton (1997) suggest examining the metaphors contained in the child's play, then incorporate this information into the session notes. Record only the themes of a child's play during a specific session. Look for commonly occurring themes in the child's play such as power and control, anger and sadness, trust or mistrust in relationships, rejection and abandonment, insecurity, and feeling violated. The child's play may include a need for protection, nurturing, boundaries, or self-empowerment.

Harter (1983) explains, "Here the theorist begins with observations, often single cases, and gradually comes to appreciate commonalities leading to a more general formulation which ties these observations together" (p. 122). Think of the therapy as putting a puzzle together. The child, parent, and others involved bring you pieces of the puzzle and as the therapist, you try to put the pieces together. Both the therapist and the parents would like to be able to fit the puzzle together to better understand the meaning behind the child's inappropriate behaviors and changes that occur during the course of therapy. However, the symbolic nature of the child's play does not always present a clear picture of its underlying meaning. The sharing of possible themes and comparing them with parent information may not complete the puzzle; nevertheless, it is important to note that resolution of issues and healing can come about for the child through the play therapy alone. The essence of play therapy is to provide an atmosphere wherein the child can play out feelings and desires without offering any direct explanation.

Homework Assignments

Begin to give general homework assignments, discussed in chapter 9, in the second or third session. Then, as you begin to assess themes in the child's play, give more specific homework assignments that are designed to help with the specific themes. According to L'Abate, Ganahl, and Hansen (1986), homework assignments enlarge the family's behavioral repertoire through the practice and establishment of new ways of interacting. It is important that the therapist monitor the homework to check progress and correct the misunderstandings parents may have. Homework assignments provide means for parents to learn and practice positive skills. They are oriented toward information about and the practice of new skills that will, hopefully, benefit the parents as well as the child.

☐ Case Studies

Case 1

Referral Concern

Jeremy, age 5, was referred by his kindergarten teacher because he cried frequently and seemed sad and withdrawn.

Theme Development

In the second session, Jeremy took three gummy dolls (two big and one little). He studied them for a minute, then placed the smaller gummy doll on top of the sand in the middle of the sandbox. In a quiet voice, he said, "The baby is alone." The therapist reflected, "It sounds like it's sad for the baby to be alone." Tears then welled in Jeremy's eyes. He shook his head affirmatively and said, "We have to find his mommy and daddy." Jeremy then took the larger gummy dolls and placed one on each side of the smaller gummy doll. His voice became excited as he announced, "Look, the mommy and daddy found the baby!"

In the third session, Jeremy played out this scene again with only slight variation. The therapist wondered what this meant, since she knew Jeremy lived with his parents and the family was, as far as she knew, intact. She questioned the mother after the fourth play session about their time together as a family. The mother said they were close, but that she and her husband worked long hours. She worked about 10 hours a day, her husband sometimes averaged 12 hours a day, and he also had to travel during some weeks. The mother related further, that before Jeremy started kindergarten her husband would sometimes take Jeremy to breakfast or spend some time with him in the mornings and go to work a little later. Now that Jeremy was in school, the morning time was impossible so the time together for the father and Jeremy had been more limited.

Possible Theme Meaning

The therapist explained that she thought Jeremy might need some extra attention and nurturing from his parents, especially his father. She talked to the mother about the importance of Jeremy having time with his mother and father that he could count on to help him feel secure, safe, and special.

Related Homework

The therapist suggested, as a general assignment, for Jeremy and his dad to have a specific date time (see *15-Minute Date* in chapter 9) each week. She also asked that Jeremy's dad take Jeremy to work with him sometimes; she thought it might be helpful to Jeremy to see where his dad worked and to spend some time with him there. The therapist also asked that Jeremy's dad call Jeremy each afternoon to tell Jeremy that he was thinking about him. Finally, she asked that Mom, Dad, and Jeremy try to set up some special family times that were very protected from being changed or interrupted. Because rituals build security and provide much joy for children, she also stressed the importance of family rituals, such as pizza night or movie night. The mother agreed to try the suggestions and felt that her husband also would.

Therapy Outcome

Jeremy played the doll scene out again in the fifth session, but once the mommy and daddy doll found the baby doll, he spent more time on the reunion of the family than he had in previous sessions. Jeremy's mother reported at the end of the fifth session that she and her husband had started incorporating the therapist's suggestions. She said she felt the three of them were already growing closer and had put more focus back on their family.

Jeremy did not play out the doll scene in the sixth, seventh, or eighth sessions. By the eighth session, he was into much more free play and his mother reported that his crying and sad demeanor had stopped, and that the teacher noted that Jeremy was participating more in class.

Case 2

Referral Concern

Kate, age 6, was brought to therapy by her mother because she was sad and withdrawn. Her mother reported that Kate seemed to worry a lot and that she cried often.

Theme Development

In the first, second, and third sessions, Kate played with a teddy bear and the medical equipment. She would tell the therapist that the bear was sick, and spent much of each session caring for the bear and administering medical care. The therapist asked the mother after the third play session if anyone in their family or friends was sick. Kate's mom replied, "No, we're all healthy, including our friends." The therapist was puzzled, but did not pursue it any further.

Kate continued to play with the bear and the medical equipment for the next six sessions. The therapist would reflect how sad and scared the bear seemed with being sick. Kate would never respond to the therapist and just kept administering medical care. Kate always referred to the bear as "the little bear" and never gave it any other name.

Possible Theme Meaning

After the ninth session, the therapist again asked the mother about anyone at all whom the family or Kate knew who was sick or had been sick. This time the mother replied, "No, really everyone we know is fine. I did have cancer two years ago, but we don't talk about that anymore—we don't even think about it." The therapist's eyes widened with this new insight. The entire family had pushed this away and had denied its significant impact upon all of them. The parents did not realize that Kate still had feelings of sadness and fear. The therapist explained that she thought Kate was still having feelings about her mother's cancer and probably needed some extra help from her mom in trying to resolve those feelings. The mother was resistant at first, insisting that no one was really concerned about it anymore. The therapist persisted, explaining that children play out something that has happened, something that is happening, or something they want to happen. The therapist expressed her concern that Kate was still trapped in some uncomfortable feelings about what her mother had experienced.

Related Homework

The therapist set up three homework assignments over the following three sessions. First, the therapist asked the mother to start doing structured play therapy activities with Kate, using dolls or stuffed animals at home. The therapist brought several stuffed animals into the office and demonstrated to the mother how to set up that one of the animals was sick and another animal was concerned about the sick animal. Second, during the structured play, the therapist began to teach the mother how to reflect feelings that Kate experienced. This was something with which the mother was unfamiliar and was not doing with Kate. The goal of the structured play was twofold: first, to help Kate's mother learn how to recognize and reflect Kate's feelings; and second, to help change the ending of the play story from being sick to being well in Kate's mind. So the mother was to work on reflecting feelings and then to play out with Kate the animal being sick, but then getting well.

Since the meeting time with the parent was limited, the therapist also gave Kate's mother a handout on reflecting feelings. Reading assignments can help expedite the learning of new skills for the parents. Use reading assignments often, especially if it is a chapter, handout, or something brief that will not take much extra time for the parent to read.

The third homework assignment the therapist suggested was for the doctor or nurse who had worked with Kate's mother during her illness, to meet with Kate and her mother and discuss her mother's illness and recovery. The therapist thought hearing it from an "official" source might dissipate some of Kate's fears. The therapist thought it might also be a good idea for Kate to actually go back to the doctor's office where she had been with her mother numerous times 2 years prior.

Kate's mother followed through on the homework assignments, although reflecting feelings was difficult for her to incorporate. She loved Kate very much, but she had been raised in an unemotional family, where feelings were not acknowledged or talked about. She and Kate met with the nurse whom the mother had seen during her cancer treatments. Kate's mother also followed through on the structured play.

Therapy Outcome

By the 12th session, Kate's affect had greatly improved, and her mother reported Kate was happier and less worried about events going on in the family or at school. Kate's mother told the therapist that she and Kate were talking about the cancer more frequently and that talking about it had helped her as well as Kate.

Case 3

Referral Concern

The school referred 5-year-old Mindy after she was diagnosed with dyslexia and had to repeat kindergarten.

Theme Development

During the first few sessions, Mindy spent the majority of time "playing school"—appointing the therapist as the student and herself as the teacher. She would write, "Do not erase!" on the dry-erase board, and was adamant as she read to the therapist out loud, "Do not erase!" As the teacher, she was strict and controlling.

In the sixth session, Mindy wrote names of "good" children and "bad" children on the board. She spent most of this session, as she had in other sessions, instructing and correcting the "student." Her tone of voice was angry and critical.

Possible Theme Meaning

When the therapist questioned Mindy's mother about school, she assured the therapist that both Mindy's first kindergarten teacher, as well as her current kindergarten teacher, were kind and nurturing. Mindy's parents both seemed kind and concerned about her, too. The therapist explained that Mindy seemed to be experiencing much fear and anxiety about school, despite the teachers' and parents' efforts. She said it is important to remember that children experience life from a phenomenological point of view—which means that how children *perceive* their world is their *reality*. As adults, we must meet children where they are in this reality and begin to help them with the conflicts and difficulties as they perceive and experience them.

Related Homework

The therapist asked Mindy's mother to sign a release of confidential information, so she could talk to the teacher about Mindy. Again, to the teacher, the therapist explained that Mindy appeared still to be experiencing fear and anxiety about school. The therapist was careful to support the teacher for her efforts with Mindy and assured the teacher that her work with Mindy was appreciated. Whenever possible, the therapist asked the teacher to spend 2 minutes in the morning with Mindy when she came into the classroom when possible. Mindy's mother agreed to bring Mindy to school a few minutes early so this assignment could be more consistent. The teacher was to explain briefly what they would be doing in school that day and then to talk to Mindy about nonthreatening events, such as Mindy's dog or extracurricular activities. The therapist wanted to lower Mindy's anxiety level and build a positive rapport between Mindy and her teacher.

The therapist also asked Mindy's mother to volunteer for field trips, school parties, and so forth in order to have more visibility at school. The therapist thought her presence might also lower Mindy's anxiety and fear.

In addition, the therapist taught Mindy's mother structured play to do at home with Mindy. The goal of the structured play was to change Mindy's perception of anxiety and fear about school to a more positive perception. Mindy's mother was to set up a mock classroom with some dolls. Sometimes Mindy would be the teacher and sometimes Mindy's mother would be the teacher. When Mindy's mother was the teacher, she was kind and nurturing and showed great concern about the students.

Mindy's teacher also agreed, at the request of the therapist, to watch for any sign of Mindy getting anxious or nervous in class. This was important because, as the teacher explained, Mindy was a model student in her behavior at school and her grades were now average with the modifications the school had made because of her dyslexia.

Therapy Outcome

Mindy's teacher reported that she and Mindy both looked forward to their few minutes together in the morning. Mindy's mother said Mindy no longer complained about going to school and was insistent that her mom gets her to school early for her time with the teacher. Mindy and her mother did the structured play a couple of times a week and Mindy would trade roles of being the teacher or one of the students with her dolls. Of course, Mindy liked her mom volunteering at school. Mindy's dad even came for one field trip and for lunch with her on occasion.

In therapy, Mindy continued to play school and continued to be strict and controlling for several more weeks. At the beginning of session 10, however, there was a change in her play. She came into the playroom and set up the classroom scenario the same way she did each week. She looked at the therapist, designated as the student by Mindy, and said, "Do you know what today is? Well, do you or don't you? What day is this?" Before the therapist could make a response, Mindy answered, "It's a day for all recess! No school!" With that announcement, Mindy began to move around the playroom in free play. She did not play out school anymore in the playroom. Therapy was terminated four weeks later.

Case 4

Referral Concern

Three-year-old Melanie was brought to therapy by her mother because Melanie had started having angry outbursts at home. Melanie's mother was confused and concerned about the change in Melanie's behavior. She reported Melanie was having no difficulty at preschool emotionally or academically, but would get very angry at home over little things that had not bothered her in the past.

Theme Development

In the first session, Melanie picked up the toy telephone. She held it to her ear and repeatedly said, "Hello. Hello. He's not there." With a sigh, she hung up the telephone. She moved about the room playing with other toys, but she would periodically come back to the telephone, pick it up and say, "Hello. Hello. He's not there." Towards the end of the first session, she handed the therapist another toy telephone. Then, Melanie picked up her phone and said, "Hello. Hello." When there was silence following her "Hello," she looked at the therapist and whispered, "You're supposed to say 'hello'." The therapist responded into her telephone, "Hello." Melanie smiled and said, "You're there."

In the second and third session, Melanie played with the telephone, but less frequently than in the first session. However, when she did play with the telephone, she would give the therapist a telephone and direct the therapist to respond with "Hello."

Possible Theme Meaning

The therapist perceived the repetitious play as significant, so she asked Melanie's mother during the 15-minute meeting about the family use of the telephone. Melanie's mother said she liked to talk on the telephone and that she talked frequently; since she did work outside the home, talking on the telephone provided social interaction for her. She did try to talk mostly when Melanie was at preschool or napping. When asked if her husband, Melanie, or Melanie's older sister talked on the phone, she said that Melanie talked to her grandparents periodically and that Melanie's dad had called her during the first few weeks of preschool to see how the schoolday had gone. The father had received a promotion at work involving working longer hours and traveling frequently, so his calls to Melanie had stopped.

The therapist thought Melanie was angry because her father was gone more and possibly experiencing feelings of abandonment. During this age, children often bond with their father and want to be with him. Melanie had been spending more time with her father, and then it was abruptly shortened. Neither of Melanie's parents had realized the impact because they were both adjusting to his workload as well, and because Melanie's mother stayed home and was very available to Melanie.

Related Homework

The therapist suggested that Melanie's father start calling Melanie again whenever possible. Because of his schedule, the times varied, but he made it a point to call her several times a week, even if it had to be late or early. He even called her from the airport one morning at 6:00 a.m. The therapist also asked that Melanie's father start sending her cards and leaving her notes. He readily agreed. When Melanie's father was in town, the therapist suggested a special date time for Melanie with him. He wrote down the time and date for her, and she was very excited. She kept the piece of paper that he had written on next to her bed, even though she could not yet read. The therapist then gave Melanie's parents a handout on reflecting feelings and asked them to read it. Lastly, the therapist discussed ways to set limits and consequences with Melanie when her anger escalated. The therapist had Melanie's mother write down Melanie's outbursts each week prior to the parent meeting. The therapist then went over ways to reflect feelings while setting limits, and providing alternative ways for Melanie to release her anger.

Therapy Outcome

Melanie's mother reported that Melanie was calmer at home after the homework assignments were incorporated. She continued to get agitated and frustrated, but it was less often and for shorter periods of time. Melanie played out the phone scene for six more sessions and then did not repeat it again until the 10th session. In sessions 11 through 14, she did not play with the phone and moved to more free play. Therapy was terminated after the 15th session.

Case 5

Referral Concern

Doug, age 9, was referred because of aggressive behavior at school.

Theme Development

During the second session, Doug spent the first 20 minutes drawing a picture of a person whom he named "the mean man." The therapist reflected that the mean man looked scary. There was no response or change in expression from Doug. As Doug drew the picture, the therapist reflected other possible feelings such as anger, sadness, and fear. Again, Doug never changed expressions or responded. When he finished the picture, he moved to the sand and spent the rest of the session playing in the sand. During the third through the sixth sessions, Doug drew the mean man, sometimes on the dry-erase board, sometimes on construction paper, and sometimes on the easel. The therapist continued to track his behaviors, emphasizing many obvious feelings. Doug never responded to these remarks by the therapist.

Possible Theme Meaning

When the therapist questioned the parents, who both attended the 15-minute meeting, they were both unaware of anything that could be frightening Doug or making him angry. The therapist did not talk specifically about the picture in order to protect the confidentiality of the session, but she did question the parents about whether or not anything traumatic or scary had happened to Doug. She even assigned them to write an 8-year timeline of Doug's life and to list all significant events that they could remember. They did, but no new information showed up to explain his drawings. The parents even had a conference with Doug's teacher, at the therapist's request, to ask about any unusual happenings at school. Again, there was no information that could explain the pictures Doug drew. The therapist realized the pictures were significant, but was puzzled about the conflict they represented for Doug.

The therapist believed, and explained to the parents, that we do not always know what the conflict is with the child. However, play therapy is a way for children to work through and master the feelings related to the conflicts and trauma they are experiencing. The therapist stressed to the parents the importance of keeping Doug in play therapy while he worked on this unknown conflict. They agreed, although Doug's father really wanted some concrete information from the therapist. He was a very involved father, and he wanted the situation cleared up at school.

Related Homework

The therapist did work with Doug's parents on limit setting and consequences regarding his behavior at school. The parents, along with the therapist, made a list of the behaviors that Doug got into trouble for at school and then prioritized their importance. The less severe infractions were to have no additional consequences at home. The top two misbehaviors on the list would have consequences at home as well at school. The therapist explained that Doug was probably discouraged due to frequent punishment at home and school. In order to try to encourage him, she asked the parents to limit their consequences to the two priority misbehaviors. She also assigned them to find something positive to say about Doug daily and to focus on his efforts, not his achievements. To help them understand the concept of encouragement more fully, the therapist also gave the parents a handout on ways to encourage children.

Therapy Outcome

Doug continued to draw the same picture during session seven through nine. He did not draw it during the 10th session, but did again during the 11th session. Then, he skipped two sessions of drawing it. In session 14, he started the picture but did not finish it. Then, in the following five sessions, he did not draw the picture at all. He continued to paint and draw, but did not draw anything resembling the mean man. His behavior also began to improve at school, but it was a slow process. The parents also continued to work on being more encouraging. It was interesting to see the changes Doug's father made as result of being more attuned to his son. Doug's father reported being more relaxed at home and work, and even tried to find more positive comments to make to his staff at work. His wife reported that Doug and her husband had grown closer and were laughing and talking more frequently. Therapy was terminated after the 19th session.

Case 6

Referral Concern

Eight-year-old Annie was brought to therapy by her stepmother. Annie's stepmother told the therapist that Annie was a very difficult child who disobeyed and misbehaved constantly. She said Annie's biological mother had died 3 years ago and that she had married Annie's father 1 year ago. She said it was a good marriage except for their constant conflicts regarding Annie, contending that Annie's father was not "firm" enough with Annie, that he let Annie manipulate him into getting whatever she wanted and did not punish her often enough. When the therapist asked Annie's stepmother what type of behaviors Annie was displaying, she reported several incidents between herself and Annie. The therapist asked if she got into trouble at school. The stepmother hedged and then said, "Yes." The therapist immediately made a mental note to confirm that information. The stepmother seemed angry as she discussed Annie's behavior. She said quite adamantly that she had never planned to have children, but now that she had married Annie's father, she not only had a child to raise, but a very difficult child at that!

Theme Development

When Annie entered the playroom, the therapist observed a quiet, shy, little girl. Annie seemed apprehensive about playing with the toys. The therapist reflected that she could play with the toys in any of the ways she wanted and that it seemed hard to decide where to start. Annie tentatively moved toward the sandbox. She had played in the sand for about 10 minutes before she accidentally spilled a small amount on the floor beside the sandbox. She quickly looked up at the therapist to see if she was in trouble. The therapist said, "Looks as if you are worried about spilling the sand. But sometimes things spill." Annie looked relieved. She still took the small broom, though, swept up the sand, and put it back in the sandbox. She continued to play cautiously with the other toys for the remainder of the session. She said very little, but did smile at the therapist several times.

During the second session, Annie played with the sand again. She then moved to the dollhouse and began to arrange the rooms of furniture and put the dolls in different rooms. The therapist heard her talking softly as Annie gave words to the dolls. In one room, there were two dolls. She heard Annie say, "Go to bed right now. And stop that crying. Stop it! Do you hear me? Do you want a spanking?"

Possible Theme Meaning

The therapist realized that there was probably much conflict between Annie and her stepmother. Annie appeared to be playing the conflict out in the playroom. The therapist asked the stepmother, during the second 15-minute meeting, to get a signed release from the father to talk to Annie's teacher (stepparents cannot sign legal papers without legal documentation of the right to do so). Then, the therapist asked about the styles of discipline that Annie's stepmother and father used. The stepmother said they used time-outs, grounding, and spanking. The therapist asked which parent usually carried out the discipline. Annie's stepmother said, "Oh, I'm almost always the one to punish Annie. Her dad works a lot and is not around much. Plus, as I told you, he lets Annie get by with things."

The therapist telephoned Annie's teacher. Just as the therapist suspected, the teacher reported that Annie was a quiet, model student with no discipline problems. She said Annie was capable of making A's, but mostly made B's. She said it was sometimes hard for Annie to concentrate and stay on task, and that affected her grades. She did not feel there were any symptoms of ADHD, but rather that Annie was anxious at times.

After the fourth session, the therapist explained to the stepmother that Annie was probably still adjusting to the loss of her mother and her father's new marriage. The therapist carefully framed her interpretation to the stepmother because she realized the stepmother was angry and could easily become resistant to therapy and remove Annie if she thought the therapist was not paying attention to her agenda, which was to change Annie's behavior. The therapist reflected that the stepmother must feel very frustrated and overwhelmed at times, making her own adjustments to marriage and raising a child all at once. The therapist also stressed that Annie's stepmother had too much of the burden of the parenting. Annie's stepmother enthusiastically agreed to that!

In trying to align and win the stepmother over, the therapist stressed the importance of taking some of the parenting pressure off the step-mother. Of course, the therapist's goal was twofold: to build rapport with the stepmother and to try to find a way to help Annie feel more loved and secure. The therapist told the stepmother it was important to get Annie's father more involved in the parenting, especially the discipline.

The stepmother liked the idea of Annie's father disciplining more and added that she wanted the therapist to tell him to stop letting Annie manipulate him. Annie's stepmother was not very sympathetic to Annie's adjustment difficulties, telling the therapist, "We have all had adjustments to make." The therapist realized, once again, the importance of trying to help Annie's father get back into more of the parenting with Annie.

Related Homework

The therapist made three immediate homework requests: (a) that Annie's father bring Annie to the next session (setting up the appointment time before work and school so he could bring Annie); (b) that Annie's stepmother and father not spank Annie for "awhile," so that the therapist could help them set up some different discipline forms that might be more effective; and (c) that Annie's time-outs be limited, since they consisted of Annie going to her room frequently for extended periods of time. The stepmother was skeptical, but agreed to try it for a few weeks. The therapist assured Annie's stepmother that she would be working with Annie's father to do more of the discipline.

The next week Annie's father brought her to therapy. Annie was obviously glad to be with him. She smiled as she introduced her father to the therapist and wanted him to see the playroom before her session started. At the end of the session, the therapist talked to Annie's father. He was a kind and sincere man who loved his daughter very much. He was also passive, very overwhelmed by his work schedule, still grieving over the death of Annie's mom, and feeling controlled by his new wife. He asked the therapist twice about the confidentiality of the session because he did not want Annie's stepmother to know how he felt. He said he felt guilty about not having more time with Annie, and because her mother had died, he did not enforce many limits or consequences with her. He said he was also gone much of the time when Annie was "getting into trouble" with her stepmother.

Because Annie's father was overwhelmed with pain, grief, and his schedule, the therapist was gentle as she explained that Annie was indeed in the middle of many adjustments, as was the rest of the family. She told Annie's father that she could see both he and Annie were discouraged and overwhelmed. Tears welled in his eyes as the therapist talked. The therapist went on to say that it was important to protect the relationship between Annie and him. She assured him that some small changes could be made that might make a very big difference for him and Annie.

The therapist asked Annie's father to have a special date time with Annie before the following session, and he agreed. She also asked Annie's father if he could bring Annie to therapy each week. He said he could if they kept the early appointment. The therapist's first goal with Annie's father was to make the relationship stronger between Annie and him.

In subsequent 15-minute parent meetings, the therapist introduced reflection of feelings that Annie experienced as well as setting limits and appropriate consequences, including using examples and hand-outs. Overall, she worked with Annie's father about being more in-volved in the discipline. She also asked him to tell his wife that he wanted to be much more involved in the discipline. He was anxious about talking to his wife, so the therapist role-played with him.

Annie's father told the therapist that Annie liked to talk about her biological mother, but that he always tried to change the subject be-cause he did not want her to "feel bad." The therapist knew it must be painful for him to talk about her, but the therapist talked about the importance of Annie being able to talk about her mother and that it could be very healing for her.

Therapy Outcome

When Annie and her father came to therapy together for the second time, Annie's affect was improved from the two previous weeks. Her play was less directed, and she had more eye contact with the thera-pist. She still played in the dollhouse, but there was no scene of a doll being punished this time. Annie told the therapist that she and her dad had stopped for a doughnut after the last session before he took her to school.

Annie's father was glad to be with his daughter. It was obvious from the way he talked about her. He told the therapist that their date time had been fun. He was glad that the therapist had told him not to spend any money during the date time because his wife did not like to spend money that was not budgeted. Also, because the *therapist* told him to have the time with Annie, his wife had willingly agreed. It was evident that his wife was really glad that the therapist had asked him to start bringing Annie to therapy because she told him, "It's about time you did more of the parenting." Annie's father was able to discuss the discipline with his wife and was eventually able to set some boundaries with her regarding the discipline of Annie. He said his wife had been skeptical at first, but after a few weeks seemed glad that he was doing the discipline. He said there were also fewer conflicts between Annie and her stepmother.

Annie's play eventually moved to more free play. She still played in the dollhouse much of the sessions, but her play moved from the critical, punishing scene to a more loving and nurturing scene. She would often name the "mommy" doll and the "baby" doll. The therapist suspected Annie was in the grieving process about the loss of her biological mother. Annie's father told the therapist that he and Annie were talking more about Annie's biological mother. He said that they had started writing down the fun memories that the three of them had shared.

The therapist periodically telephoned the stepmother to check on how things were going. The therapist did not want the stepmother to feel threatened about the increasing closeness between Annie and her dad with the possible risk that the stepmother might wield her influence and have Annie pulled from therapy or, worse, interfere in the relationship between Annie and her dad. Overall, the stepmother was pleased with the progress. There was an undertone of jealousy on occasion about the time that her husband was "finding" to spend with Annie. The therapist supported the stepmother for her efforts in bringing Annie originally to therapy and for helping her husband to become more involved in the parenting.

During the 12th session, Annie was more quiet in session than usual. About halfway through the session Annie said, "Do you think it would be okay if I quit coming here? My dad and I were thinking that we could start having breakfast together during this time."

Annie had worked through some of the grief about her mother, and she and her father had rebuilt a strong relationship. Because of the relationship, she and her stepmother were having fewer conflicts. The therapist had a termination session the following week, and then sent Annie and her dad off to breakfast!

☐ Summary

Regular meetings with parents help them to feel valuable and connected in the therapy process. These meetings are used to encourage parents, recruit their help as therapeutic agents, provide them with the therapist's understanding of what the child is expressing in the play sessions, and provide them with an overall conceptualization of the child's world.

Understanding the meaning beneath the child's play can be difficult. Careful attention to repetitive, sustained, and recurring play can assist the therapist in recognizing and identifying play themes. Combining this information with reports from parents and others, the therapist can verify intuitions and glean a more complete understanding of the issues being played out by the child. The therapist can then discuss the themes with parents and make homework assignments based on the overall conceptualization of the child. In this way, the therapist provides parents with opportunities for input into the therapy situation while maintaining confidentiality between the therapist and child.

Hopefully, the therapist will be able to meet each week for about 15 minutes, with at least one of the child's parents. The therapist can choose to have these meetings before or after each of the child's play therapy sessions, or the therapist can allow the child to choose. Frequently, young children do not wish to delay their gratification derived from playing with the therapist. However, if the therapist and parent immediately go behind closed doors following the play session, the child may envision the therapist "tattling" and experience unpleasant feelings. In play therapy, above all else, the therapist must protect the child-therapist relationship, and preserve the child's trust in the therapist.

Filial therapy is a wonderful way to involve parents in the therapy process. In this training model, parents learn child-centered play therapy concepts and procedures, and thereby assume therapeutic roles as change agents for their children. Focus is on the parent-child relationship, and benefits are numerous, with positive effects on both child and parents.

Occasionally, the therapist may sense that a parent needs additional attention and support. Many parents benefit from their own special session or even regular sessions. Some parents may readily face their own issues during a parent consultation, yet refuse to attend individual therapy. Determining whether parents need their own sessions is based primarily upon professional judgment and the parent-therapist relationship. Also, the therapist must protect the time allotted for the child and the play therapy sessions, and remember that the child is the client.

Several case studies are also presented within this chapter. These cases provide concrete examples of the development of play themes and the therapist's conceptualizations. Techniques and homework assignments are described within a contextual application. At the end of each case, the outcomes of the therapy process are discussed.

General Homework
Assignments for Parents

Homework assignments for parents are very instrumental in maximizing the outcomes of therapy. Positive results occur more rapidly, and longer-lasting benefits are derived, when assignments are completed by parents. These examples *of general homework* are applicable for all parents of children in therapy, and can be appropriately assigned regardless of the specific reasons for referral or treatment goals. These exercises keep the parents closely involved in their children's therapy, as well as help them to realize and validate their own efforts and productivity in the treatment of their children.

Putting the general homework exercises into practice is intended to increase the bonding process between parent and child. Parents are likely to become much more encouraged, and consequently much more willing to continue with their children in therapy. Often, parents need reassurance that they are getting their money's worth out of the therapy. This need can be satisfied by the "extra therapy" they can take home and do themselves. Homework improves the child's environment and by performing the exercises, through this increased effort *for* their child, parents communicate *to* the child an increased interest and belief in the importance of the child. The child benefits from added contact with, attention from, and affirmation by the parents—all supportive messages about the child's own importance. All of this usually leads to improved self-esteem, self-confidence, and self-respect for the parents and for the child.

☐ Specific Date with the Child

The *specific date* exercise involves one of the parents and the child. They plan and select an agreeable day, time, and place for their "date." The length of the date should be 15 minutes, and the parent should emphasize to the child that the date is important. The parent is urged to show genuine interest and enthusiasm. It is recommended that the parent be *slightly* more dramatic than usual in emphasizing and celebrating the importance of the date. The parent is instructed to tell the child, "You and I are going to have a date just for you and me. This is a special time together once a week for 15 minutes. Let's make our plans for our date." After the date is arranged, the parent should reemphasize its importance. "This time is very important and very special. I'm going to write it down for you and for me."

Even if the child is too young to read, the parent is asked to write "Special Date/Mommy and Justin/Tuesday at 7:00" on two small pieces of paper. One is elaborately saved by the parent, and the other is given to the child. The paper is a tangible and concrete item. The child can see, touch, feel, hold, and save the piece of paper. This accentuates the importance of the date and helps to build security for the child. It also helps in committing the parent to the appointment.

The importance of keeping the date cannot be overstressed to the parent. This is the key element in this homework assignment. Children need *the consistency of parents doing what they promise;* through this exercise they learn that Mommy and Daddy *are* trustworthy and dependable. Trustworthiness and dependability are necessary qualities in a parent; otherwise, children will grow up in a chaotic environment and develop problematic insecurity.

In addition to that risk, by not keeping the date, one of the ground rules would be broken. The ground rules for the date can be defined as follows:

1. All parties must adhere to the time limit of 15 minutes.
2. All parties, especially parents, must be committed to the time that is set.
3. "All parties" consist of one parent and one child, resulting in one-on-one time.
4. Interruptions by telephone or other members of the family are strictly forbidden.
5. The activity of the date should provide an atmosphere that allows the child to talk or share feelings.
6. The child should talk and share feelings only if he or she wants to (coaxing and pressuring the child to talk or share feelings is forbidden).

7. Watching television during the date is forbidden.
8. Flamboyant toys, activity centers, and amusement parks are not allowed.

The rules are intended to be presented in a fun, humorous, and non-intimidating fashion to parents and children. Nevertheless, adherence to the rules is also intended. The key is obviously to create the atmosphere for the child. This means that the child is permitted to be however the child wants to be and say what he or she wants to say in the presence of the parent. It is recommended for the parent to spend little or no money. Suggestions for date activities include walking around the block or walking to the park that is 15 minutes away and getting an ice cream sundae. Another recommended activity involves the parent allowing the child to lead the play, with a few toys, in a room other than the child's. If the date takes place in the child's own room, the child frequently gets too absorbed in his or her possessions and interaction with the parent is minimal or ineffective.

Strongly emphasized is the importance of not breaking this date and not allowing any interruptions. Some parents will argue that they want the date to be longer than 15 minutes and some will claim that they already have regular date-like "special times" with their children. Either way, the therapist should insist that they follow the guidelines that have been set up. The parents can extend the 15-minute time limit in the future, but in the beginning they are to adhere to it along with the other ground rules. The therapist is urged to support those parents who are already having special times with their children. After the support, the parents should be informed that they can implement this exercise in addition to their existing dates, or in lieu thereof, if necessary. Most parents will report this assignment as being different from the experience that they are already having at home. The 15-minute limit will keep many parents from feeling overwhelmed by this exercise.

If the parents do not follow through with the date, this is pertinent information about them. The first time that they fail to have the date, they should be asked to explain why the date was not kept. Typical excuses surround scheduling difficulties. This is not the time to criticize the parents. Their feelings should be reflected; then the importance of making the exercise a priority should be stressed again. If it happens again, there are likely to be underlying issues that are causing this barrier. Is the parent really interested in spending time with the child? Does the parent feel inadequate or too vulnerable? The therapist should begin to work on any underlying issues that surface with the parent.

For some parents, this special date time will facilitate a deeper bonding and stronger rapport with their child. Their confidence will grow when the outcomes are favorable. There is more encouragement, enthusiasm, and appreciation for the rewards of therapy. This is likely to inspire more involvement by the parents, more compliance with treatment, and significantly greater results.

☐ Sandwich Hug

The *sandwich hug* is characterized by multiple (more than two) family members in a big hug, while they pretend to be different parts of a sandwich. For example, the mother says, "Dad and I are the bread, and Abbie, you're the bologna. We're all a big sandwich! Mmmmmmah!" There may be several other people and many different sandwich parts (e.g., cheese, tomato, peanut butter, sprouts, tuna). Everyone tries to hug everyone. A lot of "smooshing" and "smooshing noises" are important. The goal is to have fun, while encouraging the family to hug. This exercise generates wonderful, close contact. Although some parents and children will resist, claiming it to be "corny," the sandwich hug is truly a fun, nonthreatening activity. It lasts only a few moments, and can be done frequently with little or no preparation. Some families are not in the habit of hugging and this homework gently breaks through these barriers (G. Landreth, personal communication, June, 1989).

☐ 30-Second Attention Burst

The *30-second attention burst* means having the parent stop whatever they are doing. For 30 seconds, the parent then gives the child his or her *full attention*. The mother may be on the telephone or working at her desk and the child wants her to stop and do something with him. In this case, the mother should ask the person on the telephone to excuse her for a moment, or she can stop working at her desk. She then gives the child her full attention for 30 seconds. She can hug the child, talk to the child, or get something for the child. The key is to really focus on and look at the child. This is a good technique for helping a parent to make quick, immediate contact with the child even when the parent's time is very limited. Due to the fact that it is only for 30 seconds, this technique can be used frequently. This checking-in with the child can provide security and reassurance that the child is important and loved (Landreth, 1989). However, if the child asks for more time at the moment, the parent can delay it until later. "I know you have more to show me, but I need to finish talking to Jane. I'll come and look in five minutes" or "I need to work at my desk now. I'll come back in 15 minutes and we can read one book then." It is very important that the parent come back *on time;* this will make the child more willing to accept 30-second attention bursts at other times.

☐ Notes, Cards, and Phone Calls

Notes, cards, and phone calls are effective ways to let children know that they are being thought about. This reinforces that "If I'm important enough to be thought about, then I must be important." Consider the example of a father who is a minister of a church. He frequently works long hours and gives a lot of his time to his many church members. However, he makes it a point to periodically talk on the telephone with his children. He might initiate the call or the children can do so. This makes the children feel important and gives them the security that Daddy is always accessible to them. Notes, cards, and phone calls provide a very concrete message to children that they are important enough for their parent to think about them and to talk to them, even if it is for brief moments.

☐ Structured Play Activities

Structured play therapy is described by Hambidge (1982) as a series of specific play situations that are structured to serve as a stimulus for the relative, but independent, creative play of children. According to Levy (1982), a child that has support, security, and the right play materials can re-experience—through play—a traumatic experience over and over until he or she abreacts, or can to let go of, negative feelings associated with that experience. By using the safety of play and the supportive relationship, the child can gradually approach and gain control over the traumatic experience.

Teaching the parents some of the techniques used in structured play therapy can provide children greater opportunities to continue to resolve specific issues at home beyond the play therapy session time. For example, 5-year-old Kara moved from Phoenix to Dallas. She missed her friends and was having difficulty adjusting to her new kindergarten. In addition to play therapy within the play therapist's office, Kara's mother was taught to do structured play with Kara at home. The therapist demonstrated the structured play to Kara's mother in the playroom. Using Kara's referral issue, the therapist set up the scenario that she specifically wanted the mother to work on with Kara. As the mother was willing, the therapist had her practice the structured play with her right there in the playroom. Kara's mother was then directed to set up the same scenario for the structured play activity at home.

At home, Kara's mother collected several stuffed animals that she and Kara then named. The teddy bear was named Kara, along with other animals named Nathan, Cathy, and Aaron. Mom told a story with the stuffed animals acting out Kara moving to a new city. Nathan, Cathy, and Aaron were Kara's new friends. Mom had Kara (the bear) initiate conversation with her new friends. Other times, Kara was sad and missing her friends in Phoenix. At that time, Mom had another stuffed animal talk to Kara (the bear) about her sad feelings. After asking for several repeat dramatizations over the next few days, Kara joined with her mother in making up stories for the stuffed animals.

As the therapist had requested, Kara's mother called during the week to report on the progress of the structured play at home. The therapist reflected her enthusiasm and success and encouraged her to expand the same scenario if necessary, or to set up other scenarios as needed in the future. It was important to the therapist to have some feedback, and most likely important to the mother to be supported. Also, the midweek report allowed the structured play to remain a home activity without having to make any mention of it around Kara's play therapy session. The therapist had already told the mother that she would not ask Kara about the structured play in the playroom, but would certainly reflect Kara's feelings if Kara chose to bring up the home sessions.

Structured play activities can be very helpful for a variety of issues, including separation anxiety, death of a pet, birth of a sibling, a new school, and many other life transitions. It is a great way to get the parents more involved with their children's issues and feelings in a sensitive, caring, understanding, accepting, and supportive manner.

☐ Fantasy

Grant to children in fantasy, what you cannot grant in reality (Faber & Mazlish, 1980). For example, a parent and her child pass a quick-stop store as they are driving home. The child says, "Mom, let's stop here. I want a slurpee." Mom replies, "I wish we could stop for a slurpee, but the rule at our house is no snacks this close to dinner. In fact, I wish we could take the slurpee machine home with us and have 100 slurpees. It would be so much fun to have our very own slurpee machine!" The child says, "It sure would. I bet I could drink 200 slurpees at one time!"

By granting to children in fantasy what cannot be granted in reality, you help them experience some of the rewards of the request. They will be aware that their parents *care* about their feelings and will feel more understood. In addition, children will perceive their parents as being more positive and supportive, and less punitive and critical.

Fantasy also provides a wonderful means of interaction between parents and children. Once you teach parents about sharing fantasies with children, they often expand it into many creative areas, in addition to when the parent has to deny a request.

☐ Mutual Storytelling

Capitalizing on children's natural and favorable inclination toward hearing and telling stories, Gardner (1993) conceived a mutual storytelling technique for working with children in therapy. Basically, in therapy, a child is requested to create and tell a story that has a beginning, middle, and an end. Gardner (1993) said the therapist then responds with another story involving the same characters in a similar setting, but "introduces healthier resolutions and adaptations of the conflicts present in the child's story" (p. 5). Gil (1994) expanded Gardner's technique by involving the family in adding to the child's story.

Teaching parents some of the mutual storytelling techniques allows them to continue to help their child resolve specific therapy issues at home. The therapist takes the *theme* of a story the child has told or played out in therapy (*not* the child's actual story or play activity) and creates a new story for the parents. The therapist then asks the parents, along with the child, to go home and add to the story with new, helpful solutions to the conflict of the story. The parents tell about their changes and adaptations to the story (and any possible outcomes) during the next parent meeting with the therapist.

☐ Family Meeting

The concept of the *family meeting* has been around for some time (Dreikurs and Stolz, 1964). Family meetings facilitate a sense of democracy and fairness to children. Family meetings give everyone, including the children, a voice in family decisions (Glenn & Nelsen, 1989; Weinhaus &

Friedman, 1991). Everyone deserves respect, and family meetings provide a way to both teach and model respect for children. Parents can avoid many conflicts when problems are discussed at family meetings.

Each family must establish specific rules for their family meeting such as when, where, how long, what agenda items, and who will chair the meeting. Suggest to families that they have a family meeting once a week. Stress the importance of protecting this time. As much as possible, no schedule changes should be made, no phone calls taken, and no other interruptions allowed. It is advisable to sit at the kitchen or dining room table, which fosters a work atmosphere. Usually an hour is sufficient, but may be extended if all members agree (Glenn & Nelsen, 1989).

The Chair position should rotate among all family members. Children are empowered and encouraged when they serve in that position of honor, respect, and responsibility and perceive themselves more as a vital part of the family. The leader should have an agenda. He or she is to enforce the rules of the meeting that family members have agreed to follow, such as: no interrupting when someone is talking; following through until the family has reached a consensus; and making certain that the agenda is followed.

The agenda should include decisions and problems that need to be addressed. A piece of paper on the refrigerator or a calendar are good places for members to write agenda items. Items should be written during the week as problems arise. By writing it on the agenda, family members are often able to delay complaints or arguments, since they have the assurance that their feelings and thoughts will be heard by all family members.

In addition to specific items that family members have listed, the agenda should include appreciative remarks regarding family efforts during the past week. Fun activities for the family should be planned. When it is time to discuss a problem or complaint, each person's feelings and thoughts are to be heard before solutions are discussed. The goal is to come up with a consensus among members.

☐ Summary

Homework assignments enhance play therapy for the child and help to build stronger relationships between parents and children. Homework assignments can also expedite positive changes in the child's world and facilitate longer-lasting changes. Due to homework assignments, parents tend to feel more involved in the therapy process, they are more connected with the therapist, more reassured, and they experience a sense that they are getting more for their money. Consequently, homework assignments can increase the likelihood that parents will keep their child in therapy until therapeutic goals are attained and termination is appropriate.

The homework assignments presented in this chapter can apply to most families regardless of the presenting problems for therapy. These include:

1. The Special Date;
2. The Sandwich Hug;
3. The 30-Second Attention Burst;
4. Notes, Cards, and Phone Calls;
5. Structured Play Activities;
6. Fantasy;
7. Mutual Story Telling; and
8. The Family Meeting.

These assignments are described along with implementation strategies. Numerous examples are provided, which facilitate the therapist's understanding and conceptualization of when to initiate the various tasks.

9

Special Issues

Play therapy clients carry a variety of life adjustment issues into the playroom with them, and their parents very often are able to recognize and accept the behavioral manifestations of those issues. However, the effects of divorce, school issues, and sexual abuse can be a source of enigma, frustration, and embarrassment, and seem like an exercise in futility for parents—very often undermining the parent-child relationship.

Divorce is very traumatic for parents, as well as for children. Divorce and separation leads to enormous and complex losses involving personal identity, intrapsychic welfare, interpersonal relations, and social connectedness and status. Family systems tend to be profoundly disrupted by divorce and both parents and children must make difficult adjustments. Understanding some of the effects of divorce and providing guidance for parents can make the transition period following the separation and divorce more manageable.

More and more play therapy is being provided in elementary school settings. Schools and school counselors continue to appreciate the importance of play in working with children and the tremendous impact that play therapy has on children. However, providing sufficient play therapy instruction for all school counselors is obviously beyond the scope of this or any single text. According to Kao and Landreth (1997), play therapy is one of the fastest growing disciplines within mental health. Many professionals are concerned that play therapy is not provided by expert clinicians who have training and supervised experience with established play therapy principles and practices. However, schools and school counselors also need to realize the importance of recruiting the help and involvement of parents in the therapy and other school processes of their children. Thus, issues related to play therapy in school settings are also included in this chapter.

Sexual abuse is also a powerful source of damage and disruption that can lead to a life course of problem behaviors and troubled relationships. Addressing the complications and difficulties resulting from sexual abuse can be paramount to the healing process for both children and parents.

☐ Divorce

One in every two marriages ends in divorce in the United States. Approximately one million new children become "children of divorce" each year. Divorce is more prevalent than drug abuse, teenage pregnancy, or the death of a parent and it is estimated that 37% of all American children live with a divorced parent (Neuman, 1998). The immediate and short term effects of divorce is to introduce substantial stress into the lives of related children and their parents. The effects of divorce are disruptive with negative emotional impact. Although many children seem to adequately cope with this stress through their own resources, the majority can benefit from therapeutic intervention.

Parent's Feelings

According to Jacobson (1983), marital separation is one of the most terrible events that a man or woman can face. A person's social status and role within his or her society is largely defined by marital status, along with socioeconomic status, occupation, gender, and age. Not only does marriage have legal implications, it also affects a person's interactions with family of origin, friends, and organizations such as schools and churches.

Severe life events, such as marital separation and divorce, can also cause long-term, negative psychological changes. Numerous social, interpersonal, and intrapsychic dimensions are traumatized, damaged, and lost due to divorce and separation (Jacobson, 1983).

Although the impact of divorce on children is of extreme importance, many divorced or separated parents attempt to deny their own devastating losses and feelings; by focusing on the children. Attending to issues regarding the children may appear safer and less threatening than facing many other realities of divorce. Often, both divorced parents will even join together in counseling that is on behalf of their child. Such a joint effort may be very necessary and beneficial to the child, but care must be taken to avoid the pretense of an undivided family unit. Nothing is as destructive as persistent denial of the many issues, losses, disruptions, and emotions due to separation and divorce (Jacobson, 1983). If divorcing or separating parents have greater understanding and acceptance of the many emotional issues that they themselves are experiencing, they will be strengthened and empowered as parents.

Parents need to acknowledge, understand, and accept their own issues, losses, and feelings. They should strive to prevent the effects of divorce and separation from severely impairing their psychological functioning. Otherwise, the level of functioning of these parents as providers, caregivers, and workers will suffer along with their emotional distress.

Children's Feelings

According to Berg (1989), reactions of children to divorce vary with age. Children of "preschool" age (3–5 years) experience the following: (a) confusion, sadness, and insecurity; (b) regression to earlier level of development; (c) bewilderment and loss of routine; and (d) strong sense of betrayal in security needs. Rossiter (1988) described the special difficulties presented by divorce to children unprepared for the developmental task of separating from their parents. For young children, psychological separation is embedded in everyday routines. Consequently, they have typically had fewer opportunities to practice separation and experience a sense of "wholeness" during those separations. Many young children have never stayed away from home overnight, have never walked to the corner playground alone, and have never been allowed outside unsupervised. Marital separation that precedes such experience is often emotionally overwhelming to young children and may produce fears of abandonment.

Young children, who are developmentally at a more egocentric stage, tend to see themselves as central to the break-up. Combining the child's less developed boundaries between fantasy and reality with the typical disruption in parental roles, feelings of vulnerability and fears of retribution are likely to emerge (Rossiter, 1988). Also, a recent incursion into language can render the child vulnerable, since there is no access to verbalization which can re-frame feelings of guilt, responsibility, fear, etc. The child is less likely to be provided with two-sided explanations of the separation as well as being less able to recognize parents as having good and bad qualities. Living in a one-parent household and seeing the separated parent periodically, if at all, potentiates these conflicts, and makes them more difficult to resolve.

Children of "young school" age (6–8 years) experience: (a) intense penetrating sadness; (b) guilt and self-blame; (c) confusion; (d) inhibition of anger toward the father; (e) anger toward custodial mother; (f) fantasies of reconciliation; and (g) loyalty conflicts. "Older school" age children (9–12 years) experience: (a) anger expressed toward the non-custodial parent; (b) passive-aggressive behavior and stubbornness toward custodial parent and teacher; and (c) fighting with peers (Berg, 1989).

The most obvious source of stress is the loss of the non-custodial parent, along with the resulting "suitcase" life for the child. The intensity of stress varies, depending on the amount of contact with both parents before and after the divorce. Stress is most severe when extreme closeness existed, followed by no contact whatsoever (Berg, 1989).

According to Chethik (1989), divorce can be viewed as a developmental interference, which creates considerable internal stress in a child. Four major affective reactions stimulated by marital disruption will need to be worked through by the child. First, anger/rage occurs because the child feels cheated by the disruption in the family and the loss of a sense of security. The anger or rage may be acted out and expressed by defiance or direct antisocial trends. The expression of anger may leave the child feeling threatened, and fearing further loss. Feelings of anger may then be intensely defended against, emerging in symptoms such as phobias.

A second major affective reaction is loss/grief. The quality of the relationship with the non-custodial parent changes, as well as a major loss in the sense of family (Chethik, 1989). A child's ego is not sufficiently developed to handle grieving or mourning for the absent parent. Consequently, the child will often attempt circumvention through defenses such as infantile regression or omission of affect. Mendell (1983) maintains that, "the multitude of developmental processes cannot come to a halt in order for the child to do the work of mourning" (p. 324).

Third, guilt/self-blame is exacerbated, and often has several sources. Many children have the egocentric fantasy that they are responsible for the divorce. This type of self-blame frequently causes loss of self-esteem (a sense of badness) and a need for punishment. Loyalty conflicts can foster feelings of guilt (Chethik, 1989). There is often a great deal of acrimony between the parents, and many children feel torn between them. Children often feel pressure to side with one parent, against the other, while internally trying to maintain a loving connection with both. This can produce a powerful sense of disloyalty and guilt.

A fourth major affective reaction is the fear that abounds within children during marital disruption and divorce. Children typically fear abandonment by the separated parent (Chethik, 1989). They may also fear that the custodial parent will take a similar abandonment course. Marital disruption can lead to emotional loss of the separated parent, with regressive withdrawal from the custodial parent. Thus, symptoms of separation anxiety and clinging behavior are often exhibited. Fears of survival are prominent, often expressed by preoccupations with food or money concerns.

Therapeutic Interventions

According to Mendell (1983), "the therapist can best serve such children as a 'developmental facilitator' who helps the child renegotiate necessary developmental tasks while simultaneously helping the child tolerate the pain of grieving the lost relationship" (p. 353).

Chethik (1989) reported a case study in which the impact of play therapy was seen to resolve much of the impact of divorce on the male child, and reduce impediments to his ongoing development. At the beginning of therapy, the child seemed paralyzed in his development. This was commensurate with the age at which he experienced interference of the parental divorce and emotional loss of his father. The child exhibited regressive withdrawal from his mother and the inability to use his intellect at school.

Through play, the child was able to create stories that involved fighting between a mother and a father. A male baby listened to the rancor while still in the mother's stomach. The father did not want the baby, however the mother did. This was the basis of the fighting. The baby came out, hit the father with his fist, and then ran away with the mother to a special house. The stories sometimes ended with happy endings. One story included the police coming to the special house, putting a chain around the baby's neck, and taking him away—even though the mother fought desperately to save the baby. Play assisted the child to clarify many of the realities of the history of the difficult marriage and parental fighting. The stories began to take a more empathic view. In one, a father image was trapped in a fire, then rescued and nurtured. The stories included a wise owl soothing the impulsiveness of an irrepressible monkey. The owl also soothed the viciousness of a primitive father-tiger who was out to tear the monkey apart. The wise owl effected continuous compromises, showing the monkey how to acquire many treasures, while teaching the tiger to have some pleasure from the playfulness of the immature monkey. Through play, the child became increasingly comfortable with his own aggression. He became more cooperative and more able to apply his energies toward learning.

The therapist can share some of the themes of play therapy with the parents and make suggestions to the parent based on those themes. In addition, the following interventions may be helpful when working with divorced parents:

1. Encourage the parent(s) to seek individual therapy if there is continuing conflict between the divorced couple and/or unresolved grief. Jacobson (1983) said, "the extent and nature of the post-separation and divorce relationship between (former) spouses are important" (p. 113).
2. Encourage parents to work toward a decent working relationship as parents (Ricci, 1997). Children benefit tremendously when parents can maintain an amiable relationship. Ricci suggests divorced parents to view themselves in a "parent-business" relationship. Applying business principals may help calm down the relationship.
3. Stress the importance of the child having a place to live that "feels" like home (Blaine, 1969). Children will probably be going between two homes, so it is important to establish a permanent place, preferably in each home, where the child can always go. Blaine stated that a child needs "a sanctuary where his own private possessions are kept, a refuge which keeps away the rootless, floating feeling that can be so terrifying to a youngster" (p. 79).
4. Teach parents to respond empathetically to the anger the child may be feeling and acting out. Parents may be tempted to punish the child when the child is angry. While setting limits may be necessary, it is important for the parent to show understanding regarding the child's anger and rage over the divorce. Parents should listen to the child about his pain, fears, and animosity (Grollman, 1969). Neuman (1998) suggests the parent help the child make a "angry hat or jacket." Decorate a hat or jacket that represents images of anger. Tell the child to wear the hat or jacket when she is angry. This will notify the parent of the child's feelings and the parent can then talk to the child.
5. Teach parents to be sympathetic to the child's sadness and grief. The parents may be deep into their own pain, making it difficult for them to tolerate their child's pain. However, the child needs to grieve and needs support when sad. Gardner (1970) stresses it is a necessity for the child to cry and grieve in order to heal.

6. Request that the parents tell the child, time and time again, that he is not responsible for the divorce. Reiterate frequently that parents only are responsible for the divorce. Neuman (1998) suggests decorating a "not-guilty shirt." The child can put any message that he wants, such as, "I did not cause my parents to divorce" or "it's not my fault." Neuman stated that, "Clear, repetitive statements validating the idea that the child is not at fault will increase the likelihood that he will integrate and believe this message" (p. 237).

☐ Play Therapy in Elementary School Settings

According to Landreth (1987) "play therapy in the elementary school is considered to be a vital and integrated part of the total educational process" (p. 260). Play therapy in elementary schools helps children develop positive emotional, physical, intellectual, and social awareness and skills. Play therapy is an especially valuable and beneficial experience for children who are unsuccessful in school, have poor self-concepts, and have difficulty relating to others. Although there appears to be a recent rise in the appreciation and use of play therapy being applied in schools, the benefits have been acknowledged and evidenced for decades. As stated by Landreth, "it is not a question of whether the elementary school counselor should use play therapy but, instead, how play therapy procedures and skills should be used in the schools" (p. 255).

Crow (1989) found that the self-concept of first graders, who had been retained, was improved through the process of child-centered play therapy in the school setting. Play therapy, according to Bishop (1971):

is an integral part of the methods elementary school counselors employ in their work with school children. . . . Learning cannot occur without full participation on the part of the learner. Children need to be involved with their hands, ideas, feelings and elbows. . . . Hence methods used by counselors should provide structures from which activities take on new perspectives and feelings have new meanings. (p. 41)

Alexander (1964) studied how play therapy affected a child who had been exhibiting adjustment difficulties and reported that:

there are times when a sensitive, responsive teacher is able to have a therapeutic relationship with a child. This is frequently quite difficult for teachers because of the large number of children in the class and the teacher's lack of awareness and experience with the possibilities of such an experience. . . . (Whereas) the school play therapist can offer his undivided attention for a 50-minute period once a week. (p. 257)

Alexander concluded from his case study that the therapist's acceptance of the child led to the establishment of a close, trusting relationship, and the child's feeling of freedom in the therapist-child relationship led toward growth and self-actualization. Also, the child was able to use what was learned during the experience of this relationship with the therapist in everyday life and relationships outside of the playroom.

Through interactions with the therapist in Alexander's (1964) study, the teacher developed increased levels of understanding and acceptance of the child. Also, the impact of the therapist-child relationship on the child resulted in the child becoming a catalyst in an enhanced teacher-child relationship. White, Flynt, and Draper (1997) report the effective use of "Kinder Therapy" which creates an "opportunity for the teacher and child to make a meaningful connection on an emotional level that will change their relationship, the child's behavior, and the teacher's behavior outside of the classroom" (p. 37). Teachers have inherent importance in the lives of children and can assume therapeutic roles as a positive change agents in the lives of children. Similar to Filial Therapy, which is discussed in chapter 7, Kinder Therapy was shown to have positive effects with the child including improved self-control, social skills, and ability to deal appropriately with difficult emotions. Teachers also developed skills that could be transferred from the therapy sessions to the classroom, and even outside of the school setting. These skills in relating to children included tracking, accepting, understanding, encouraging, and limit-setting.

Baggerly (1999) studied the effects of play sessions facilitated by fifth grade students who had been trained in child-centered play therapy skills and procedures. These procedures resulted in positive change in kindergarten children who had adjustment difficulties. Improvement was observed in several areas including self-control, self-acceptance, self-confidence, interrelationships, and somatic complaints.

School counselors need to have similar interactions and training sessions with parents. Similar to teachers, parents can enhance their understanding, acceptance, and appreciation of their children. Children need to experience (and perceive) unconditional acceptance directly from their parents, and not only from teachers and counselors. When children sense that their feelings are accepted and validated, then tension, anger, fear, and anxiety decrease (Guerney, 1983). When parents apply basic therapy (and parenting) skills, such as reflecting and empathic understanding, children feel completely accepted by their parents (VanFleet, 1994). Parent-child interactions and relationships will thereby be greatly enhanced, children will have more understanding and trust of their parents, and children will develop more trust, respect, and appreciation for themselves.

☐ Sexual Abuse

Sexual abuse is defined by Faller (1988) as "any act occurring between people who are at different developmental stages which is for the sexual gratification of the person at the more advanced developmental stage" (pp. 11–12). Sexual abuse can range from a child being fondled by another child to more intense and extreme sexual acts being forced upon a child by an adult. A child may experience non-contact sexual abuse whereby the perpetrator engages in "sexy talk, exposure, or voyeurism" (p. 12). Whatever the range of sexual acts and age of the perpetrator, the child victim can be affected in a negative way emotionally. Fergusson and Mullen (1999) said exposure to child sexual abuse is associated with increased risks of mental health and adjustment problems.

There are two key ways the therapist can be instrumental in working with the parents of sexually abused children in therapy: first, the therapist can look for themes of playroom activities, discuss the presumed themes with the parents, and make suggestions and homework assignments based on the themes; second, the therapist can educate the parents about predictable issues the child is facing or will face as a result of the sexual abuse. For example, issues children are apt to encounter include, but are not limited to, loss of trust, altered body image, guilt and responsibility, anger, depression, and self-destructive behavior (Faller, 1988; Long, 1986; Schetky & Green, 1988; Walker, Bonner & Kaufman, 1988).

Loss of Trust

Betrayal is a traumagenic factor often apparent in victims of sexual abuse. The sense of betrayal can be monumental and is significantly related to the child's relationship with the perpetrator (Homeyer, 1994). The child's sense of trust is manipulated by the offender, causing the normal expectation of safety and security to be damaged (Walker, Bonner & Kaufman, 1988). Rencken (1989) said, "the child loses trust, security, and, as a result, the essence of childhood" (p. 4).

The sexually abused child may develop the inability to form trusting relationships, especially with caretaking figures. The impact of being exploited by someone who should have protected and nurtured the child can be devastating. The child may be confused and overwhelmed; especially when there is a plot to silence the child about the abuse. When a child has experienced abuse by an adult of one sex, most often a man, the child tends to distrust adults of that sex (Faller, 1988).

Trust issues must be addressed immediately in therapy. Johnson (1989) said, "Children and their families need to feel a trusting relationship with the therapist" (p. 101). One way parents or caregivers can help ameliorate loss of trust is to provide the victim opportunities to interact and form relationships with people who can be trusted. It is crucial for the people involved in trying to build a trusting relationship with the sexually abused child to be dependable and honest. This includes the parents and the therapist. Appointments and promises should be kept, and the child needs to know that information from the parents and therapist is straightforward and direct. The victim also needs to feel supported by the parents and therapist despite rejection or acting-out behavior by the victim (Faller, 1988). When parents understand the impact that loss of trust can have on the sexually abused child, they are more inclined to be consistent in their support and promises to the child, and parents may be able not to take the child's rejection of them so personally.

Mandy, age 6, was abused by her 15-year-old stepbrother for several months before Mandy told her friend, Ellen. Ellen told her mother who, in turn, told Mandy's mother. Intervention was made quickly by Mandy's parents. They believed her and immediately took Mandy for a medical examination and to therapy. The therapist reported the abuse, and an investigation was conducted by the child protective services personnel. The investigation revealed that Mandy's stepbrother had been abused by a babysitter several years prior to coming to live with his biological father, stepmother, and Mandy. Therapy was also set up for Mandy's stepbrother. The caseworker and therapist helped set up guidelines for the parents to protect Mandy from further abuse.

Several weeks into therapy, Mandy's parents reported that Mandy had been hostile and antagonistic to her mother and did not want to participate in the usual activities with her father, such as going to McDonald's or to the park. Mandy's parents were bewildered by her behavior and felt discouraged. The therapist explained that Mandy's acting-out behavior could be expected as she most likely was having difficulty trusting anyone, especially her father, since he was male. The therapist worked with the mother on reflecting Mandy's feelings as well as setting boundaries to protect herself when Mandy's behavior was too hurtful. Mandy's mother responded well to reflecting feelings, but her own guilt feelings about her daughter's abuse made it difficult for her to set boundaries with Mandy. The therapist assigned Mandy's mother to write down the verbal exchanges between her and Mandy for the next session. The next week, during the parenting meeting, the therapist and Mandy's mother role-played in order to help the mother set boundaries to protect herself while maintaining support and empathy for her daughter.

Mandy's father was very sad at the rejection from his daughter. The therapist had him write down the usual activities that he and Mandy did together. The therapist helped him modify those activities in order for Mandy and her father to still have some time together, with the intent that Mandy experiences less stress and anxiety. For instance, they usually went to McDonald's on Saturday morning while Mandy's mother slept late. Mandy would play for about an hour before they ate and returned home. The therapist suggested that Mandy and her father drive-through and not stay to play, or that Mandy invite a friend to go with them. The therapist stressed that time spent with Mandy was an important way for Mandy to know her dad loved and supported her. However, the loss of trust that Mandy experienced as a result of her stepbrother's abuse was now projected onto others, such as her father. The goal for the modified activities between Mandy and her father was intended to give them a chance to rebuild that trust.

Altered Body Image

Children who have been sexually abused often have a distorted perception of their body. As stated by Faller (1988) "they feel they are physically damaged, dirty, ruined, or no longer whole or perfect" (p. 290). Sgroi (1982) states that this distorted perception causes many child victims to view themselves as damaged goods. The child has reason to believe that he or she has been damaged as a result of physical injury or pain. Long (1986) expanded the damaged goods syndrome definition for the younger sexually abused child. Long said the child may perceive him or herself as different, used, pitiful, vulnerable, and partly to blame. Sexually abused children may think people can tell, just by looking at them, that something terrible has happened. They need constant reassurance and support by their parents. Therapists can help the parents to aid the child in rebuilding a positive regard toward their body and self.

Seven-year-old Erica was fondled several times by her uncle, who lived in the same city. Erica told her mother one night when her mother was getting her ready for bed. Erica's parents reported the abuse and filed charges against the uncle. A number of extended family members lived in the same city. There was animosity and division among family members as a result of the abuse and the charges being filed by the parents. While most family members supported Erica, several were angry that she had caused a public scandal for the family.

In play therapy, Erica drew several pictures of a little girl with no arms—possibly an indication that she had felt powerless against her uncle and his sexual gestures. Erica's mother reported that Erica did not want to take her bath at night and was uninterested in her overall appearance. She was no longer excited about shopping for new clothes as she had been in the past, and she did not want to brush her hair.

The therapist asked Erica's mother to make a collage at home with Erica. Erica's mother took a large piece of poster-board and put a picture of Erica in the middle. Then, Erica and her mother started in the top left corner, adding pictures with different themes that the therapist had suggested. Themes included people (relatives, friends, teachers) who were supportive of Erica; clothes and accessories cut out of catalogs and advertisements that were representative of what Erica had enjoyed wearing in the past; activities that Erica had participated in or was currently participating in, such as dance, Brownies, and the church choir; and strong people in Erica's life who could help support and protect her, such as her parents, police, and teachers. The collage activity was executed without Erica's mother specifically mentioning the abuse. Erica's mother reported that Erica looked forward to the poster-board activity. Erica's drawings eventually began to change in play therapy. Gradually, she took more pride in her appearance. Her mother also paced shopping sprees with Erica; they went for shorter periods of time and Erica's mother carefully watched for cues from Erica.

One reason the therapist included activities Erica was involved in, such as dance, was to help build her self-esteem through feeling confident and prideful about what she did well. This also helped enhance Erica's feelings about herself and helped move her toward acceptance of her body again.

Guilt and Responsibility

Guilt is a major repercussion experienced by victims of sexual abuse (Faller, 1988). If the child experiences some pleasure during the sexual contact or in some way feels responsible for the sexual abuse, there is a greater probability that the child will feel guilt (Gil, 1991). The perpetrator may use tactics such as telling the child victim that she was too pretty to resist or that her hair or clothes made him want her sexually. He may tell the child victim that he will go to jail if she exposes what has happened between them, that he will tell everyone that she really wanted him to do the sexual things, or that it would break up the family. There are many ways the perpetrator can hold the victim hostage by making the victim feel guilty and responsible for the sexual acts between them (MacFarlane & Korbin, 1983; Sanford, 1982).

The therapist can teach the parent about *cognitive restructuring*, and thereby help the sexually abused child to *think differently* about the events that have happened to her. The goal is to correct illogical beliefs such as, "it's my fault because I held Uncle John's hand while crossing the street." The molested child must come to the conclusion that the abuse is not his or her fault. This awareness can greatly help the child's self-esteem and psychological development (Damon, Todd, & MacFarlane, 1987). Parents can play a strategic role in helping the child release the feelings of guilt and responsibility. It can take resourcefulness and skill to help the child place blame on the perpetrator where it belongs. It is a complicated process because sometimes what the perpetrator has said becomes a reality for the child, such as the family breaking up or the perpetrator going to jail. It is even more arduous when the perpetrator is a parent and the other parent also blames the child (Faller, 1988).

The therapist can help parents devise concrete ways to aid the victims in shifting responsibility for the abuse to the perpetrator. Most important is to reassure children that *all* of the responsibility for the abuse belongs to the perpetrator. Parents can verbalize this message to their children frequently. The parents and children can write down feelings the children express such as, "It's my fault Uncle Henry lost his job at the school." Then, they can rewrite the message and post it somewhere for the children to see: "It's Uncle Henry's fault that he lost his job at the school." Parents can also make a list of the children's strengths and place such lists in a highly visible area where the children can see them often. Structured play can be a great avenue to help children change the messages of guilt and responsibility, and it can be a nonthreatening way for parents and children to process feelings and information about the abuse. Structured play can be centered on nonsexual themes when children and/or parents are too uncomfortable to discuss it directly, with the benefit of still helping children recognize where blame should be placed.

For example, 9-year-old Angie was sexually abused by a Sunday school teacher while on a weekend campout with her Sunday school class. Later, when the abuse was exposed, the Sunday school teacher was asked to leave the church. Angie felt very guilty about this since the teacher had told her he would not be able to go to church if she told. In play therapy, Angie spent the majority of her time playing with the puppets. She had the puppets act silly and funny for a little while, and then abruptly changed the theme to something more serious, such as the main puppet, Catherine, getting in trouble for all sorts of behaviors ranging from talking in class to stealing. The therapist perceived that as Angie playing out her feelings of guilt and responsibility for the abuse in a nonsexual way. The therapist taught Angie's mother how to do structured play at home with Angie around this theme. Angie's mother said Angie enjoyed playing with her dollhouse at home, so the therapist set the structured play around the dollhouse and a doll that Angie's mother named Anna. Angie's mother set the stage for the structured play the first few times by having Anna acting out behaviors that were serious *and* silly. Angie's mother watched for cues when Angie looked stressed or distracted, and switched back to a silly theme to relieve the pressure. After a few sessions with the structured play, Angie began to join in making up the stories for Anna to play out. Angie's mother always took the opportunity to reflect Anna's feelings and to verbalize when Anna was not responsible for something. About six weeks later, Angie invited her father to "come watch the plays" that she and her mother were doing.

Sexually abused children need to hear *many* times and in *many* ways that they are not responsible for the sexual abuse. Parents, with the therapist's help, can be instrumental in communicating this message to their children.

Anger

Anger is another common reaction that victims of sexual abuse experience (Finkelhor, 1986). The anger may be directed at the perpetrator, the other parent, other adults who are viewed as unprotective, professionals who have intervened, siblings, friends, teachers, and so forth. Caretakers and parents must be forewarned that the sexually abused child may target their anger toward them. The child's anger may be displayed directly or indirectly in noncompliance, talking back, negative attention-seeking behaviors, and claims that the caretaker or parent does not care about them (Damon, et al., 1987). The goal is to provide *places* and *means* whereby the victims can express the anger (Faller, 1988).

First, the therapist can *normalize the anger*. The therapist explains to the parents that the anger is a normal, expected, and necessary reaction to the abuse. Most parents will nod in agreement, but often have difficulty when they see the expression of their children's anger. They may be afraid of the anger or just not know how to respond to the anger; it can be helpful for the therapist to process with the parents their own reactions to the anger. In an effort to teach parents appropriate and beneficial ways to respond to the anger, the therapist can model and role-play with them (Damon, et al., 1987).

Second, in addition to normalizing the anger, the therapist should help parents set up viable places and means for the anger to be expressed. This can range from hitting pillows and punching bags to yelling. Both parents and children need definite parameters about where and when intense anger can be displayed. The parents need preparation for times when children display anger in an inappropriate place over a seemingly trivial incident, such as a child's food order being cooked incorrectly in a restaurant. Parents can recognize this type of outburst as a cue that the child is feeling angry about deeper issues such as, possibly, the abuse. Once parents identify the cue, they can intervene with supportive responses and safe places for expression of the anger (Faller, 1988).

Third, other creative interventions may be suggested to the parents to facilitate resolution of the child's anger. The parents may help the child write a letter to the perpetrator or to other adults the child felt were unprotective. The child and parent can have an assigned playtime at home (i.e., filial therapy) where the parent lets the child lead the play and responds accordingly. It is important for the therapist to assess the parents' ability and availability in regard to the child's anger. The therapist must cautiously and carefully integrate the child and parents working together, must move slowly and gauge the tolerance of both parents and child in carrying out an assignment, and try to measure its effectiveness.

Parents or other adults can be beneficial agents in helping children release and resolve their anger. If the parents are unable to tolerate or facilitate expression of their children's anger, the therapist can look for other adults who might be available to the child. Anger can be destructive, with long-term effects, when not channeled appropriately.

Depression and Self-destructive Behavior

In clinical studies, the most commonly reported effect of child sexual abuse is depression (Briere & Runtz, 1991; Browne & Finkelhor, 1986).

In addition to symptoms of depression, self-destructive tendencies may also be result of sexual abuse (Finkelhor, 1986) and often surface before the abuse is exposed. Depression may be centered around guilt, feeling responsible for the abuse, anger toward the perpetrator or other adults, confusion, or fear (Faller, 1988).

Depression may surface through somatic complaints by the child, such as headaches or stomachaches. It may be disguised through destructive acting out behaviors such as getting into fights at school, arguing, or being non-compliant. Even small children may exhibit suicidal tendencies, that may escalate or worsen as they reach adolescence (Faller, 1988).

Helping the child feel better about oneself is necessary to counteract the feelings of depression (Pearce & Pezzot-Pearce, 1997). Interventions for depression and self-destructive behavior also include, the *family acting metaphorically as a team*, the *me badge*, and the *imaginary feelings x-ray machine*. When there are identified symptoms of the depression, such as not wanting to go to school, the therapist can request that the family members of the sexually abused child "act metaphorically as a team." The parents and other family members act as if the problem (not wanting to go to school) is on one side and the family is on the other side (ways to encourage the child about going to school). Each member makes a contribution to dealing with the problem (Freeman, Epston, & Lobovits, 1997).

Originally developed by Cunningham and MacFarlane (1991) to work with children who molest other children, the *me badge* is an effective activity that parents can use to bolster the self-esteem of sexually abused children. In this activity, the parent divides a circular piece of cardboard into four sections. The child then draws or identifies four positive characteristics about oneself in the quadrants. These characteristics might include something that is very special to the child, something the child does to help the family, something the child likes to do, and something she is good at doing. This visual and concrete depiction should be kept and shown periodically to encourage the child with the reminder of his or her strengths.

For children who have difficulty expressing their feelings, Selekman (1997) devised the *imaginary feelings x-ray machine*. Selekman says to the parents and child: "If I had an imaginary feelings x-ray machine that could show me what feelings you have inside, what would I see in the x-ray pictures?" (p. 108). The child is instructed to lie down on a large piece of paper on the floor. The parent then draws an outline of he child's body on the paper. Once the contour of the child's body has been drawn, the child draws or paints pictures within the lines of feelings that would be picked up by the x-rays. When finished, the child and parents can talk about the feelings. This activity helps the child and parents become more aware of the child's emotional world.

Raising children's self-esteem through activities that build self-confidence and facilitate the release of the child's anger can help alleviate depression. Some children may need medication for the depression. By helping the parents recognize the signs of depression, parents can then empathize with their children and inform the therapist of the symptoms. The therapist can then make a plan based on the information of the parents.

Seven-year-old Candy complained to her mother about frequent stomachaches. After a couple of months of Candy's complaints, her mother took her to the pediatrician. The pediatrician found no physical cause for the stomachaches and suggested therapy for Candy because he suspected there was an underlying reason for them. Candy's mother reluctantly took her to play therapy. Candy's mother worked part-time, went to school, and also had three other children; Candy's father worked long hours as an electrician. Finances were strained for the family and absorbed much energy from Candy's parents as they tried to stay financially afloat. Candy revealed to the therapist that her father would come into her room sometimes at night and "do things" to her. As the abuse was revealed, Candy's mother staunchly denied it and refused to believe Candy. As a result, Candy was removed from her home and placed with foster-parents while the trial for Candy's father was pending.

Candy refused to participate in school, whether it was answering a question or completing assignments in class. Her complaints of stomachaches increased. One week in therapy, as she played with the dolls, she said, "This baby, Susan, wants to go to sleep. She hopes she never wakes up again because nobody loves her."

Candy appeared to be feeling rejected, confused, and afraid. Her entire life had been turned upside down as a result of telling about the abuse. Her mother's refusal to believe her exacerbated these feelings. Candy's foster-mother was supportive and available both in time and emotionally when Candy needed her. The therapist set up a psychiatric evaluation to assess the suicidal ideation and any possible necessity for medication. The psychiatrist prescribed an antidepressant, and slowly the therapist set up interventions for Candy and her foster-mother to do outside the play therapy sessions.

Interventions included Candy writing her mother a letter describing how sad and mad she was at her mother for not believing her and for "letting those people" take her away from her mother. Candy told her foster-mother what to write. As she wrote, the foster-mother reflected Candy's feelings, which helped Candy express her feelings and also increased the bond between Candy and her foster-mother. Over the next few months, Candy's foster-mother had special play sessions at home implementing filial therapy. The antidepressant, play therapy, and support of her foster-parents helped Candy work through some of the abuse.

☐ Summary

Divorce affects many areas of life for the parents and children and often includes deep emotional feelings of sadness, anger and hopelessness. By understanding how the parents and children are affected by divorce, they can begin to work through these various levels, stage-by-stage. Interventions include: encouraging the divorced parents to get individual therapy if there continues to be emotional pain and conflict between them; encourage parents to strive toward a decent working relationship as parents; teach parents to be empathetic to the child's sadness and anger; and reiterate to the child that the divorce is not his or her fault.

Play therapy in the elementary schools helps children develop positive emotional, physical, intellectual, and social awareness skills. Play therapy can be a valuable and beneficial experience for children in the school setting. The therapist has the advantage of interacting with the child's teacher and parents. Whether the contact with the parents and/or teacher is frequent or sporadic, the therapist can make suggestions that will be beneficial to the child.

Likewise, sexual abuse can be profoundly traumatizing for children *and* their parents. Sexual abuse involves a betrayal of the most basic trust between a child and another person, and a betrayal of the cornerstone of childhood: innocence. This chapter also addresses numerous issues and consequences of sexual abuse including:

1. Loss of trust;
2. Guilt;
3. Responsibility;
4. Altered body image;
5. Anger;
6. Depression; and
7. Self-destructive behavior.

The subtle, pervasive, and socially stigmatizing nature of sexual abuse leaves the child victims incredibly confused and their parents terribly frightened. Therapy and education addressing the complexities of sexual abuse can be pivotal to the healing process for both children and parents.

Incorporating Brief Therapy and Managed Care

Managed care is growing across the United States and will continue to influence the mental health field. Private practices and agencies will be affected. Whether or not you agree with the concept of managed care, you need to know how to work within the system.

When working in a managed care system, the therapist will usually be working under more time restraints in regard to the number of therapy sessions. There is an emphasis on brief therapy under managed care. According to Hoyt (1995) brief therapy is defined as, "the intention of helping patients make changes in thoughts, feelings, and actions in order to move toward or reach a particular goal as time-effectively as possible" (p. 1). Budman and Gurman (cited in Hoyt) strongly attest that it is important to be *time-sensitive*.

In order to be time-sensitive, it is imperative to set clearly defined goals quickly and move into problem solving strategies as soon as possible. For therapy to be brief and effective, clear goals must be defined, key problems identified, and an effective treatment plan formulated and executed. Many therapists believe they must know an immense amount about the client before they can intervene with a treatment plan (Lazarus, 1997).

When integrating play therapy with brief therapy, the theoretical foundation of the therapist becomes vitally important. For instance, if you use child-centered play therapy, setting goals in the playroom with children is as out of the question as hurrying the therapy process. Children lead the therapy and the therapist follows. The therapist makes no attempt to lead the conversations or actions of children (Axline, 1969). The key to maintaining the integrity of the therapy for children is to set goals with the parents and other caregivers. The managed care group may be able to control the number of sessions with children, but the therapist can control the therapeutic content through which the goals that are established.

According to Dr. Chris Sheldon (personal communication, August 20, 1997), clinical administrator for MCC Behavioral Care, "It is essential to have parents or caregivers involved. The managed care company wants to see that there is an appropriate treatment plan from the therapist, and the vast majority of time, the treatment plan should include interventions in the child's environment."

If, on the other hand, you use more direct or interpretative therapy in the playroom, you may feel comfortable setting goals and treatment plans with children. Either way, you can incorporate brief therapy without compromising your theoretical values. By incorporating work with the parents of your child clients, you can enhance your value to managed care companies.

Lazarus (1997) stresses that *time-effective therapy* should not be based on a prearranged number of sessions. However, many therapists hold to the range of 6 to 12 sessions. While many problems or disorders are able to be treated briefly, there are some clients who require additional sessions. Sheldon (1997) said that, in terms of the relationship between the managed care company and the therapist, and in terms of overall cost to the managed care company, the focus is on the overall pattern of the therapist. Does the therapist request additional sessions on all clients, or is it a subset?

The most important rule in brief therapy is to be very goal-oriented. According to Araoz and Carrese (1996) "a treatment must be specific for resolving a specific type of impairment within a specific time frame" (p. 2).

☐ Phases of Brief Therapy

Brief therapy can be reflected in five stages: (a) pretreatment selection criteria, (b) beginning phase, (c) middle phase, (d) end phase, and (e) follow-through phase (Hoyt, 1995).

Pretreatment Selection Criteria

How motivated is the client to change? How willing is the client to follow through on homework assignments? What indications are there to support that this client is suitable for short-term therapy? The therapist should look for contraindications such as severe depression, active psychosis, suicidal ideation, and so forth (Hoyt, 1995). Deciding whether child clients are suitable for therapy can be difficult because children are often good candidates for therapy, or brief therapy, while their parents or caregivers may not be good candidates. The parents may be resistant or have contraindications, but if they can tolerate their children coming to therapy, the therapist can focus on the children. If the parents are willing participants and/or have no other contraindications, then the therapy process will not only be enhanced, but the therapist will also have greater success when doing brief therapy under managed care.

Beginning Phase

In this phase, the focus is on establishing rapport and a working alliance with clients. To obtain a solid understanding of the complaints and the goals of the clients, it is essential to clarify why they are seeking therapy at the particular time. The parameters of the therapy must also be clearly defined. For instance, if clients are limited to 6 or 12 sessions, the therapist must make sure they are informed of this at the beginning of treatment (Hoyt, 1995). In addition, whether providing short- or long-term therapy, therapists are urged to start giving homework assignments beginning with the first session.

Middle Phase

The middle phase is the *working through* phase. As the therapist, look for patterns and choices that clients are making, while maintaining focus on the primary goals that were set in the beginning phase (Hoyt, 1995). Because parents are most often the ones looking for change (rather than their children), this phase often necessitates extra attention to the themes of the children's play and changes that are occurring to minimize resistance and transference on the parents' part. On the other hand, this phase can be especially helpful in working with the parents and in expediting the therapy process. The therapist can monitor the progress of the homework assignments and gauge the resistance of the parents based on the playroom themes expressed by their children.

End Phase

Although the termination of therapy is acknowledged and begun, continued work on the therapy goals is stressed to both the children and their parents. Separation and dependency issues are explored, as well as possible mourning of the therapy ending (Hoyt, 1995). Developmentally, children need transition time. It is especially important to inform children of termination in advance, so they can have time to process the ending of therapy. It is also important to tell the parents and be aware of their reaction to the termination of the therapy. Emphasize to both parents and children that they can come back to therapy at a later time if needed. Most managed care companies allow for a return to therapy in the future.

During the end phase, it is beneficial for the therapist to include embedded messages about the abilities and skills that the families and children have been able incorporate during the therapy process. One of the goals as a therapist is to elicit the strengths from the family system that will benefit the children long after the therapy has ended.

Follow-through Phase

Change may begin in therapy, but continues outside therapy (Hoyt, 1995). Likewise, change and problem solving will hopefully continue beyond the formal termination of therapy. In working with the parents, this information may be vital in aiding them to continue what has been started in therapy. When the number of therapy sessions is limited, the parents can try to assess whether or not progress is continuing with their children in terms of the goals set at the beginning of therapy. The parents need to know they can call the therapist and the managed care company if their children encounter the same or new problems in the future.

☐ Setting Goals in Brief Therapy

It is paramount to set *specific* goals and to *stay focused* on those goals when providing short-term therapy. The goals should be set by the clients or parents and the therapist together. Usually, it will be the parents who set the goals for therapy. The parents will report the problems and what they want changed in regard to the behaviors of their children. The therapist can use these goals in the treatment plan and can immediately begin to make homework assignments based on these goals. If there are more than one or two goals, the therapist must prioritize. Working on numerous goals may not be possible when therapy sessions are limited. According to Araoz and Carrese (1996):

> The practitioner must be very clear about what she or he is asked to help correct, modify, or cancel. The list of impairments is not a vague, theoretical, or interpretative series of concepts (e.g., anal retentive personality traits), but a precise, concrete, measurable definition of behaviors (e.g., extremely possessive of what belongs to her, unwilling to share anything material with others; becomes upset when family or friends "borrow" small things, like ordinary weekly magazines without "asking her permission"). (p. 33)

When attempting to set concise goals with the parents, ask questions such as the following:

1. What behavior(s) do you want changed in your child?
2. When did the behavior(s) or problem(s) start?
3. Do you know of any catalyst for the behavior(s) or problem(s)?
4. What do you worry about regarding your child?
5. If you had a magic wand, what would life look like for your child?
6. Why do you want this behavior(s), problem(s), or stressor(s) changed?
7. When your child leaves therapy, what do you want to be different?

You can pose some or all of these questions to the parents, depending on the information you are receiving. Do not be hesitant about asking all of them even though some are similar. The more detailed information you have about children's problems or behaviors, the more quickly and succinctly you can set goals regarding the problems or behaviors.

Focusing Principles

In the context of linking parents to the play therapy process, Bloom (1981) provides several principles for helping the therapist stay focused on the goals of therapy, and recommends the following focusing principles:

1. Identify a problem on which to focus.
2. Do not underestimate the strengths of the client.
3. Be prudently active.
4. Explore the client's dynamics, then provide interpretations in a tentative fashion (be prudently active).
5. Encourage the client to express emotions.

6. Begin the problem solving process during the interview.
7. Diligently monitor the time.
8. Do not be overambitious.
9. Minimize the number of fact-seeking questions.
10. Pay attention to the client's current functioning—do not focus only on the precipitating event.
11. Try to avoid getting side-tracked.
12. Do not overestimate a client's insight or self-awareness—it is often appropriate to state the obvious.

☐ Treatment Plan

Most managed care companies will require a treatment plan from the therapist following the assessment of clients by the therapist. The treatment plan should include the specific problems the clients are experiencing. According to Sheldon (1997), "If the child is having behavioral problems at school, the treatment plan should specify the behavioral problem that the family, therapist, and child are trying to address. The managed care company wants something that an independent observer could agree on whether or not improvement has occurred."

For example, a child is referred to therapy because he is not sleeping well at night. The therapist should work towards a specific behavioral goal that will either help the client sleep through the night or at least sleep seven hours for five nights of the week. There needs to be a specified intervention that is geared toward addressing the problem or desired behavioral change. The interventions depend on the cognitive and emotional state of the parent and the child, as well as the nature of the presenting problem. Sheldon (1997) said managed care companies want to ensure that follow-up treatment reports are linked to the initial treatment plan. The interventions that the therapist is implementing in the follow-up sessions should be in alignment with the interventions that were suggested in the treatment plan. This is especially important when the therapist is requesting additional sessions.

From the therapist's perspective, it may seem that the managed care company is arbitrarily imposing a great many requirements in the treatment planning and treatment reporting process. Understandably, the paperwork that is involved is burdensome for therapists to complete and often takes much time. However, the more treatment plans a therapist writes, the more proficient the therapist will become in writing them. Sheldon (1997) stated, "I am personally convinced that writing the treatment plan is in fact very helpful for the treatment itself. It really does keep the therapist, and therefore the family system, focused on what they are doing."

The elements in a treatment plan that are being requested by the managed care company are elements that regulatory agencies have given to the managed care company. Sheldon (1997) said the two private, not-for-profit agencies—The National Committee for Quality Assurance (NCQA) and Joint Commission for the Accreditation of Healthcare Organizations (JCAHO)—were set up to improve the quality of health care and monitor managed care companies in order to ensure effective treatment for clients. The agencies require managed care companies and therapists to have explicit goals that are directly related to specified behavioral changes within a specified period of time. This is a reflection of the mental health field moving toward a more medical model. As the mental health field is evolving, it is important to maintain a focus on quality and on outcomes of the therapy. Sheldon (1997) stated "it is incumbent on the mental health professions to demonstrate that what they do is helpful." He further stressed the importance of connecting play therapy with specific behavioral treatment plan goals to be pursued outside the therapy room. The therapist can help accomplish this by setting specific goals and working closely with the parents of child clients.

☐ Interventions with the Parents

Homework Assignments

From the managed care companies' point of view, homework assignments are a tangible demonstration that the therapist is involving the whole system in achieving progress. Homework assignments also provide some very useful information on whether progress and improvement are actually occurring. The therapist has the opportunity to see if the parents have an investment in their children improving by whether or not they complete the homework assignments.

Reframing

When recommending interventions and/or homework assignments, the therapist should remember that the parents may be experiencing a range of feelings regarding their children's behaviors or problems (e.g., helpless, hopeless, overwhelmed, sad, or angry). The first intervention with the parents is to reflect the parents' feelings and then begin to help them reframe how they perceive their children. Frames are the rules by which people construct their reality (de Shazer, 1982). "Reframing, then, is a process that involves helping the client transform his or her 'rules' for developing meaning out of a particular problematic situation" (p. 101).

The therapist shows acceptance of children and parents by listening intently as problems and behaviors are described. The therapist then searches "for a piece of the frame's construction upon which a solution can be built" (de Shazer, 1982, p. 102). Therapists are urged to find ways to give the parents hope about solutions and try to help them perceive their children differently.

Support System

Accessing support for children and/or families can be one of the most beneficial interventions a therapist can employ outside the playroom, especially in brief therapy. Accessing the *support system* means integrating and incorporating individuals that are in the child's or family's life who might help with solutions or encouragement. This might include grandparents, close friends of the family, teachers, daycare providers, or many others. The therapist should be proactive in finding out who is close and supportive of the child and/or family. For example, if the child has depression, the therapist might recruit the help of a supportive teacher to provide needed acceptance, flexibility, and special group experiences for the child. Grandparents can be encouraged to focus intense attention on the child or take the child on an adventure (i.e., to the zoo). Grandparents and others can be of tremendous support, not only to the child, but also in providing parents with needed respite and time to relax—especially during stressful periods. Parents need time to themselves and opportunities to take care of themselves.

The parents can sign a release of confidential information to allow the therapist to talk to these people within the child's support system. Members of the support system can even be requested to attend the 15-minute parent meeting (assuming that parent's consent is obtained). Appreciation for the valuable role that they play in the child's life should be expressed, and they should be asked to do something specific with, or for, the child that the therapist thinks might be helpful.

Many managed care companies look closely at the support systems available to clients. The more you can access those support systems, the more likely the case manager is to authorize necessary sessions. Anything outside the therapy session that can help children or families reach the goals that have been set can aid the therapy process and facilitate the authorization of sessions.

Support Groups

Support groups follow the same theory as support systems, with the difference that support groups are community resources available to children or families, ranging from self-help groups such as *Alcoholics Anonymous* to *Parents Without Partners* to church activities. They are usually free or have a minimal charge for participants, and they can be very useful in supporting people in times of difficulty.

The support group forum allows people to listen and to obtain valuable reality testing that contribute support and education (Burt & Burt, 1996). "Clinicians should be aware of the support group resources in their communities and use them as adjuncts to their intervention" (p. 174). The therapist should spend time researching what is available and help clients and/or families access it. This includes groups for the family as well as the child clients. For instance, the school counselor might conduct a group for children whose parents are divorced. Perhaps the client could benefit from a *Big Sister* or *Big Brother* group. The single mother or father of your client might benefit from a *Parents Without Partners* group or a divorce recovery group at a church or synagogue.

Your treatment plan should include recommendations that utilize community resources. Managed care companies are more willing to authorize your services when you maximize outside free resources (Friedman, 1997). When the child is the client, managed care companies look carefully at what resources the therapist employs in addition to the child. There is an emphasis on exercising the options available outside the therapy session since the child does not necessarily have control of many areas in his or her life.

Coin Flip Task

The *coin flip task* is effective in helping people get into a more playful mode that may interrupt outmoded, unproductive patterns (Friedman, 1997). For example, when parents are dealing with trying to get their Attention Deficit Hyperactive Disorder (ADHD) child to do her homework, the therapist might suggest that the parents flip a coin. When the coin comes up heads, the parents are instructed to do something different than they usually would do in trying to get the child to finish her homework. If it comes up tails, they are to respond the way they usually respond in trying to get her to finish her homework. According to Friedman,, "this kind of task can be effective in encouraging client creativity while allowing the client to not entirely give up the old way of managing the situation. Just stopping the action to find a coin can be enough to unbalance the situation in ways that create change" (p. 82). The coin flip task can be a positive means of interceding between the child and parents when the parents are stuck in a form of discipline that is not working effectively. It is often beneficial when working with resistant parents because they can try something different without committing to it indefinitely.

Cheerleading

Cheerleading is a form of support and encouragement for positive things clients are doing and for their changing and solving of problems (Walter & Peller, 1992). "Cheerleading may be emotional support that comes across through raised voice tone, gestures, excited expressions, or word choice. In the session, we want to respond immediately to any mention of change, however small" (p. 106).

Parents may be cognitively aware of their making changes that result from their following through with homework assigned by the therapist, or they may think changes occur spontaneously with children through therapy. However they perceive the therapy process, there is an enormous advantage for parents in receiving positive feedback for their efforts and changes. The parents may be experiencing confusion, fear, or uncertainty, so encouragement, support, and endorsement from the therapist can be reassuring.

One form of cheerleading is to ask the parent, "How did you make the decision to do that?" The therapist usually asks this question with excitement and curiosity (Walter & Peller, 1992). The parents may not have realized that they intentionally decided to do something different or made a change, but the therapist wants the parent to see the reality of the conscious change they have made. For example, the parents may not have realized they were doing something that was different and substantive for the children. "How did you do that?" helps point out the parents' action and imbeds the ideas of action and change. The parents may make excuses, or not take responsibility for their actions, but this question is a non-confrontational way of making them aware of what they are doing differently and positively with their children.

Other examples of cheerleading are "That is really great!" (Walter &

Peller, 1992) or "Good for you!" Any form of complimentary encouragement can be supportive of new or positive behavior, and it is a way for the therapist to point out changes the parents are making with their children. This kind of support is empathic and heartwarming for the parents and also helps facilitate a good rapport between the therapist and parents. The parents are more likely to see the therapist as an ally and not as someone criticizing them for the difficulties with their children. Be sincere when implementing these phrases; overuse may make the parents think you are being insincere and phony and you will lose the effectiveness of these phrases. Nevertheless, whenever there is positive change or effort on the part of the parents to help their children, or whenever they follow through with suggestions you make, give them credit.

Supporting Changes

Small changes lead to larger changes (Walter & Peller, 1992). When parents take a small step toward solving problems in their children's lives, and when they can see positive results from that effort, the parents are more encouraged and empowered to make changes simultaneously in other areas. According to Walter and Peller, "saying that small change is generative also means that we hold to the belief that a client who has experienced some success at achieving something manageable is, therefore, in a more resourceful state to find solutions to other, more difficult problems" (p. 19).

The therapist can help the parents realize that problems are solved one step at a time. The therapist points out the small changes to the parents with the hope that they will courageously begin to make other changes. So point out changes, no matter how insignificant or small they may seem.

☐ Summary

Due to the impact of insurance and managed care companies, therapists face increasing demands to plan concrete and measurable treatment strategies and complete extensive treatment and billing reports. Managed care case managers tend to request therapists to be increasingly problem-focused, goal-directed, and time-sensitive in the services provided. This can prove to be especially challenging for play therapists. However, by gaining a greater understanding of the complexities of managed care and by involving parents in the therapy process, play therapists can move forward successfully in this endeavor, protect the integrity of the children and parents, and preserve the therapeutic relationships. Appendix D contains a table delineating an example of the managed care format.

Described in this chapter are phases of brief therapy. These phases include pretreatment and selection criteria, the beginning phase, middle phase, end phase, and follow-through phase. Strategies to set goals within the brief therapy environment are presented. Brief therapy requires therapists to apply specific, concrete, and measurable strategies when describing treatment plans. Therapists must also remain focused on the treatment plan when providing services and especially when describing treatment progress in the managed care reports. Therapists are also encouraged to search for social support and positive influences from the community that fall outside of the formal and clinical (paid for) purview of treatment.

Specific parental interventions are also addressed in this chapter. These interventions include:

1. Reframing;
2. Support systems;
3. Support groups;
4. Homework;
5. The Coin-flip task;
6. Cheerleading; and
7. Supporting changes.

In addition, it is important to keep the parent informed and involved regarding managed care issues and processes. Even in the complex and demanding environment of managed care therapy and reimbursement processes, the stability of an open and trusting parent-therapist relationship can help to preserve the professional level of care provided to the child. (See Appendix D for Table 1: Eight Characteristics of Managed Behavioral Health Care.)

APPENDIX A: Sample Professional Disclosure Statement and Informed Consent

Therapist's Name and Title
Agency Name
Street Address
City, State, ZIP
Telephone Number(s)

Professional Disclosure Statement

Professional Qualifications: [sample] M.Ed., Counseling Psychology, Temple University, 1990. National Certified Counselor (#1234); Licensed Marriage and Family Therapist (#3456); Registered Play Therapist (#5678). My formal education has prepared me to counsel individuals, groups, parents, families, and children.

Experience: [sample] During my master's program, under supervision, I gained experience in group and individual counseling with children, adults, and families. I have also gained experience at the Family Therapy Clinic, and in private practice.

Areas of Competence: [sample] In addition to providing individual and group counseling for adults, adolescents, and children, I also provide workshops regarding parenting and developmental concerns.

Informed Consent

Counseling Relationship

During the time we work together, we will meet weekly, or as scheduled, in sessions lasting approximately 50 minutes. Although our sessions

190

may be very intimate psychologically, ours is a professional relationship rather that a social one. Our contact will be limited to the counseling sessions you arrange with me except in case of emergency when you may page me through the above number. Please do not invite me to social gatherings, offer me gifts, ask me to write references for you, or ask me to relate to you in any way other than in the professional context of the counseling sessions. You will be best served if our sessions concentrate exclusively on your goals and concerns.

Effects of Counseling

At any time, you may initiate a discussion of possible positive or negative effects of entering, not entering, continuing, or discontinuing counseling. While benefits are expected from the counseling process, specific results cannot be guaranteed. Counseling is a personal exploration and may lead to major changes in your life perspectives and decisions. These changes may affect significant relationships, your job, and your understanding of yourself. Some of these life changes could be temporarily distressing. The exact nature of these changes cannot be predicted. Together we will work to achieve the best possible results for you.

Client Rights

Some clients need only a few counseling sessions to achieve their goals; others may require months or years of counseling. As a client, you are in complete control and may end our counseling relationship at any time, although I do ask that you participate in a termination session. You also have the right to refuse or discuss modification of any of my counseling techniques or suggestions that you believe might not be helpful.

I assure you that my services will be rendered in a professional manner consistent with accepted legal and ethical standards. If at any time for any reason you are dissatisfied with my services, please let me know. If I am not able to resolve you concerns, you may report your complaints to the:

National Board for Certified Counselors, Inc.
3 Terrace Way, Suite D
Greensboro, NC 27403-3660
(336) 547-0607

Postponement and Termination

I reserve the right to postpone and/or terminate counseling of clients who come to their session under the influence of alcohol or drugs. I also reserve the right to discontinue counseling of clients who do not comply with the medication recommendations of their psychiatrist or physician.

Cancellation

Your session is reserved for you. In the event that you will be unable to keep an appointment, please notify my office at least 24 hours in advance, so that someone else may utilize this time. In the absence of your notification, you will be billed for the missed session. Also, if you are absent for two consecutive sessions, I may ask to terminate our counseling relationship, and provide you with appropriate referrals.

Referrals

I realize that I am not able to provide appropriate treatment for all of the conditions that clients may have. For this reason, you and/or I may believe that a referral is needed. In that case, I will provide you with some alternatives including programs and/or people who may be able to assist you. A verbal exploration of alternatives to counseling will also be made available to you at your request. You will be responsible for contacting and evaluating those referrals and/or alternatives.

Fees

In return for a fee of $_____ per session, I agree to provide counseling services for you. If the fee is a hardship for you, please let me know. Cash or personal checks are acceptable, or with prior authorization, I will file for reimbursement from your health insurance company. The fee for each session, or the insurance co-payment for which you are responsible, will be due and must be paid at the beginning of each session.

Records and Confidentiality

All of our communication becomes part of the clinical record. Records are my property, but you have a right to the information within your record. Adult client records are disposed of seven years after termination of the counseling relationship. Records of minor clients are disposed of seven years of the client's 18th birthday. Most of our communications are confidential, but the following limitations and exceptions exist: (a) you provide me with your consent to release information; (b) I have reasonable suspicion that you are a danger to yourself or someone else; (c) you disclose abuse, neglect, or exploitation of a child, elderly, or disabled person; (d) you disclose sexual contact with another mental health professional; (e) I am ordered by a court to disclose information; (f) you involve me in a lawsuit; (g) I need to release specific information in order to receive compensation for services rendered; or (h) I am otherwise required by law to release information. If I see you in public, I will protect your confidentiality by acknowledging you only if you approach me first.

Marriage or Family Counseling

I will keep confidential (within the limits cited above) anything you disclose to me without your family member's knowledge. However, I encourage open communication between family members, and I reserve the right to terminate our counseling relationship if I judge any secret to be detrimental to the therapeutic progress.

By your signature below, you are indicating that you read and understood this statement, and any questions you had about this statement were answered to your satisfaction. By my signature, I verify the accuracy of this statement and acknowledge my commitment to conform to its specifications.

Printed Name of Client or Child   Date

Signature of Client or Legal Guardian   Signature of Counselor

APPENDIX B: Sample Play Therapy Parent Intake Session Checklist

Play Therapy Parent Intake Session

1. Open the session with your Professional Disclosure Statement. (Give a copy to the parents to follow along as you address the main points.)
2. Invite the parents to discuss their reasons for bringing their child for play therapy; how you might be able to help their child; or, if appropriate, how you will help with a referral for other services.
3. Provide an explanation of the nature of play therapy.
4. Have the parents sign your Professional Disclosure Statement. (Offer them a copy.)
5. Have the parents complete the Client Intake Form and sign the Authorization for Treatment at the end of the form.
6. If the presenting problem seems to be school-related or medical, have the parents sign a Release of Confidential Information form that you deem appropriate. This will allow you, for example, to discuss issues with school personnel or medical professionals. You should get a release to consult with current or previous mental health professionals from whom the client has received services.
7. If the parents are divorced, the managing conservator, or legal guardian, must sign all of the forms. A copy of the most recent court order regarding custody and conservatorship issues must be received by you before services with the child can be provided (i.e., a stepparent cannot sign for the spouse event if the spouse has legal authority to consent for mental health services).
8. Clarify any procedural details (i.e., session time and length, fees, taping, supervision, next appointment, parent meetings, etc.).

9. Have the parents sign any other forms that are pertinent to your particular services.
10. If a parent seems particularly stressed or brings up numerous personal issues, discuss the possibility of a separate appointment for the parent meeting.
11. If available, show the playroom to the parents at the end of the intake session.

APPENDIX C: Sample Child Client Intake Form and Authorization for Treatment

CHILD CLIENT INTAKE

Therapist Name
Street Address, City, State, ZIP
Telephone Number(s)

Child Information

Name _____   Date of First Visit _____

Address _____   City, State, ZIP _____

Gender _____ Date of Birth _____   Social Security # _____

Home Phone _____ OK to Call? _____   Leave Message? _____

Emergency Contact _____   Relationship _____

Address _____   Phone Numbers _____

Referred by _____   OK to Contact? _____

Reason for Visit _____

Other Concerns (check all that apply):   Anger Control: _____

School/Work Problem: _____ Attention Problem: _____ Impulsivity: ____

Frequent Fights: ___ Sudden Behavior Changes: ___ Family Problems: ___

Isolating: _____ Family Problems: _____ Alcohol/Drug Use: _____

Trouble with the Law: _____   Other: _____

Child's Natural Mother Information

Name of Mother ——————————— Date of Birth ———————

Address ——————————— City, State, ZIP ———————

Home Phone ——————— OK to Call? ——————— Leave Message? ———————

Work Phone ——————— OK to Call? ——————— Leave Message? ———————

Marital Status (give dates of all that apply): Married: ———————

Never Married: ——————— Widowed: ——————— Separated: ———————

Divorced: ——————— Remarried: ———————

Child's Natural Father Information

Name of Father _____ Date of Birth _____

Address _____ City, State, ZIP _____

Home Phone _____ OK to Call? _____ Leave Message? _____

Work Phone _____ OK to Call? _____ Leave Message? _____

Marital Status (give dates of all that apply): Married: _____

Never Married: _____ Widower: _____ Separated: _____

Divorced: _____ Remarried: _____

Legal Guardian Information (if the child does not reside with natural or adoptive parents, a copy of the most recent court order assigning conservatorship/custody is required)

Name of Legal Guardian _____ Relation to Child _____

Guardian's Gender ___ Date of Birth _____ Social Security # _____

Address _____ City, State, ZIP _____

Home Phone _____ OK to Call? _____ Leave Message? _____

Work Phone _____ OK to Call? _____ Leave Message? _____

Primary Household Information (list all persons residing at household—oldest to youngest)

Name	Age	Gender	Relation to Client

Secondary Household Information (list all persons residing at household—oldest to youngest)

Name	Age	Gender	Relation to Client

Other Treatment Information

Current Medications _____ Do These Help? _____

Current Medications _____ Do These Help? _____

Current Medications _____ Do These Help? _____

Prescribing Physician _____ OK to Contact? _____

Previous Medications _____ Why discontinued? _____

Previous Medications _____ Why discontinued? _____

Previous Therapist _____ Dates _____

Reason for Visit _____ Outcome of Therapy _____

Previous Therapist _____ Dates _____

Reason for Visit _____ Outcome of Therapy _____

Insurance Information

Name of Child Client _____

Name of Insured _____ Relation to Child Client _____

Insured's Social Security _____ Date of Birth _____

Insurance Company _____ Phone _____

Insurance Company Address _____

Insurance ID #_____ Group # _____

Employer _____

Release for Insurance

I, the undersigned, assign directly to [therapist's name and credentials] medical benefits otherwise payable to me directly. I understand that I am financially responsible for all charges whether or not paid by insurance. I hereby authorize [therapist's name and credentials] to release all necessary information in order to receive payment for services. I authorize the use of this signature on all of my insurance claim submissions.

Signature of Insured/Guardian _____Date _____

Authorization for Treatment

Therapist's Disclosure

I, [therapist's name and credentials], am committed to the confidentiality and privileged communications of all clients. There are, however two exceptions. According to law, any evidence of physical or sexual child abuse must be reported. Also, if an individual intends to take harmful, dangerous, or criminal action against oneself or another human being, it may be my duty to report such action or intent.

Full payment of the session is the client's responsibility and is requested at the beginning of each session. If you use insurance and your insurance requires that that you pay a co-payment amount, that amount should be paid at the beginning of each session. Any other agreements must be made and agreed to in advance.

Your session is reserved for you. If you are unable to make your appointment, you are asked to notify this office at least 24 hours in advance, so someone else may use this time. In the absence of your notification, you will be responsible for payment for the missed session.

Parent/Guardian's Authorization

I, the undersigned, hereby authorize [therapist's name and credentials] to render necessary treatment or to make an appropriate referral for:

[name of child client]: _____

My signature below indicates that I have read and understand the above information.

Signature of Parent/Guardian _____ Date _____

APPENDIX D: Managed Care Format

Table 1. Eight Characteristics of Managed Behavioral Health Care

Features	Comments
1. Specific problem solving	Why has the patient come to therapy now? Identification with patient of achievable, measurable goals.
2. Rapid response and early intervention	Therapy begins right away, engaging the patient as soon as possible, including amplifying useful pre-treatment progress.
3. Clear definition of patient and therapist responsibilities, with an emphasis on patient competencies, resources, and involvement	The therapist structures treatment contacts, conducts particular interventions, and involves significant others as needed. The patient is encouraged to participate actively, including doing "homework assignments" and making behavioral changes outside of therapy sessions.
4. Time is used flexibly and creatively	The length, frequency, and timing of sessions vary according to patient needs with the ideal being the most parsimonious intervention likely to have positive effects in a given situation.
5. Interdisciplinary cooperation	Medical and psychological involvement blends into a more holistic view of the patient. Allied health professionals may be used as indicated, as may appropriate psychopharmacology.

(*continued on next page*)

Table 1. Eight Characteristics of Managed Behavioral Health Care (*Continued*)

Features	Comments
6. Multiple formats and modalities	Individual, group, and/or marital/family therapy may be used in sequential or concurrent combinations, and participation in various community resources (including self-help, twelve-step, and support groups) may be vigorously encouraged.
7. Intermittent treatment or a "family practitioner" model	The idea of a once-and-for-all "cure" gives way to a more realistic view that patients can return for "serial" or "distributed" treatment as needed, often focused around developmental issues throughout the life cycle. The therapist-patient relationship may be long-term although frequently abeyant.
8. Results orientation and accountability	Is treatment helping? Outcomes measurement helps define what works best. Utilization review and quality assurance function as complementary procedures, efficacious relief of symptoms being in the best interests of the patient and the company.

Hoyt, copyright 1995 in *Brief Therapy and Managed Care*. Reprinted with permission of Jossey-Bass, Inc., a subsidiary of John Wiley & Sons, Inc.

APPENDIX E: National and State Protective Services and Advocacy Agencies

National Organizations

National Association for Protection
and Advocacy Systems
220 1 Street N. W., Suite 150
Washington, D.C. 20001
(TTD) (202) 546-8206
(Telefax) (202) 546-7354

State and Local Organizations

Alabama
Alabama Disabilities Advocacy
Program
University of Alabama
P.O. Box 870395
Tuscaloosa, AL 35487-0395
(205) 348-4928
(800) 826-1675

Alaska
Advocacy Services of Alaska
615 E. 82nd Avenue, Suite 101
Anchorage, AK 99518
(907) 344-1002
(800) 478-1234

American Samoa
Client Assistance and Protection
Advocacy Program
P.O. Box 3937
Pago Pago, American Samoa 96799
(10) 288-011-684-633-2441

Arizona
Arizona Center for Law in the
Public Interest
3724 North 3rd Street, Suite 201
Phoenix, AZ 85012
(602) 274-6287

Arkansas
Advocacy Services, Inc.
Evergreen Place, Suite 201
1100 N. University
Little Rock, AR 72207
(501) 324-9215
(800) 482-1174

California
California Protection and
Advocacy, Inc.
191 Howe Avenue, Suite 185N
Sacramento, CA 95825
(916) 488-9950
(800) 776-5746
(818) 546-1631
(510) 839-0811

Colorado
The Legal Center
455 Sherman Street, Suite 130
Denver, CO 80203
(303) 722-0300

Connecticut
Office of P&A for Handicapped
  and DD Persons
60 Weston Street
Hartford, CT 06120-1551
(203) 297-4300
(203) 566-2102
(800) 842-7303
  (statewide toll-free)

Delaware
Disabilities Law Program
144 E. Market Street
Georgetown, DE 19947
(302) 856-0038

District of Columbia
Information Protection and
  Advocacy Center for
  Handicapped Individuals, Inc.
4455 Connecticut Avenue, N.W.
Suite B100
Washington, DC 20008
(202) 966-8081

Florida
Advocacy Center for Persons
  with Disabilities
2671 Executive Center, Circle West
Webster Building, Suite 100
Tallahassee, FL 32301-5024
(904) 488-9071
(800) 342-0823

Georgia
Georgia Advocacy Office, Inc.
1798 Peachtree Street, N.W.
Suite 505
Atlanta, GA 30309
(404) 885-1234
(800) 282-4538

Guam
The Advocacy Office
Micronesia Mall, Office A
West Marine Drive
Dededo, Guam 96912
10288-011-(671)-632-7233

Hawaii
Protection and Advocacy Agency
1580 Makaloa Street, Suite 1060
Honolulu, HI 96814
(808) 949-2922

Idaho
Co-Ad, Inc.
4477 Emerald, Suite B-100
Boise, ID 83706
(208) 336-5353

Illinois
Protection and Advocacy, Inc.
11 E. Adams, Suite 1200
Chicago, IL 60603
(312) 341-0022

Indiana
Indiana Advocacy Services
850 N. Meridian Street, Suite 2-C
Indianapolis, In 46204
(317) 232-1150
(800) 622-4845

Iowa
Iowa P&A Service, Inc.
3015 Merle Hay Road, Suite 6
Des Moines, IA 50310
(515) 278-2502

Kansas
Kansas Advocacy and Protection
  Services
2601 Anderson Avenue
Manhattan, KS 66502
(913) 776-1541
(800) 372-2988

Kentucky
Office for Public Advocacy
Division for P&A
100 Fair Oaks Lane, 3rd Floor
Frankfort, KY 40601
(502) 564-2967
(800) 372-2988

Louisiana
Advocacy Center for the Elderly
and Disabled
2100 O'Keefe, Suite 700
New Orleans, LA 70112
(504) 522-2337
(800) 662-7705

Maine
Maine Advocacy Services
32 Winthrop
P.O. Box
Augusta, ME 04338
(207) 626-2774
(800) 233-7201

Massachusetts
DD Law Center for Massachusetts
11 Beacon Street, Suite 925
Boston, MA 02108
(617) 723-8455

Michigan
Michigan P&A Service
106 W. Allegan, Suite 210
Lansing, MI 48933
(517) 487-1755

Minnesota
Minnesota Disability Law Center
430 First Avenue North, Suite 300
Minneapolis, MN 55401-1780
(612) 332-1441

Mississippi
Mississippi P&A System for DD, Inc.
5330 Executive Place, Suite A
Jackson, MS 39206
(601) 981-8207

Missouri
Missouri P&A Service
925 S. Country Club Drive, Unit B-1
Jefferson City, MO 65109
(314) 893-3333

Montana
Montana Advocacy Program
316 N. Park, Room 211
P.O. Box 1680
Helena, MT 59624
(406) 444-3889
(800) 245-4723

Nebraska
Nebraska Advocacy Services, Inc.
522 Lincoln Center Building
215 Centennial Mall South
Lincoln, NE 68508
(402) 474-3183

Nevada
Office of Protection and Advocacy,
Inc.
Financial Plaza
1135 Terminal Way, Suite 105
Reno, NV 89502
(702) 688-1233
(800) 992-5715

New Hampshire
Disabilities Rights Center
P.O. Box 19
18 Low Avenue
Concord, NH 03302-0019
(603) 228-0432

New Jersey
Client Assistant Program
NJ Department of the Public
Advocate
Division of Advocacy for the DD
Hughes Justice Complex CN850
Trenton, NJ 08625
(609) 292-9742
(800) 792-8600

New Mexico
P&A System Inc.
1720 Louisiana Boulevard, N.E.
Suite 204
Albuquerque, NM 87110
(505) 256-3100
(800) 432-4682

New York
New York Commission on Quality
of Care for the Mentally Disabled
99 Washington Avenue, Suite 100
Albany, NY 12210
(518) 473-4057
(518) 473-7378

North Carolina
Governor's Advocacy Council for
Persons with Disabilities
1318 Dale Street, Suite 100
Raleigh, NC 27605
(919) 733-9250
(800) 821-6922

North Dakota
North Dakota Protection and
Advocacy Project
400 E. Broadway, Suite 515
Bismarck, ND 58501
(701) 224-2972
(800) 472-2670
(800) 642-6694 (24-hour line)

Northern Marian Islands
Karidat
P.O. Box 745
Saipan, CM 96950
(670) 234-6981

Ohio
Ohio Legal Rights Service
8 East Long Street, 6th Floor
Columbus, OH 43215
(614) 466-7264
(800) 282-9181

Oklahoma
Protection and Advocacy Agency
for DD
4150 South 100th East Avenue
210 Cherokee Building
Tulsa, OK 74146-3661
(918) 664-5883

Oregon
Oregon Advocacy Center
625 Board of Trade Building
310 Southwest 4th Avenue
Suite 625
Portland, OR 97204-2309
(503) 243-2081

Pennsylvania
Pennsylvania Protection and
Advocacy, Inc.
116 Pine Street
Harrisburg, PA 17101
(717) 236-8110
(800) 692-7443

Puerto Rico
Planning Research and Special
Projects
Ombudsman for the Disabled
P.O. Box 5163
Hato Rey, PR 00919-5163
(809) 766-2333
(809) 766-2388

Rhode Island
Rhode Island P&A System, Inc.
(RIPAS)
151 Broadway, 3rd Floor
Providence, RI 02903
(401) 831-3150

South Carolina
South Carolina P&A System for the
Handicapped, Inc.
3710 Landmark Drive, Suite 208
Columbia, SC 29204
(803) 782-0639
(800) 782-0639

South Dakota
South Dakota Advocacy Services
221 South Central Avenue
Pierre, SD 57501
(605) 224-8294
(800) 658-4782

Tennessee
Tennessee Protection and
  Advocacy, Inc.
P.O. Box 121257
Nashville, TN 37212
(615) 298-1080
(800) 342-1660

Texas
Advocacy, Inc.
7800 Shoal Creek Boulevard
Suite 171-E
Austin, TX 78757
(512) 454-4816
(800) 252-9108

Utah
Legal Center for People with
  Disabilities
455 East 400 South, Suite 201
Salt Lake City, UT 84111
(801) 363-1347
(800) 662-9080

Vermont
Vermont DD Law Project
12 North Street
Burlington, VT 05401
(802) 863-2881

Citizen Advocacy, Inc.
Chase Mill, 1 Mill Street
Burlington, VT 05401
(802) 655-0329

Virginia
Department for Rights of Virginians
  with Disabilities
James Monroe Building
101 North 14th Street, 17th Floor
Richmond, VA 23219
(804) 225-2042
(800) 552-3062

Virgin Islands
Virgin Islands Advocacy Agency
7A Whim Street, Suite 2
Fredericksted, VI 00840
(809) 772-1200
(809) 776-4303
(809) 772-4641 (TDD)

Washington
Washington Protection and
  Advocacy System
1401 E. Jefferson, Suite 506
Seattle, WA 98122
(206) 324-1521

West Virginia
West Virginia Advocates, Inc.
1524 Kanawha Boulevard East
Charleston, WV 25301
(304) 346-0837
(800) 950-5250

Wisconsin
Wisconsin Coalition for Advocacy
16 N. Carroll Street, Suite 400
Madison, WI 53703
(608) 267-0214

Wyoming
Wyoming P&A System, Inc.
2424 Pioneer Avenue, Suite 101
Cheyenne, WY 82001
(307) 632-3496
(800) 328-1110
(800) 632-3496
(800) 624-7648

Native American
DNA People's Legal Services, Inc.
P.O. Box 306
Window Rock, AZ 86515
(602) 871-4151
(Reprinted with permission
  of Guy D. Ogan.)

APPENDIX F: Parenting Manual: Essential Skills and Practical Suggestions

☐ Contents

Introduction **208**
Reflective Listening **209**
Encouragement **213**
Limit Setting... **215**
Summary **220**
References **221**

☐ Introduction

Through our years of working with parents and children, we have learned that consistent use of three main parenting skills can provide the environment for children to learn love, respect, self-control, responsibility, and self confidence. These three skills are reflective listening, encouragement, and limit setting.

Reflective listening involves paying attention to your children's messages. This skill communicates to your children that they must be very important, because you are interested in them and you want to understand their world. Being encouraged is the opposite of being discouraged. Encouragement is a powerful tool that you, as parents, can use to help your children realize many of their own abilities and strengths, and recognize favorable values and behaviors. By setting realistic limits, you can help your children learn to accept responsibility for their choices (and behaviors). The children are then able to develop the self-control they need in order to have positive outcomes, as a result of their choices.

208

Your children each bring a unique set of characteristics into the world. Each child has a distinctive disposition, personality, and potential for intellectual, physical, emotional, and social development. The interaction between you and your children can influence the degree to which they realize their full potential. By incorporating and using reflective listening, encouragement, and appropriate limit setting, consistently, you can become more comfortable with your parenting ability (Bartz & Rasor, 1983). You will reduce stress for yourselves and your children. They will know where you stand because you will know where you stand (Helmstetter, 1989). It takes strength and courage to do what you know is best. These three principles can help you be a more effective parent as well as have a close, bonded relationship with your children. Though it may be many years before your children realize and appreciate your efforts, we appreciate them—you will too!

☐ Reflective Listening

Listening, really listening to your children means that you *identify* the feelings behind what the children are saying, and not saying (Guerney, 1988). Listening to your children requires letting them know that you recognize their feelings. This communicates your acceptance of your children and validates their feelings. You are like a mirror to your children so that they can see themselves more clearly and gain more understanding about themselves and their feelings (Eyre & Eyre, 1995).

We know that a person who is upset tends to lose perspective. By listening reflectively, we can help a child think through an upsetting problem. That is, we can reflect and clarify the child's feelings to help lay a foundation for the child to resolve the problem. Here is an example of reflective listening:

> **Child**: That teacher is unfair! I'll never do well in tha' ᴊass!
> **Parent**: You're feeling angry and disappointed, and you feel like giving up.

Thus, reflective listening involves grasping what the child feels and means, and then stating this meaning so the child feels understood and accepted. Reflective listening provides a sort of mirror for the child to see himself of herself more clearly. Reflective listening is an active process that involves both verbal and nonverbal behaviors. It involves an empathic response, thus validating and accepting the other person's (child's) experience. It does not introduce new content, opinions, nor offer advice. In other words, it gives the child feedback.

Communication between you and your children is facilitated by *open responses*. An open response signifies that you have heard and understand what your child has said—that *you heard the feelings behind the words* (Dinkmeyer & McKay, 1982). A *closed response* is one that indicates that the listener has neither heard nor understood what was said. Closed responses tend to cut off communication.

Examples of closed and open responses following a child's remark:

Child: I'm so mad at Billy and the other kids! They didn't come over and play with me. There's nothing to do.

Closed Response: Well, things don't always go the way we want them to. That's part of life.

Open Response: It seems as if no one cares, and you're feeling left out.

The first response does not accept the child's feelings; it says that what he or she feels does not matter. This subtle type of put-down blocks communication and may leave the child feeling rejected. As parents, we *do not want our children to hurt*. We often try to protect them by redirecting their feelings. This redirection tends to interfere with the child learning how to understand, cope with, manage, and appropriately express his or her own feelings—responsibility for the child's feelings is taken over by the parent.

The second response recognizes what the child is feeling. It shows acceptance and concern, which opens the communication pathway. Knowing of your acceptance, the child will feel more free, and may decide to tell you more. Reflective listening means that we produce open responses that reflect the child's feelings and meaning. It is not simply parroting or repeating the child's actual words. It requires understanding and sensitivity to a wide variety of feelings, plus the ability to express them. *Reflective listening is non-judgmental.* It is an indication that you are trying to understand the feeling and the meaning of the child's message. Consequently, reflective listening allows the child to feel heard and accepted, encourages the child to understand and accept his or her own feelings, and encourages the child to keep talking (Dinkmeyer & McKay, 1982).

Communication processes are always nonverbal as well as verbal. More than half of communication is nonverbal. Our actions, facial expressions, and tone of voice communicate whether or not we are listening. We can communicate nonverbally through a smile, a frown, or a pat on the back. Deciding to be silent, and not overprotect, nag, or interfere, communicates acceptance. When we respond non-judgmentally by accepting our child's feelings and meanings, both verbally and non-verbally, we show empathy, improve communication, and strengthen the relationship.

Although children sometimes send messages directly (i.e., "I hate that kid"), usually the feeling is expressed by body language and tone of voice, rather than by words. For example: A child is crying and says, "All the kids pick on me!" The child's tone of voice and tears tell you of the hurt, yet the child did not say, "All the kids pick on me— I feel hurt and rejected."

Children tend to be more able to understand their emotional experiences, while they have not yet developed their thinking and rationalizing abilities. *A good listener is sensitive to the accompanying feeling* and reflects it: "You're hurt when the kids pick on you." *When you catch the feeling and reflect it, the child knows you understand.* Also, your child will have increased self-understanding, and words to describe what he or she experiences.

When children send their feelings directly (i.e., "I hate that kid") you can respond by simply acknowledging the feeling: "You are really angry with him!" Notice that the response was different from parroting. Parroting would be just bouncing back the child's words with no indication that you care or understand.

Since reflective listening will be as new to the child as it is to you, expect a startled reaction to your first attempts. Be honest with your child. It is OK to say, "I *am* talking differently. That's because I'm trying to be the best Mommy (or Daddy) that I can be."

Never try to force your children to share their feelings. Your well-intentioned responses may be seen as an invasion of privacy. A power struggle could result. Your children must feel free to accept or reject your offer to help or talk. They will talk when they have the need and feel safe—when they know that you will accept their feelings and try to understand them. Waiting patiently for your children to disclose feelings can be difficult and frustrating; but a *key to reflecting* your children's feelings is to *follow their lead.*

Children will want to continue talking with you about their feelings. This is especially true if they harbor intense feelings such as anger, hurt or sadness. Your response may open the door for a dramatic exchange. For example, your child may charge, "You never let me do anything!" You respond with, "You're angry and feel I'm unfair." The child may come back with, "Yeah, you sure are! You treat me like a baby!" Now what do you do? *Don't panic—keep reflecting*: "It seems to you that I don't trust you." Then continue reflecting until it seems as if the problem is worked out or until the child's tone and behavior indicate a desire to stop.

Don't be discouraged if the child does not respond quickly. Remember that this is a new experience for the child too. He or she may be uncomfortable at first, simply because you are talking different. There will be many opportunities to try again, if you make attempts to respond to the child's invitations. Children don't always work through their problems during these listening sessions. Your patience and efforts will often help them to handle their problems later, on their own.

Don't be concerned about listening and reflecting "just right." You don't have to do it perfectly. *Your attempt to understand is much more important than accurate understanding.* When the child knows that you want to understand, he or she is more likely to help you by providing more information. If you are sincere in an attempt to understand, but mis-identify the feeling, the child will let you know, and you can try again. If you find yourself wishing that you had said something different, say just that (i.e., "That didn't sound right. I wish that I had said . . .").

Parents sometimes find it difficult to think of words to explain feelings. Dinkmeyer and McKay (1982) use the following range of feeling words to describe two common emotions.

To reflect *upset feelings*:

accused	disrespected	left out
angry	doubt	put down
anxious	embarrassed	sad
bored	feel like giving up	unfair
defeated	guilty	unhappy
difficult	hate	unloved
disappointed	hopeless	worried
discouraged	hurt	worthless

To reflect *happy feelings*:

accepted	encouraged	happy
appreciated	excited	love
better	glad	pleased
capable	good	proud
comfortable	grateful	relieved
confident	great	respected

Parents sometimes find themselves blocked when they want to respond to the child's feelings and meanings. *Reflective listening is a skill that requires effort and practice.* Like any skill, it becomes easier and more natural as you practice it more. It is OK if you are not an expert, especially when you are first learning. The most important thing is that you are trying.

When you are about to respond to your child, think to yourself: "What is my child feeling?" Think of a feeling word that describes the emotion being experienced and expressed by the child. For example, if your son says, "I'll sure be glad when school's out! It's stupid!" (Question: "What is he feeling?" Possible answer: "bored"). Now put the feeling word into a sentence: "You seem to be really bored with school." If you concentrate on asking yourself the question, "What is my child feeling?" you will find that your listening and accurate reflecting gets easier and easier.

☐ Encouragement

Encouragement can be a key element in helping your child build self-esteem. However, encouragement can be tricky. *The single most important rule is that encouragement deals only with the child's efforts and accomplishments, not with his or her character and personality attributes.* When a boy cleans up the yard, it is only natural to comment on how hard he has worked, and on how good the yard looks. It is highly unrelated, unhelpful, and inappropriate to tell him that he is a "good boy."

Similar to reflecting, words of encouragement should not be judging of the child; rather they should *mirror* for the child a realistic picture of his efforts and accomplishments (Ginott, 1956). Avoid words of value and judgment, such as good, bad, pretty, ugly, excellent, great, and the like. The use of value-laden words by parents sets children up to become "pleasers" and "approval junkies." The long term-result is that their self-concept and self-confidence are dependent upon the approval of others (Nelsen, 1981). By avoiding value– and judgment–laden words, you help your children develop positive self-image and appreciation of their own efforts. By stating only what you see the children have done (are capable of doing), they can conclude that they are accepted and have capabilities.

As Nathaniel Branden (cited in Faber & Mazlish, 1980) has said in his book, *The Psychology of Self-Esteem*, "There is no value judgment more important to man, no factor more decisive in his psychological development and motivation—than the estimate he passes on himself" (p. 173). Self-evaluation has profound influence on a child's (or adult's) emotions, thought processes, values, wishes, goals, choices, and behaviors.

Your comments should be phrased so that the child draws positive inferences about himself or herself. For example: Kenny, age ten, helped his father fix up the basement. In the process he had to move heavy furniture.

> **Father:** The workbench is so heavy. It is hard to move, but you did it.
> **Kenny (with pride):** I did!
> **Father:** That took a lot of strength.
> **Kenny:** I'm pretty strong, huh!

In this example, Father commented on the difficulty of the task. *It was the child himself who came to his own conclusions about his personal power.* It is important how parents and others communicate with children. Through this communication, children make conclusions about themselves. Had his father said, "You are so strong" then Kenny might have replied, "No, not really." A fruitless, if not bitter argument might have followed, which would probably have discouraged both Kenny and his father.

Encouragement has two parts: (1) our word, and (2) the child's conclusions. Our words should state clearly that we appreciate the child's effort, work, achievement, help, consideration, or creation. Our words should be framed so that the child will almost invariably draw a positive, yet realistic, conclusion about his or her personality. Our words should be like a magic canvas upon which children cannot help but to paint positive pictures of themselves.

Follow these steps in giving encouragement:

1. Describe what you see.

> **Mother:** I see a clean floor, a smooth bed, and books neatly lined up on the shelf.

2. Describe what you feel.

> **Mother:** It's a pleasure to walk into this room.

3. Sum up the child's favorable behavior with one word.

> **Mother:** You sorted out your pencils, crayons, and pens. That's what I call organized!

Examples of phrases that recognize effort and show acceptance:

"I like the way you handled that."
"I'm glad you're pleased with it."
"You've really worked hard on that."
"It looks like you spent a lot of time on that."

In summary, encouragement should contain the following:

1. Valuing and accepting children, as they are, not putting conditions on acceptance.
2. Pointing out the positive aspects of behavior ("I like the way you handled that").
3. Showing faith in children so they can come to believe in themselves ("I know you and your sister can work that out.")
4. Recognizing effort and improvement, rather than requiring achievement.
4. Showing appreciation for contributions.

☐ Limit Setting

Limit setting helps the child with his or her feelings and conduct. The parents allow the child to express what he or she feels, but limit and direct inappropriate behavior. The limits are set in a manner that preserves the self-respect of the parent as well as that of the child. The limits are neither arbitrary nor capricious, but educational and character-building (Reynolds, 1990).

Limits are applied without violence and without excessive anger. The child is likely to resent the restrictions or limits, and is not punished additionally for not liking the prohibitions.

In the setting of limits, the outcome depends on the process. A limit should be stated in a way that tells the child clearly what constitutes unacceptable conduct, and what substitute(s) will be accepted.

Mother: Your brother is not for hitting. It is OK to hit that pillow.

A limit must be stated firmly, so that it carries only one message to the child: "This prohibition is for real. I mean business." In setting limits, the one who hesitates is lost in endless arguments. Restrictions, invoked haltingly and clumsily, become a challenge to children and evoke a battle of wills, which no one can win. A limit must be stated in a manner that is deliberately calculated to minimize resentment and to save self-esteem. The very process of limit-setting should convey authority, not insult. It should deal with a specific event.

Example: Six-year-old Cindy went with Mother to the department store. While Mother made a purchase, Cindy roamed around the toy section and selected three toys that she wanted. When mother came back, Cindy asked confidently, "Mom, can I have these?" Mother blurted out, "More toys? You already have more toys than you know what to do with. Everything you see, you want. I am not made of money!"

A minute later, Mother realized the source of her daughter's anger and tried to pacify her by buying her a cookie. But the sorrowful look on Cindy's face remained.

When a child requests something that we must deny, we can at least show respect by granting him or her the satisfaction of having the wish for it. Thus, Cindy's mother might have said: "You wish you could take these toys home. I bet you wish you could take home all of the toys in this store. But there is no money in the budget for toys today. You can have some ice cream or a cookie though. Which do you choose, ice cream or a cookie?"

Perhaps Cindy would choose the latter, and the whole incident might be concluded with Mother buying a cookie for Cindy. Or perhaps Cindy would cry. In either case, Mother would stick to her decision, and to the choices she offered. She may again show understanding by mirroring her daughter's desire for toys, but the limit is upheld. "You wish you could have the toys. You want them very much, but we can't buy toys today."

When a parent is not sure of what to do, it is best to do nothing except to think and clarify one's own attitudes. It is always OK to say, "I need a few minutes to think about this." Following is Landreth's (1991) A, C, T model which is a respectful and effective way to set limits:

1. The parent *acknowledges what the child is feeling* and reflects this using simple words: "You wish you could go to the movies tonight."
2. The parent clearly *communicates the specific limit*: "But the rule in our house is no movies on school nights."
3. The parent *targets appropriate alternative ways in which the feelings can be expressed*: "You may go to the movies on Friday or Saturday night. Which do you choose?"

It is also helpful if the parent subsequently reflects the child's resentment that is likely to arise when restrictions are imposed. This validates the child's feelings and helps the child learn to express his or her own feelings (i.e., "It is obvious that you don't like the rule. You wish that there weren't such a rule. You wish the rule said that every night is movie night.").

It is not always necessary or feasible to phrase the limit in this pattern. At times, it is necessary to state the limit first and mirror feelings later. For example, when a child is about to hit his sister with a bat, the mother should say, "Not her, the ball!" She will do well to deflect the child by pointing to the ball. The mother may even need to grab the bat. She can then get at the angry feelings and suggest some appropriate and less dangerous ways of expressing them. For example:

> "You may be as angry as you want at your sister. You may be furious. Inside yourself, you may dislike her, but there will be no hurting. If you want to, you can hit the ball, but your sister is not for hitting."

Limits are accepted more willingly when they point out the function of an object. "The chair is for sitting, not for standing" is much better than "don't stand on the chair."

At times, children will continue to break limits after the limits have been clearly and respectfully communicated. Children may need to have the limits communicated two or three times. The primary goals or reasons that children misbehave, break rules, and exceed limits are to seek attention, revenge, power, or display inadequacy (Dinkmeyer and McKay, 1982). The first three are relatively easy to understand. However, it is difficult for some parents to believe that their child breaks rules just to prove that he or she "always fails" or is "the problem child."

If limits continue to be broken, then *natural or logical consequences* need to occur in order for the child to learn to take responsibility for his or her choices and to enhance self-control. Often, parents will remind, coax, nag, threaten, punish, or excuse their child for not following through on certain rules, or breaking the certain limits. Such reactions by parents often reinforce the misbehavior. To remedy this, do the unexpected, and *respond rather than react*. Responding involves a planned, rational (logical) decision. Reacting refers to emotional and reflexive behavior.

An effective way of responding is to *allow natural and logical consequences to occur, which has advantages over rewards and punishment*. First, it holds children, not their parents, responsible for their own behavior. Discipline, in its truest sense, is teaching. Punishment, however, is simply designed to stop an unwanted behavior. Second, it allows children to make their own decisions about which behaviors are appropriate. Third, it permits children to learn from the natural order of events and the social order of events, rather than forcing them to comply with the wishes of others. When using natural or logical consequences, remember to remain calm, communicate manner-of-factly, show goodwill, behave respectfully, give choices, and be willing to accept the child's decision (Nelsen, 1981).

The child who refuses to eat, gets hungry. The child who refuses to wear mittens, gets cold hands. These are examples of natural consequences. Many situations do not provide the opportunity for natural consequences to occur. Logical consequences must then be applied—especially in instances of danger to the child. (It would not be appropriate to allow a child to kick a wild bear and then experience the natural consequence.)

Logical consequences must be *respectful, reasonable, and related.* Nelsen (1981) describes these as the three Rs of logical consequences. They also must be manageable by the parent. For example, it is not reasonable to ground a child for six months, because many events that parents want the child to experience will arise during that time frame. *It is better to have a very small consequence that can be complied with 100% than to have a severe consequence that is partially and inconsistently experienced.*

Logical consequences permit a child to learn from social experiences, by acknowledging mutual respect and mutual rights. For the consequences to be effective, the child must see them as logically related to their misbehavior. In other words, *the consequences must "fit" their behavior in a logical way.* For example:

> **Father:** (TV is Blaring) Jim, I realize it's Saturday morning and you enjoy your cartoons, but Mom and I are trying to sleep. So, you may choose to turn the TV down, or to play outside. Which do you choose?

Logical consequences are related to the misbehavior:

> **Mother:** Susan, I am going to vacuum the carpets today. I can't vacuum in your room if there are toys and clothes lying on the floor. So, you can choose to pick up your toys and clothes, or you can choose for me to place them in bags and put them in your closet.

Logical consequences are impersonal—they imply no element of personal or moral judgment by the parent:

> Without permission, Hugh borrowed his father's hammer, and then lost it. Dad handled the situation by focusing on the impersonal fact that the hammer must be replaced:

> **Father:** How will you replace the hammer, Hugh?

Logical consequences are concerned with present and future behavior and do not focus on past mistakes:

> **Mother:** (The next time Ralph asks to go out after coming home late) Ralph, you can't go, because you chose not to take responsibility for coming home on time. We'll try again tomorrow.

When logical consequences are invoked, the parent's voice is friendly and implies goodwill:

Charles: Mom, I'm going to play with Champ now.
Mother: (Matter-of-factly) No, Charles—You haven't taken time to give him his food and water today. We'll try again tomorrow.

Logical consequences permit choice:

Father: You may choose to sit quietly at the table or you may choose to leave the table.

The purpose of allowing natural consequences to occur and designing logical consequences is to encourage children to take responsibility for their choices, not to force children's submission. This mode of discipline permits a child to choose and then be accountable for the decision—whether or not it turns out well. You must permit your children to make poor decisions, because they will learn from the consequences.

Remaining matter-of-fact and non-punishing is extremely important. This means separating the deed from the doer. If you can view misbehavior objectively, rather than regarding it as a personal affront, you will be much more effective. If you were trying to teach your child a new skill, such as an athletic or musical skill, you would probably be patient. You would expect and accept mistakes. If you can learn to approach any sort of mistake this way, you will find it easier to regard misbehavior as a learning experience, rather than a violation of parental authority.

When limit setting and logical consequences do not work, look for natural causes for rebellion such as hunger, fatigue, and extreme stress. Take care of the physical needs and crises before expecting cooperation.

Remain in control, respecting yourself and your child. You are not a failure if your child rebels, and your child is not bad. Set reasonable consequences if your child disobeys. Let your child choose to behave appropriately or inappropriately, but set a reasonable consequence for misbehavior. Emphasize the fact that it is the child's choice. This is how the child will learn effective and appropriate decision-making skills. For example:

Mother: If you choose to leave your toys on the floor, then you choose to not play with them tomorrow.

If your child refuses to choose, you choose for him or her. The child's refusal to choose is also a choice. Set the consequences:

Father: If you choose not to turn the TV off, or turn it down, then you choose for me to pick the one that is most convenient to me.

Finally, enforce the consequences. Do not back down. The most important component of limit setting and discipline is consistency. You must say what you mean, and mean what you say. If your child is upset, it is OK to briefly and respectfully remind him or her "You chose not to play with those toys when you chose to leave them on the floor." If you give in to your child's anger or tears, then you will lose your role as a parent, lose your power, communicate that you do not need to be respected, and help your child to learn techniques to better manipulate you. Consistent, reasonable, respectful, and related consequences to your child's choices will help him or her to learn to respect others, to be accountable for his or her actions, to enhance self-control, and to make better choices. Also, it will decrease the need for you to set limits and discipline your child.

☐ Summary

Reflective listening can help promote a warm and trusting relationship between you and your children. According to Guerney (1988):

> Showing understanding helps your child to understand his own feelings and to learn how to cope with them. It helps him to build self-confidence by increasing his ability to solve his own problems. Accepting a child's feelings is so powerful a method that it can often help children see things more clearly, and therefore, they are able to solve things themselves without your having to tell them what to do or how to do it. (p. 22)

Encouragement is a crucial link in helping your children develop autonomy, self-reliance, and self-esteem. It may feel awkward at first when you are trying to think of *encouraging statements* to say to your children, but it is a skill that will greatly benefit them by enhancing their self-confidence and belief in themselves.

Limits and choices give children the security of knowing what is expected of them. Just imagine if you and your child were staying on the 51st floor of a hotel. Outside your hotel room is a balcony that overlooks the city. Now imagine going out on that balcony to look at the city. Imagine that there is not a railing of any kind around the balcony. Would you go out on the balcony? Would you sit or stand on the balcony for an hour? Limits provide, for children, the railing of security and safety around the balcony outside life's experiences. Remember that the next time you are tempted not to follow through on a limit. The sense of safety and security you give your children through limits will benefit them for a lifetime; they will be prepared to make choices that will benefit them as adults because you took the risk of letting your children make choices and live with the consequences.

When limit setting does not work, look for natural causes for children's unacceptable behavior. For example, a child who persistently rebels and does not respond cooperatively to limits may be hungry, stressed, or emotionally concerned about bullying from peers. Take care of your child's physical needs and crises before expecting cooperation.

Parenting is demanding and, at times, exhausting. It depends on intelligence, heart, soul, and especially perseverance. It is very important to be kind to ourselves, even when we do not live up to our expectations. Remember that it is OK to make mistakes. However, you must acknowledge your mistakes, and if appropriate, apologize. Then explain that you are trying to be the best parent that you can be. Being good at anything requires patience and hard work, but the rewards of success are worth it. There is nothing more important than being successful at parenting, and nothing more rewarding. The suggestions in this parenting manual may take patience and practice, but they can be rewarding to you and your children. Give children your attention, acceptance, love, respect, and understanding that they deserve and need. They will reward you by being loving, caring, self-confident, respectful, and responsible.

☐ References

Bartz, W. R., & Rasor, R. A. (1983). *Surviving with Kids* (4th ed.). San Luis Obispo, CA: Impact.

Dinkmeyer, D. & McKay, G. D. (1982). *The Parent's Handbook*. Circle Pines, MN: American Guidance Service.

Eyre, L., & Eyre, R. (1995). *Teaching your Child Sensitivity* (2nd ed.). New York: Fireside.

Faber, A. & Mazlish, E. (1980). *How to Talk So Kids Will Listen and Listen So Kids Will Talk*. New York: Rawson Wade.

Ginott, H. (1956). *Between Parent and Child*. New York: Avon.

Guerney, L. (1988). *Parenting: A Skills Training Manual* (2nd ed.). State College, PA: Institute for the Development of Emotional and Life Skills.

Helmstetter, S. (1989). *Predictive Parenting: What to Say When You Talk to Your Kids*. New York: William Morrow.

Landreth, G. L. (Ed.) (1991). *Play Therapy: The Art of the Relationship*. Muncie, IN: Accelerated Development.

Nelsen, J. (1981). *Positive Discipline* (2nd ed.). New York: Ballantine.

Reynolds, E. L. (1990). *Guiding Young Children: A Child-Centered Approach*. Mountain View, CA: Mayfield.

REFERENCES

Achenbach, T. M., Howell, C. T., Quay, H. C., & Conners, C. K. (1991). National survey of problems and competencies among four- to sixteen-year-olds. *Monographs of the Society for Research in Child Development, 56*(3, serial no. 225).

Albano, A. M., Chorpita, B. F., & Barlow, D. H. (1996). Childhood anxiety disorders. In E. J. Mash & R. A. Barkley (Eds.), *Child psychopathology* (pp. 196-241). New York: Guilford Press.

Alexander, E. D. (1964). School centered play-therapy program. *Personnel and Guidance Journal, 43,* 256-261.

American Association for Marriage and Family Therapy. (1991). *AAMFT code of ethics.* Washington, DC: Author.

American Counseling Association. (1995). *Code of ethics and standards of practice.* Alexandria, VA: Author.

American Psychiatric Association. (1994). *Diagnostic and statistical manual of mental disorders* (4th ed.). Washington, DC: Author.

American Psychological Association. (1995). *Ethical principles of psychologists and code of conduct.* Washington, DC: Author.

Araoz, D. L., & Carrese, M. A. (1996). *Solution-oriented brief therapy for adjustment disorders: A guide for providers under managed care.* New York: Brunner/Mazel.

Arthur, G. L., & Swanson, C. D. (1993). *Confidentiality and privileged communication.* Alexandria, VA: American Counseling Association.

Axline, V. (1969). *Play therapy.* New York: Ballantine.

Baggerly, J. N. (1999). *Adjustment of kindergarten children through play sessions facilitated by fifth grade students trained in child-centered play therapy procedures and skills.* Unpublished doctoral dissertation, University of North Texas, Denton.

Barber, B. K., & Olsen, J. A. (1997). Socialization in context: Connection, regulation, and autonomy in the family, school, and neighborhood, and with peers. *Journal of Adolescent Research, 12,* 287–315.

Barkley, R. A. (1995). *Taking charge of ADHD: The complete, authoritative guide for parents.* New York: Guilford Press.

Barkley, R. A. (1996). Attention-deficit/hyperactivity disorder. In E. J. Mash & R. A. Barkley (Eds.), *Child psychopathology* (pp. 63–112). New York: Guilford Press.

Barkley, R. A. (1997). *Defiant children: A clinician's manual for assessment and parent training.* New York: Guilford Press.

Bartz, W. R., & Rasor, R. A. (1983). *Surviving with kids* (4th ed.). San Luis Obispo, CA: Impact.

Berg, B. (1989). Cognitive play therapy for children of divorce. In P. Keller & S. Heyman (Eds.), *Innovations in Clinical Practice: A Source Book* (Volume 8) (pp.143–173). Sarasota, FL: Professional Resource Exchange.

Bergman, J. S. (1985). *Fishing for barracuda: Pragmatics of brief systemic therapy.* New York: W. W. Norton.

Bernard, J. M., & Goodyear, R. K. (1998). *Fundamentals of clinical supervision.* Boston: Allyn & Bacon.

Bernstein, B. E. & Hartsell, T. L. (1998). *The portable lawyer for mental health professionals.* New York: Wiley.

Bishop, J. K. (1971). Play therapy in the schools. *Alberta Counsellor, 2,* 41–44.

Blaine, G. B. (1969). The effect of divorce upon the personality development of children and youth. In E. A. Grollman (Ed.), *Explaining divorce to children.* Boston: Beacon Press.

Blalock, R. (1997). Personal communication, August 17, 1997.

Blatt, S. J., & Homann, E. (1992). Parent-child interaction in the etiology of dependent and self-critical depression. *Clinical Psychology Review, 12,* 47–91.

Bloom, B. L. (1981). Focused single-session therapy: Initial development and evaluation. In S. H. Budman (Ed.), *Forms of brief therapy.* New York: Guilford Press.

Bowlby, J. (1969). *Attachment and loss.* New York: Basic Books.

Bowlby, J. (1980). *Loss: Sadness and depression.* New York: Basic.

Braswell, L., & Bloomquist, M. L. (1991). *Cognitive-behavioral therapy with ADHD children.* New York: Guilford Press.

Bratton, S. C. (1994). Filial therapy with single parents. (Doctoral dissertation, University of North Texas, Denton, TX, 1993). *Dissertation Abstracts International, 54(8),* A2890.

Brazelton, T. B. (1995). *Touchpoints* (4th ed.). Menlo Park, CA: Addison-Wesley.

Brazelton, T. B., & Cramer, B. G. (1990). *The earliest relationship: Parents, infants, and the drama of early attachment.* Reading, MA: Perseus Books.

Briere, J., & Runtz, M. (1991). The long-term effects of sexual abuse: A review and synthesis. *New Directions on Mental Health Services, 51,* 3–13.

Brody, V. (1997). Developmental play therapy. In K. J. O'Connor & L. M. Braverman (Eds.), *Play therapy theory and practice: A comparative presentation* (pp. 160–181). New York: Wiley.

Bromfield, R. (1992). *Playing for real: The world of a play therapist.* New York: Dutton.

Browne, A., & Finkelhor, D. (1986). Impact of child sexual abuse: A review of the research. *Psychological Bulletin, 99,* 66–77.

Burt, M. S., & Burt, B. B. (1996). *Stepfamilies: The step by step model of brief therapy.* New York: Brunner/Mazel.

Carroll, F. & Oaklander, V. (1997). Gestalt play therapy. In K. J. O'Connor & L. M. Braverman (Eds.), *Play therapy theory and practice: A comparative presentation* (pp. 184–203). New York: Wiley.

Carkhuff, R. J. (1969). *Helping and human relations: A primer for lay and professional helpers.* New York: Holt, Rinehart, & Winston.

Chethik, M. (1989). *Techniques of child therapy: Psychodynamic strategies.* New York: Guilford Press.

Clarke, J. I. (1978). *Self-esteem: A family affair.* New York: HarperCollins.

Cole, M., & Cole, S.R. (1996). *The development of children* (3rd ed.). New York: W. H. Freeman.

Copley, B., Ferryan, B., & O'Neill, L. (1987). Play therapy and counseling children. *British Journal of Occupational Therapy, 50,* 413–416.

Corey, G. (1991). *Theory and practice of counseling and psychotherapy* (4th ed.). Pacific Grove, CA: Brooks/Cole.

Corey, G., Corey, M. S., & Callanan, P. (1998). *Issues and ethics in the helping professions* (5th ed.). Pacific Grove, CA: Brooks/Cole.

Craig, G. J. (1983). *Human development* (3rd ed.). Englewood Cliffs, NJ: Prentice-Hall.

Crow, J. (1989). *Play therapy with low achievers in reading*. Unpublished doctoral dissertation, University of North Texas, Denton.

Cunningham, C., & MacFarlane, K. (1991). *When children molest other children: Group treatment strategies for young sexual abusers*. Orwell, VT: Safer Society Press.

D'Amico, P. J., & Friedman, A. G. (1998). General fears. In C. E. Schaefer & A. R. Eisen (Eds.), *Helping parents solve their children's behavior problems* (pp. 39–66). Northvale, NJ: Aronson.

Damon, L., Todd, J. & MacFarlane, K. (1987). *Child Welfare, LXVI*(2), 125–137.

Davenport, Y. B., Zahn-Waxler, C., Adland, M. L., & Mayfield, A. (1984). Early child-rearing practices in families with a manic-depressive parent. *American Journal of Psychiatry, 141*, 230–235.

de Shazer, S. (1982). *Patterns of brief family therapy: An egosystemic approach*. New York: Guilford Press.

de Shazer, S. (1988). *Clues: Investigating solutions in brief therapy*. New York: W. W. Norton.

Dinkmeyer, D., & McKay, G. D. (1982). *The parent's handbook: Systematic training for effective parenting*. Circle Pines, MN: American Guidance Service.

Dreikurs, R., & Stolz, V. (1964). *Children: The challenge*. New York: Hawthorn.

Epstein, R. S. (1994). *Keeping boundaries: Maintaining safety and integrity in the psychotherapeutic process*. Washington, DC: American Psychiatric Press.

Erikson, E. H. (1963). *Childhood and society* (2nd ed.). New York: W. W. Norton.

Erikson, E. H. (1964). *Insight and responsibility*. New York: W. W. Norton.

Eyre, L., & Eyre, R. (1995). *Teaching your child sensitivity* (2nd ed.). New York: Fireside.

Faber, A., & Mazlish, E. (1980). *How to talk so kids will listen and listen so kids will talk*. New York: Avon.

Faller, D. C. (1988). *Child sexual abuse: An interdisciplinary manual for diagnosis, case management, and treatment*. New York: Columbia University Press.

Fallone, G. P. (1998, April). Parent training and ADHD. *The ADHD Report*, 9–12.

Fergusson, D. M., & Mullen, P.E. (1999). *Childhood sexual abuse: An evidence-based perspective*. Thousand Oaks, CA: Sage Publications.

Finkelhor, D. (1986). *A sourcebook on child sexual abuse*. Newbury Park, CA: Sage.

Freeman, J., Epston, D. & Lobovits, D. (1997). *Playful approaches to serious problems*. New York: Norton.

Friedman, S. (1997). *Time-effective psychotherapy*. Needham Heights, MA: Allyn & Bacon.

Friedman, R. J., & Doyal, G. T. (1992). *Management of children and adolescents with attention deficit-hyperactivity disorder* (3rd ed.). Austin, TX: Pro-ed.

Gardner, R. A. (1970). *The boys and girls book about divorce*. New York: Bantam.

Gardner, R. A. (1993). *Story-telling in psychotherapy with children*. Northvale, NJ: Aronson.

Gil, E. (1991). *The healing power of play: Working with abused children*. New York: Guilford Press.

Gil, E. (1994). *Play in family therapy*. New York: Guilford Press.

Gilliland, B. E., James, R. K., Roberts, G. T., & Bowman, J. T. (1984). *Theories and strategies in counseling and psychotherapy*. Englewood Cliffs, New Jersey: Prentice Hall.

Ginott, H. G. (1956). *Between parent and child*. New York: Avon.

Glenn, H. S., & Nelsen, J. (1989). *Raising self-reliant children in a self-indulgent world*. Rocklin, CA: Prima.

Glover, G. (1996). *Filial therapy with native americans on the flathead reservation*. Unpublished doctoral dissertation, University of North Texas, Denton, TX.

Green, M. (1980). *Pediatric diagnosis* (3rd ed.). Philadelphia: W. B. Saunders.

Greenspan, S. I. (1991). *The clinical interview of the child*. Washington, DC: American Psychiatric Press.

Grollman, E. A. (Ed.). (1969). *Explaining divorce to children.* Boston: Beacon Press.

Guerney, B. G. (1976). Filial therapy used as a treatment method for disturbed children. *Evaluation, 3,* 34–35.

Guerney, B. G., Guerney, L. F., & Stover, L. (1972). Facilitative therapist attitudes in training parents as psychotherapeutic agents. *The Family Coordinator, 21,* 275–278.

Guerney, L. (1983). Client-centered (nondirective) play therapy. In C. E. Schaefer & K. J. O'Connor (Eds.), *Handbook of play therapy* (pp. 21–64). New York: Wiley.

Guerney, L. (1988). *Parenting: A skills training manual* (2nd ed.). State College, PA: Institute for the Development of Emotional and Life Skills.

Gupta, V. B. (1999). *Manual of developmental and behavioral problems in children.* New York: Marcel Dekker.

Hambidge, G. (1982). Structured play therapy. In G. L. Landreth (Ed.), *Play therapy* (pp. 105–119). Springfield, IL: Thomas.

Hammen, C. (1991). *Depression runs in families: The social context of risk and resilience in children of depressed mothers.* New York: Springer-Verlag.

Hammen, C., & Rudolph, K. D. (1996). Childhood depression. In E. J. Mash & R. A. Barkley (Eds.), *Child psychopathology* (pp. 153–195). New York: Guilford Press.

Harris, Z. (1995). *Filial therapy with incarcerated mothers.* Unpublished doctoral dissertation, University of North Texas, Denton, TX.

Harter, S. (1983). Cognitive-developmental considerations in the conduct of play therapy. In C. E. Schaefer & K. J. O'Connor (Eds.), *Handbook of play therapy* (pp. 89–127). New York: Wiley.

Hartsell, T. (1997). Personal communication, July 24, 1997.

Helmstetter, S. (1989). *Predictive parenting: What to say when you talk to your kids.* New York: William Morrow.

Hendrix, D. H. (1991). Ethics and intrafamily confidentiality in counseling with children. *Journal of Mental Health Counseling, 13,* 323–333.

Herlihy, B. & Corey, G. (1997). *Boundary issues in counseling: Multiple roles and responsibilities.* Alexandria, VA: American Counseling Association.

Homeyer, L. E. (1994). Play therapy behaviors of sexually abused children. Unpublished doctoral dissertation, University of North Texas, Denton.

Hoyt, M. F. (1995). *Brief therapy and managed care.* San Francisco: Jossey-Bass.

Jacobs, E. H. (1998). *Fathering the ADHD child.* Northvale, NJ: Aronson.

Jacobson, G. F. (1983). *The multiple crises of marital separation and divorce.* New York: Grune & Stratton.

James, O. (1997). *Play therapy: A comprehensive guide.* Northvale, NJ: Aronson.

Johnson, K. (1989). *Trauma in the lives of children.* Alameda, CA: Hunter House.

Kagan, J. (1994). *Galen's prophecy: Temperament in human nature.* New York: Basic Books.

Kale, A. (1997). *Filial therapy with parents of children experiencing learning difficulties.* Unpublished doctoral dissertation, University of North Texas, Denton, TX.

Kao, S., & Landreth, G. L. (1997). Evaluating the impact of child-centered play therapy training. *International Journal of Play Therapy, 6*(2), 1–20.

Kell, B. L., & Mueller, W. J. (1966). *Impact and change: A study of counseling relationships.* New York: Appleton-Century-Crofts.

Kennedy, E., Spence, S. H., & Hensley, R. (1989). An examination of the relationship between childhood depression and social competence amongst primary school children. *Journal of Child Psychology and Psychiatry, 30,* 561–573.

Kochanska, G. (1991). Patterns of inhibition to the unfamiliar in children of normal and affectively ill mothers. *Child Development, 62,* 250–263.

Kottman, T. (1995). *Partners in play: An Adlerian approach to play therapy.* Alexandria, VA: American Counseling Association.

L'Abate, L., Ganahl, G., & Hansen, J. C. (1986). *Methods of family therapy.* Englewood Cliffs, NJ: Prentice-Hall.

Landreth, G. L. (1987). Play therapy: Facilitative use of child's play in elementary school counseling. *Elementary School Guidance & Counseling, 21,* 253–261.

Landreth, G. (1989). Personal communication, June 21, 1989.

Landreth, G. L. (1991). *Play therapy: The art of the relationship.* Muncie, IN: Accelerated Development.

Landreth, G. L., Homeyer, L. E., Glover, G. & Sweeney, D. S. (1996). *Play therapy interventions with children's problems.* Northvale, NJ: Aronson

Landreth, G. L., & Sweeney, D. S. (1997). Child-centered play therapy. In K. J. O'Connor & L. M. Braverman (Eds.), *Play therapy theory and practice: A comparative presentation* (pp. 17–43). New York: Wiley.

Lazarus, A. A. (1997). *Brief but comprehensive psychotherapy.* New York: Springer.

Levy, D. M. (1982). Release therapy. In G. L. Landreth (Ed.), *Play therapy* (pp. 92–104). Springfield, IL: Thomas.

Lockwood, J., & Harr, B. (1973). Psychodrama: A therapeutic tool with children in group play therapy. *Group Psychotherapy and Psychodrama, 26*(3–4), 53–67.

Long, S. (1986). Guidelines for treating young children. In K. MacFarlane & J. Waterman (Eds.), *Sexual abuse of young children* (pp. 220–243). New York: Guilford Press.

MacFarlane, K., & Korbin, J. (1983). Confronting the incest secret long after the fact: A family study of multiple victimization with strategies for intervention. *Child Abuse and Neglect, 7,* 225–240.

Mash, E. J., & Dozois, J. A. (1996). Child psychopathology: A developmental-systems approach. In E. J. Mash & R. A. Barkley (Eds.), *Child psychopathology* (pp. 3–60). New York: Guilford Press.

McCarney, S. B. (1992). *Emotional or behavior disorder intervention manual.* Columbia, MO: Hawthorne Educational Services.

McCarney, S. B., & Bauer, A. M. (1990). *The parent's guide: Solutions to today's most common behavior problems in the home.* Columbia, MO: Hawthorne Educational Services.

Mendell, A. (1983). Play therapy with children of divorced parents. In C. Schaefer & K. O'Connor (Eds.), *Handbook of play therapy* (pp. 320–354). New York: Wiley.

Mercer, L. (1997). Personal communication, September 30, 1997.

Merriam-Webster, Inc. (1984). *Webster's ninth new collegiate dictionary* (9th ed.). Springfield, MA: Author.

Milos, M. E., & Reiss, S. (1982). Effects of three play conditions on separation anxiety in young children. *Journal of Counseling and Consulting Psychology, 50*(3), 389–395.

Morrison, J. D., (Ed.). (1948). *Masterpieces of religious verse.* New York: Harper.

Moustakas, C. (1997). *Relationship play therapy.* Northvale, NJ: Aronson.

National Association of Social Workers. (1996). *Code of ethics.* Washington, DC: Author.

Nelsen, J. (1981). *Positive discipline* (2nd ed.). New York: Ballantine.

Neuman, M. G. (1998). *Helping your kids cope with divorce the sandcastles way.* New York: Random House.

Norton, C. C., & Norton, B. E. (1997). *Reaching children through play: An experiential approach.* Denver, CO: Publishers Cooperative.

O'Connor, K. J. (1991). *The play therapy primer: An integration of theories and techniques.* New York: Wiley.

Ogan, G. D. (1994). *Can anyone help my child?* Abilene, TX: Faith Publishing.

Olweus, D. (1979). Stability of aggressive reaction patterns in males: A review. *Psychological Bulletin, 86,* 852–875.

Osherson, S. (1995). *The passions of fatherhood.* New York: Fawcett.

Pearce, J. W. & Pezzot-Pearce, T. D. (1997). *Psychotherapy of abused and neglected children*. New York: Guilford Press.

Pope, K. S. (1991). Dual relationships in psychocounseling. *Ethics and Behavior, 1*, 21–34.

Radke-Yarrow, M., Cummings, E. M., Kuczynski, L., & Chapman, M. (1985). Patterns of attachment in two- and three-year-olds in normal families and families with parental depression. *Child Development, 56*, 884–893.

Rief, S. (1997). *The ADD/ADHD checklist: An easy reference for parents and teachers*. Paramus, NJ: Prentice Hall.

Rencken, R. H. (1989). *Intervention strategies for sexual abuse*. Alexandria, VA: American Association for Counseling and Development.

Reynolds, E. L. (1990). *Guiding young children: A child-centered approach*. Mountain View, CA: Mayfield.

Ricci, I. (1997). *Mom's house, dad's house: A complete guide for parents who are separated, divorced, or remarried*. New York: Simon & Schuster.

Ries, A., & Trout, J. (1986). *Positioning: The battle for your mind* (2nd ed.). New York: McGraw-Hill.

Rogers, C. (1951). *Client-centered therapy*. Boston: Houghton Mifflin

Rossiter, A. (1988). A model for group intervention with preschool children experiencing separation and divorce. *American Journal of Orthopsychiatry, 58*(3), 387–396.

Ryan, V., & Wilson, K. (1996). *Case studies in non-directive play therapy*. Philadelphia: Balliere Tindall.

Sanford, L. T. (1982). *The silent children*. New York: McGraw-Hill.

Schaffer, S. J. (1997). Don't be aloof about record-keeping; it may be your best liability coverage. *The National Psychologist, 6*, 21.

Schetky, D. H., & Green, A. H. (1988). *Child sexual abuse*. New York: Brunner/Mazel.

Sears, W., & Sears, M. (1993). *The baby book: Everything you need to know about your baby—From birth to age two*. Boston: Little, Brown & Co.

Selekman, M. D. (1997). *Solution-focused therapy with children*. New York: Guilford Press.

Sgroi, S. M. (1982). *Handbook of clinical intervention in child sexual abuse*. Lexington, Massachusetts: Lexington.

Sheldon, C. (1997). Personal communication, August 20, 1997.

Silver, L. B. (1999). *Attention-deficit/hyperactivity disorder: A clinical guide to diagnosis and treatment for health and mental health professionals*. Washington, DC: American Psychiatric Press.

Tatum, R. (1997). Personal communication, August 14, 1997.

Texas State Board of Examiners of Professional Counselors (1994). *Licensed professional counselor act*. Austin, TX: Author.

Thomas, A., & Chess, S. (1977). *Temperament and development*. New York: Brunner/Mazel.

Thomas, A., Chess, S., & Birch, H. G. (1968). *Temperament and behavior disorders in children*. New York: New York University Press.

Van der Zande, I. (1993). *1, 2, 3 . . .The toddler years*. Santa Cruz, CA: Santa Cruz Toddler Care Center.

Van der Zande, J. W. (1996). *Human development* (6th ed.). New York: McGraw Hill.

VanFleet, R. (1994). *Filial therapy: Strengthening parent-child relationships through play*. Sarasota, FL: Professional Resource Press.

Vasey, M. W. (1995). Social anxiety disorders. In A. R. Eisen, C. A. Kearney, & C. A. Schaefer (Eds.), *Clinical handbook of anxiety disorders in children and adolescents* (pp. 131–168). Northvale, NJ: Aronson.

Walker, C. E., Bonner, B. L., & Kaufman, K. L. (1988). *The physically and sexually abused child*. New York: Pergamon Press.

Walter, J. L., & Peller, J. E. (1992). *Becoming solution-focused in brief therapy*. New York: Brunner/Mazel.

Weinhaus, E., & Friedman, K. (1991). *Stop struggling with your child*. New York: HarperCollins.

Weiss, L. (1979). *Emotionally yours*. Dallas, TX: I. T. Productions.

White, J., Flynt, M., & Draper, K. (1997). Kinder therapy: Teachers as therapeutic agents. *International Journal of Play Therapy, 6*(2), 33–49.

Whitman, B. Y., & Smith, C. (1991). Living with a hyperactive child: Principles of families, family therapy, and behavioral management. In P. J. Accardo, T. A. Blondis, & B. Y. Whitman (Eds.), *Attention deficit disorders and hyperactivity in children* (pp. 187–221). New York: Marcel Dekker.

Winnicott, D. W. (1965). *The family and individual development*. London: Tavistock.

Woods, S. K., & Ploof, W. H. (1997). *Understanding ADHD: Attention deficit hyperactivity disorder and the feeling brain*. Thousand Oaks, CA: Sage.

Zahn-Waxler, C., Cummings, E. M., McKnew, D. H., & Radke-Yarrow, M. (1984). Altruism, aggression, and social interactions in young children with a manic-depressive parent. *Child Development, 55*, 112–122.

INDEX

Abuse
  reporting, 40, 46–47
  sexual, 40, 46–47, 54–55, 168–177
Acceptance, 21
Achenbach, T. M., 63
Adderall, 68
Adland, 95
Advocacy agencies, 203–207
Al-Anon, 119
Albano, A. M., 62, 87
Alexander, E. D., 166–167
American Assn. of Marriage & Family
    Therapists, 35, 54
  Code of Ethics, 36, 41
American Counseling Assn., 9, 35, 44,
    47, 54, 57, 60
  Code of Ethics and Standards of Practice,
    36–41
American Psychological Assn., 35, 65–
    66, 84, 87–90
  *Ethical Principles of Psychologists and
    Code of Conduct,* 48–49
Anger
  divorce, 163–164
  normalizing, 174
  sexual abuse, 173–174
Angry parents. *See* Resistant parents
Antidepressants
  ADHD, 68
  anxiety disorders, 90–91
  depression, 85
Anxiety disorders, 63, 87–93
  assessment, 87–90
  generalized anxiety disorder, 87–88
  graded exposure, 92
  obsessive-compulsive disorder, 89–90
  parenting skills, 91–93
  peers, 92
  pharmacology, 90–91

  play, 92
  separation anxiety disorder, 88–89
  social phobia, 89
Araoz, D. L., 179, 182
Arguing
  ADHD, 82
  grade-schoolers, 32
Arthur, G. L., 42
Assessment
  ADHD, 64–70
  anxiety, 87–90
  depression, 83–85
  generalized anxiety disorder, 87–88
  obsessive-compulsive disorder, 89–90
  separation anxiety disorder, 88–89
  social phobia, 89
Atarax, 90
Attachment, 22
  infancy, 26
  parental depression, 98
Attention burst technique, 154–155
Attention spans, 28
Attention-deficit/hyperactivity disorder,
    62–84
  antecedent phase of behavior, 73–74
  coin flip task, 186–187
  core symptoms, 66–67
  diagnosis/assessment, 64–70
  inheritability, 93–94
  interventions, 72–83
  managed care issues, 67
  parenting skills, 70–72
  pharmacology, 72–73
  relationship structure, 79–83
  situational structure, 77–79
  structure/routine, 74–77
  treatment/medication, 67–70
Audiotaping sessions, 54
Authorization for treatment form, 200

Autonomy
  toddlers, 26–30
Axline, V., 14–15, 179

Baggerly, J. N., 167
Barber, B. K., 98
Barkely, R. A., 64–66, 69, 80–83, 87
Barlow, D. H., 62, 87
Bartering, 55–57
Bartz, W. R., 209
Bauer, A. M., 76
Benzodiazepines, 90–91
Berg, B., 162–163
Bergman, J. S., 120–121
Bernard, J. M., 8, 44
Bernstein, B. E., 41–42, 44–47
Bipolar disorder
  attachment, 98
  effects on children, 96–97
  inheritability, 97–98
  inhibition, 99–100
  parental, 93–100
  socialization, 99
Birch, H. G., 26
Bishop, J. K., 166
Biting, 27
Blaine, G. B., 165
Blalock, R., 64–65, 67–71, 74, 80
Blatt, S. J., 84, 97–98
Bloom, B. L., 182
Bloomquist, M. L., 73
Bonner, B. L., 168
Boundaries
  setting, 39
  with resistant parents, 121–122
Bowlby, J., 34, 95, 98
Bowman, J. T., 109
Branden, N., 213
Braswell, L., 73
Bratton, S. C., 130
Brazelton, T. B., 22, 29, 31
Breach of confidentiality, 40
Brief therapy, 178–189
  cheerleading, 187–188
  coin flip task, 186–187
  focusing principles, 182–182
  goal setting, 181–183
  homework assignments, 184
  interventions with parents, 184–188
  phases, 179–181
  reframing, 184–185
    support groups, 186
    support system, 185–186
    supporting change, 188
    treatment plan, 183–184
Briere, J., 174
Brody, V., 133
Bromfield, R., 1, 18
Browne, A., 174
Burt, B. B., 186
Burt, M. S., 186
Buspar, 91

Callanan, P., 8, 36
Career parents, 105–106
Carkhuff, R. J., 2
Carrese, M. A., 179, 182
Carroll, F., 133
Case studies, 134–148
Chapman, M., 95
Cheerleading, 187–188
Chess, S., 25–26
Chethik, M., 163–164
Child client intake form, 196–199
Chorpita, B. F., 62, 87
Clarifying, 216
  parents' expressions, 6
Clarke, J. I., 28
Client questionnaires, 7–8
Cognitive restructuring, 172
Cole, M., 86
Cole, S. R., 86
Communication
  encouragement, 213–215
  parent/child, 22
  play as, 13–16
  reflective listening, 209–213
  resistant parents, 102–104
  teaching skills, 12
  with children, 16–18
Comparisons, 30
Compensation issues, 56–57
Competency
  preschoolers, 30
Confidentiality, 40–45
  adolescents, 43
  breach of, 40
  child clients, 41–43
  defining parameters, 8–9
  duty to warn, 40, 43–45
  exceptions, 40–41
  in court, 52–53

in family therapy, 41
privacy, 40
privileged communication, 40
Confrontation, 119–120
Confused technique, 103
Conners, C. K., 63
Copley, B., 4
Corey, G., 8, 36, 24, 30, 39–44, 46, 48–
    50, 120
Corey, M. S., 8, 36
Countertransference, 109–110
Craig, G. J., 30–32
Cramer, B. G., 22
Crow, J., 166
Crying
    in infancy, 24–25
Cummings, E. M., 95–96
Cunningham, C., 175
Custody issues
    legal right for therapy, 47–48
    therapists and lawsuits, 51–52

Damon, L., 172–174
"Dates" with parents, 106–107, 152–153
Davenport, Y. B., 95
De'Amico, P. J., 91–92
Depression, 63, 83–87
    academic successes, 86
    conflict, 86–87
    diagnosis/assessment, 83–85
    inheritability, 94–95
    parental, 93–100
    parenting skills, 86–87
    pharmacology, 85
    sexual abuse, 174–177
    social successes, 86
    symptoms, 83–85
deShazer, S., 185
Developmental issues, 21–34
    disruption by divorce, 163–164
    father's role, 33–34
    grade-schoolers, 31–32
    infancy, 24–26
    parent education, 12
    parental expectations, 21–22
    play therapy, 13–16
    preschoolers, 30–31
    stages, 23–33
    teenagers, 32–33
    toddlers, 26–30
    young adults, 33

Dexedrine, 68
Dinkmeyer, D., 210, 212, 217
Discipline, 22–23
Divorce, 108–109, 161–166
    absent fathers, 33–34
    children's feelings, 162–164
    custody issues, 47–48
    lawsuits, 51–52
    legal right for therapy, 47–48
    parents' feelings, 161–162
    therapeutic interventions, 164–166
Documentation, 39
    clinical notes, 49–51
    treatment plans, 183–184
Doyal, G. T., 70
Dozois, J. A., 63, 94, 98
Draper, K., 167
Dreikurs, R., 157
Drombooble, W. A., xx
DSM-IV, 64–66, 84, 87–90
Dual relationships, 45–46
    bartering, 56–57
    gifts, 60
    hugging, 55, 58–59
    sexual exploitation, 54–55
Duty to warn, 40, 43–45
    Tarasoff case, 44

Elavil, 90
Empathic listening, 2–3
Empathizing, 5
    resistant parents, 103–104
Encouragement, 213–215
Epstein, 37–38, 51
Epston, D., 175
Erikson, E., 24, 27, 30–31, 33
Ethical issues, 35–61
    audiotaping sessions, 54
    compensation, 55–57
    confidentiality, 40–43
    custody issues, 47–48
    documentation, 39, 49–51
    dual relationships, 45–46
    duty to warn, 43–45
    gifts, 60
    guidelines, 35–36
    hugging, 55, 58–59
    informed consent, 48–49
    length of sessions, 58
    licensing, 35–36
    non-office settings, 57–58

Ethical issues (*Cont.*):
  parent manipulation, 51–52
  professional judgment, 38–40
  responding to complaints, 53–54
  sexual abuse, 46–47
  sexual exploitation, 54–55
  standard of care, 38–40
  subpoenas, 52–53
  telephone calls, 59
  therapist responsibility, 36–37
  therapists' fears, 37–38
  videotaping sessions, 54
Expectations, parental, 21–22
Externalizing behaviors, 62–63
  ADHD, 64–83
Extracurricular activities, 31–32
Eyre, L., 209
Eyre, R., 209

Faber, A., 156, 213
Faller, D. C., 168–175
Fallone, G. P., 65, 93
Family meetings, 157–158
Family therapy
  confidentiality, 41
Fantasy, 156–157
Fathers' role, 33–34
Fergusson, D. M., 168
Ferryan, B., 4
Filial therapy, 124, 130–133
Finkelhor, D., 173–175
Flynt, M., 167
Forms, 190–200
  authorization for treatment form,
    200
  child client intake form, 196–199
  informed consent form, 190–193
  intake session checklist, 194–195
  professional disclosure statement,
    190
Freeman, J., 175
Friedman, A. G., 91–92
Friedman, K., 157–158
Friedman, R. J., 70
Friedman, S., 186–187

Ganahl, G., 134
Gardner, R. A., 157, 165
Gender differences, 63
Generalized anxiety disorder, 87–88

Gestalt therapy, 133
Gifts, 60
Gil, E., 157, 172
Gilliland, B. E., 109
Ginott, H. G., 213
Glenn, H. S., 157–158
Glover, G., 92, 130
Goals
  brief therapy, 181–183
  parents', 9–10
Goodyear, R. K., 8, 44
Grade-schoolers
  and divorce, 163–164
  arguing, 32
  developmental issues, 31–32
  extracurricular activities, 31–32
  peer approval, 32
Grandparents, 110–111
Green, A. H., 168
Green, M., 28, 83–84
Greenspan, S. I., 4, 6
Grollman, E. A., 165
Guerney, B. G., 4, 130
Guerney, L. F., 4, 167, 209, 220
Guilt
  divorce, 163–164
  preschoolers, 30–31
  sexual abuse, 171–173
Gupta, V. B., 71–72

Haldol, 91
Hambidge, G., 155
Hammen, C., 83, 86, 94
Hansen, J. C., 134
Harr, B., 11
Harris, Z., 130
Harter, S., 134
Hartsell, T. L., 36–54, 59–60
Helmstetter, S., 209
Hendrix, D. H., 43
Hensley, R., 86
Herlihy, 39, 46
Highlighting technique, 111
Homann, E., 84, 97–98
Home offices, 57–58
Homework, 134
  30-second attention burst, 154–155
  ADHD, 75–76
  brief therapy, 184
  family meetings, 157–158
  fantasy, 156–157

mutual storytelling, 157
notes, 155
parent assignments, 151–159
parent dates, 152–154
samples, 135–148
sandwich hugs, 154
structured play, 155–156
telephone calls, 155
Homeyer, L. E., 92, 168
Howell, C. T., 63
Hoyt, M. F., 178–181, 202
Hugging, 55, 58–59
sandwich, 154
Humor, 121

Identity issues
teenagers, 32–33
Imaginary friends, 29–30
Industriousness
grade-schoolers, 31–32
Infancy
attachment, 26
crying, 24–25
developmental issues, 24–26
difficult babies, 25–26
temperament, 25–26
Inferiority issues
grade-schoolers, 31–32
Information gathering, 7–11
client questionnaire, 7–8
questioning cycle, 7
Informed consent, 48–49
form, 190–193
minors, 41
videotaping sessions, 54
Inhibition, 99–100
Initial contact, 2–3
explaining therapy, 12–18
intake interview, 4–11
parent education, 11–12
referrals, 3
Initiative
preschoolers, 30–31
Insomnia, 84–85
Intake interview, 4–11
authorization for treatment form,
200
checklist, 194–195
child client form, 196–199
clarifying, 6
client questionnaire, 7–8

defining goals, 9–10
defining parameters, 8–9
forms, 48–49
information gathering, 7–8
reflecting feelings, 4–6
supporting parents, 10–11
with children, 17–18
Internalizing behaviors, 62–63
International Assn. for Play Therapy,
13
Interviews, 4–11

Jacobs, E. H., 33, 64, 66, 70, 75–82
Jacobson, G. F., 161–162, 165
James, B. E., 109
James, O., 4, 12
Johnson, K., 169
Joint Commission for the Accreditation
of Healthcare Organizations, 184

Kagan, J., 25
Kale, A., 130
Kao, S., 160
Kaufman, K. L., 168
Kell, B. L., 126
Kennedy, E., 86
"Kinder therapy," 167
Klonopin, 91
Kochanska, G., 96, 99–100
Korbin, J., 172
Kottman, T., 4
Kuczynski, L., 95

L'Abate, L., 134
Landreth, G. L., 14–15, 59, 92, 131–
133, 154–155, 160, 166, 216
Lazarus, A. A., 178–179
Legal issues, 35–61
audiotaping sessions, 54
clinical notes, 49–51
compensation, 55–57
confidentiality, 40–43
custody issues, 47–48
dual relationships, 45–46
duty to warn, 43–45
gifts, 60
guidelines, 35–36
hugging, 58–59
informed consent, 48–49

Legal issues (*Cont.*):
  length of sessions, 58
  licensing, 35–36
  non-office settings, 57–58
  parent manipulation, 51–52
  professional judgment, 38–40
  responding to complaints, 53–54
  sexual abuse, 46–47
  sexual exploitation, 54–55
  standard of care, 38–40
  subpoenas, 52–53
  telephone calls, 59
  therapist responsibility, 36–37
  therapists' fears, 37–38
  videotaping sessions, 54
Levy, D. M., 155
Licensed Professional Counselor Act
  (Texas), 37–38
Licensing boards
  complaints to, 37–38, 53–54
  power of, 37–38
Limit setting, 215–220
  logical consequences, 217–219
Lobovits, D., 175
Lockwood, J., 11
Logical consequences, 217–219
Long, S., 168, 170
Love, infancy, 26
Luvox, 91

MacFarlane, K., 172, 175
Managed care
  ADHD assessment, 67
  brief therapy, 178–189
  sample format, 201–202
  treatment plans, 183–184
Marital therapy, 118–119
Mash, E, J., 63, 94, 98
Masturbation
  preschoolers, 30
Mayfield, 95
Mazlish, E., 156, 213
McCarney, S. B., 76, 86–87, 92
McKay, G. D., 210, 212, 217
McKnew, D. H., 96
Medical issues, 62–101
  ADHD, 64–83
  anxiety, 87–93
  depression, 83–87
  parents', 93–100
Mellaril, 91

Mendell, A., 163–164
Mercer, L., 89–91, 93
Merriam-Webster, Inc., 56, 113
Metaphors, 133
Milos, M. E., 92
Moustakas, C., 11, 13
Mueller, W. J., 126
Mullen, P. E., 168
Mutual storytelling, 157

National Assn. for Protection and
  Advocacy Systems, 203
National Assn. of Social Workers, 46
National Board for Certified
  Counselors, 191
National Committee for Quality
  Assurance, 184
National organizations, 203–207
Natural consequences, 217–218
Nelsen, J., 80–81, 87, 157–158, 213,
  217–218
Neuman, M. G., 161, 165–166
Norton, B. E., 4, 133
Norton, C. C., 4, 133

O'Connor, K. J., 10
O'Neill, L., 4
Oaklander, V., 133
Obsessive-compulsive disorder, 89–90
Ogan, G. D., 64, 74–75, 77–80
Olsen, J. A., 98
Olweus, D., 63
Osherson, S., 33

Parent education, 11–12
  explaining therapy, 12–18
  pharmacology, 93
Parent meetings, 127–150
  case studies, 134–148
  children's involvement, 128–129
  determining themes, 133–134
  filial therapy, 130–133
  parents' involvement, 129–130
  scheduling, 127–128
  weekly, 127–130
Parental depression, 93–100
  attachment, 98
  effects on children, 96–97
  filial therapy, 130–133

inheritability, 95, 97–98
inhibition, 99–100
socialization, 99
Parenting skills
ADHD, 70–72
anxiety disorder, 91–93
closed/open responses, 210
depression, 86–87
encouragement, 213–215
filial therapy, 130–133
limit setting, 215–220
logical consequences, 217–219
manual, 208–220
reflective listening, 209–213
support groups, 82
team concept, 81–82
Parents
brief therapy interventions, 184–188
career, 105–106
cheerleading, 187–188
coin flip task, 186–187
grandparents, 110–111
homework assignments, 151–159,
    184
not seeking counseling, 109–110
recently separated/divorced, 108–109
reframing, 184–185
resistant, 102–104, 113–126
single, 107–108
supporting, 185–186, 188
two-career, 106–107
Passive-aggressive behavior, 163
Paxil, 91
Pearce, J. W., 175
Peer approval
anxiety, 92
grade-schoolers, 32
Peller, J. E., 187–188
Pezzot-Pearce, T. D., 175
Pharmacology
ADHD, 72–73
anxiety disorders, 90–91
depression, 85
parental resistance, 93
Phenomenological perceptions, 15–16
Play therapy
determining themes, 133–134
educating children, 16–18
educating parents, 12–16, 130–133
principles, 13–16
school setting, 160–161, 166–168
Ploof, W. H., 71, 81

Pope, K. S., 45
Positioning, 122–126
Pregnancy, 21
Preschoolers
and divorce, 162–163
comparisons, 30
competency, 30
developmental issues, 30–31
masturbation, 31
teasing, 30
Privacy, 40
Privileged communication, 40
Professional disclosure statement, 190
Professional judgment, 38–40
Protective service agencies, 203–207
Prozac, 85, 91

Quay, H. C., 63
Questioning cycle, 7

Radke-Yarrow, M., 95–98
Rasor, R. A., 209
Referrals, 3
Reflecting
in questioning, 7
parents' feelings, 4–6
resistant parents, 103
single parents, 108–109
Reflective listening, 209–213
Reframing, 119–120, 184–185
Reiss, S., 92
Rencken, R. H., 168
Resistant parents, 102–104, 113–126
acknowledging their agenda, 115–
    116
covertly, 117
gentle confrontation, 119–120
helping supportive parent, 117–118
individual therapy, 118–119
marital therapy, 118–119
overtly, 117
protecting yourself, 121–126
reflecting with, 103–104, 114–115
reframing, 120–121
targeted changes, 116–117
Responsibilities of therapist, 36–37
Reynolds, E. L., 28, 215
Ricci, I., 165
Rief, S., 74, 77, 80
Ries, A., 121–122

Risperdal, 91
Ritalin, 68
Roberts, G. T., 109
Rogers, C., 22, 34
Role confusion
  teenagers, 32–33
Rossiter, A., 162
Rudolph, K. D., 83, 86, 94
Runtz, M., 174
Ryan, V., 133

Sanford, L. T., 172
Santa Cruz Toddler Care Center, 27
Schaffer, S. J., 50
Schetky, D. H., 168
School settings, 160–161, 166–168
Sears, M., 22, 25
Sears, W., 22, 25
Selective serotonin reuptake inhibitors,
  91
Selekman, M. D., 175
Self-confidence
  toddlers, 26–27
Self-control
  ADHD, 78–80
Separation anxiety disorder, 88–89
Sexual abuse, 168–177
  anger, 173–174
  body image, 170–171
  depression, 174–177
  guilt, 171–173
  loss of trust, 168–170
  reporting, 40, 46–47
  self-destructive behavior, 174–177
Sgroi, S. M., 170
Shame
  ADHD, 94
  sexual abuse, 171–173
  toddlers, 26–30
Sheldon, C., 179, 183–184
Silver, L. V., 79
Sinequan, 90
Single parents, 107–108
Small change technique, 106–108
Smith, C., 70–72
Social phobia, 89
Socialization
  parental depression, 99
Spence, S. H., 86
Standard of care, 38–40
State agencies, 203–207

Stolz, V., 157
Storytelling
  divorce, 164–165
  mutual, 157
Stover, L., 4
Structured play, 155–156
Subpoena notice, 52–53
Suicide risk
  confidentiality, 8–9
  sexual abuse, 174–177
Supervision, 39
  seeking advice, 122
Support groups, 185
Supporting parents' efforts, 10–11
Swanson, C. D., 42
Sweeney, D. S., 92, 133

Tantrums
  toddlers, 27–28
Tarasoff v. Regents of California, 44
Tatum, R., 62–63, 65, 67–70, 72, 83–
  85, 90
Teachers, 92
Teasing
  preschoolers, 30
Teenagers, 32–33
Telephone calls, 2–3, 59
  parent/child, 155
Temperament
  infancy, 25–26
Texas State Board of Examiners of
  Professional Counselors, 37–38
Theme development, 133–134
  examples, 135–148
Therapeutic relationship
  defining parameters, 8–9
  legal/ethical issues, 35–61
  parameters, 55–61
  play therapy, 14–16
  protecting, 36–55
Thomas, A., 25–26
Todd, J., 172
Toddlers
  attention span, 28
  autonomy, 28–29
  biting, 27
  developmental issues, 26–30
  imaginary friends, 29–30
  tantrums, 27–28
  toilet training, 28
Tofranil, 90

Toilet training, 28
Tranquilizers, 91
Tranxene, 91
Trout, J., 122–123
Trust
    establishing with children, 16–18
    establishing with parents, 12–18
    in infancy, 24
    sexual abuse, 168–170
Two-career parents, 106–107

Valium, 91
Van der Zanden, J. W., 25, 27–28, 31, 60
VanFleet, R., 131–132, 168
Vasey, M. W., 89
Videotaping sessions, 54

Walker, C. E., 168
Walter, J. L., 187–188

Weinhaus, E., 157–158
Weiss, L., 23, 29
White, J., 167
Whitman, B. Y., 70–72
Wilson, K., 133
Winnicott, D. W., 23, 26
Woods, S. K., 71, 81
Working through phase, 180

Xanax, 91

Young adults
    developmental issues, 33

Zahn-Waxler, C., 95–99
Zoloft, 91

Printed in Great Britain
by Amazon